WOMEN PHILOSOPHERS OF THE SEVENTEENTH CENTURY

In this rich and detailed study of early modern women's thought, Jacqueline Broad explores the complexity of women's responses to Cartesian philosophy and its intellectual legacy in England and Europe. She examines the work of thinkers such as Mary Astell, Elisabeth of Bohemia, Margaret Cavendish, Anne Conway, and Damaris Masham, who were active participants in the intellectual life of their time and were also the respected colleagues of philosophers such as Descartes, Leibniz, and Locke. She also illuminates the continuities between early modern women's thought and the anti-dualism of more recent feminist thinkers. The result is a more gender-balanced account of early modern thought than has hitherto been available. Broad's clear and accessible exploration of this still unfamiliar area will have a strong appeal to both students and scholars in the history of philosophy, women's studies, and the history of ideas.

JACQUELINE BROAD is a Lecturer in Philosophy in the School of Philosophy and Bioethics at Monash University Victoria. She has published on women's philosophy in the *Dictionary of Literary Biography* volume on *British Philosophers, 1500–1799*, and in the *Australasian Journal of Philosophy*.

WOMEN PHILOSOPHERS OF THE SEVENTEENTH CENTURY

JACQUELINE BROAD

Monash University

PUBLISHED BY THE PRESS SYNDICATE OF THE UNIVERSITY OF CAMBRIDGE
The Pitt Building, Trumpington Street, Cambridge CB2 1RP, United Kingdom

CAMBRIDGE UNIVERSITY PRESS
The Edinburgh Building, Cambridge, CB2 2RU, UK
40 West 20th Street, New York, NY 10011-4211, USA
477 Williamstown Road, Port Melbourne, VIC 3207, Australia
Ruiz de Alarcón 13, 28014 Madrid, Spain
Dock House, The Waterfront, Cape Town 8001, South Africa

http://www.cambridge.org

First published 2002

Printed in the United Kingdom at the University Press, Cambridge

Typeface Baskerville Monotype 11/12.5 pt   *System* LaTeX 2ε [TB]

A catalogue record for this book is available from the British Library

Library of Congress Cataloguing in Publication data

Broad, Jacqueline.
Women philosophers of the seventeenth century / Jacqueline Broad.
p. cm.
Includes bibliographical references and index.
ISBN 0 521 81295 X
1. Women philosophers. 2. Philosophy, Modern – 17th century. I. Title.
B105.W6 B76 2002 190′.82′09032 – dc21 2002067376

ISBN 0 521 81295 X hardback

For my mother, Sandra

But to what Study shall we apply our selves? Some Men say that Heraldry is a pretty Study for a Woman, for this reason, I suppose, That she may know how to Blazon her Lord and Master's great Achievements! They allow us Poetry, Plays, and Romances, to Divert us and themselves; and when they would express a particular Esteem for a Womans Sense, they recommend History; tho' with Submission, History can only serve us for Amusement and a Subject of Discourse. For tho' it may be of Use to the Men who govern Affairs, to know how their Fore-fathers Acted, yet what is this to us, who have nothing to do with such Business? Some good Examples indeed are to be found in History, tho' generally the bad are ten for one; but how will this help our Conduct, or excite in us a generous Emulation? since the Men being the Historians, they seldom condescend to record the great and good Actions of Women; and when they take notice of them, 'tis with this wise Remark, That such Women *acted above their Sex*. By which one must suppose they wou'd have their Readers understand, That they were not Women who did those Great Actions, but that they were Men in Petticoats!

Mary Astell, *The Christian Religion* (1705)

Contents

Acknowledgements

I am extremely grateful to the many wonderfully supportive friends and colleagues who assisted in the writing of this book. Special thanks must go to Sarah Hutton for her invaluable advice and suggestions on my research; Karen Green and Rae Langton, for their perceptive criticisms and comments on numerous rough drafts; Richard Watson for his many excellent stylistic suggestions; and both Sarah Hutton and Eileen O'Neill for their helpful examiners' comments on my doctoral dissertation, 'The Impertinencies of a Woman's Pen: A Study of the Metaphysical Views of Four Seventeenth-Century Women Philosophers', on which this book is based. I was also extremely fortunate to have the financial assistance of the Monash Postgraduate Publications Award, and the Australian Federation of University Women, who awarded me a fellowship to carry out archival research in England and Europe. In addition, I would like to express my gratitude to librarians at the Bodleian Library, the University of Oxford, the British Library, London (particularly Frances Harris in the MSS Department), the Amsterdam University Library (UvA), the Niedersächsische Landesbibliothek, Hanover, and the Rare Books Room at the Matheson Library, Monash. Thanks must go to the Mauritshuis Museum, The Hague, for their kind permission to reproduce Samuel van Hoogstraten's painting of Anne Conway on the dust jacket of this book; and to the *Dictionary of Literary Biography*, who permitted me to reproduce parts of an essay on Mary Astell that I wrote for *British Philosophers, 1500–1799*. Finally, I would like to acknowledge the generous assistance of Susan Beer, Jillian Britton, Stephen Clucas, Hilary Gaskin, Guido Giglioni, Anne Kelley, Neil Levy, Luisa Simonutti, Patrick Spedding, and Jo Wallwork, and to give a special, warm thanks to Jeremy Aarons and my family, for their support and encouragement.

Introduction

There are few scholars outside of the history of philosophy who have heard of Elisabeth of Bohemia (1618–80), Margaret Cavendish (1623–73), Anne Conway (1631–79), Mary Astell (1666–1731), Damaris Masham (1659–1708), and Catharine Trotter Cockburn (1679–1749). These women philosophers are now mere footnotes to the standard historical–intellectual accounts of the early modern period. There is no history of scholarship on their works, and there are no long-standing disagreements or controversies about interpretations of their views. Although a number of their works have been reprinted, the bulk of their writings can be found only in rare-book rooms, and a few of their manuscripts still remain unpublished. Yet in the seventeenth century, these women were the friends and correspondents of famous philosophers of their time, such as René Descartes (1596–1650), Thomas Hobbes (1588–1679), John Locke (1632–1704), and Gottfried Wilhelm Leibniz (1646–1716). Some women discussed philosophy with these men, they raised philosophical questions in letters, and they wrote and published their own thoughts on metaphysics. Male colleagues dedicated books to them, and many of their contemporaries acknowledged their influence or praised their understanding.

Feminist philosopher Mary Astell is a notable case in point. In 1693, Astell took the bold step of writing to the English philosopher-divine, John Norris (1657–1711), to present her criticisms of his views. 'Sir', she writes,

Though some morose Gentlemen wou'd perhaps remit me to the Distaff or the Kitchin, or at least to the Glass and the Needle, the proper Employments as they fancy of a Womans Life; yet expecting better things from the more Equitable and ingenious Mr. *Norris*, who is not so narrow-Soul'd as to confine Learning to his own Sex, or to envy it in ours, I presume to beg his Attention a little to the Impertinencies of a Womans Pen.[1]

Astell then proceeds to highlight inconsistencies in Norris's theory of love. In the seventeenth century, the term 'impertinent' had at least two meanings: it had the modern sense of being 'bold' or 'insolent', but it also had the sense of being 'irrelevant' or 'not pertinent' (*OED*). In 1696, feminist author Judith Drake remarks that her fellow women are often considered 'impertinent', or given to 'a humour of busying our selves about things trivial, and of no Moment in themselves'.[2] Astell probably intends her comment about women's 'impertinencies' in this sense, to blunt the sharp edge of her objections.

Today the supposed irrelevance or 'impertinence' of early modern women's thought is offered as an explanation for their absence from the history books.[3] The philosophical issues that these women debated have passed out of the intellectual mainstream. Philosophy as a discipline no longer primarily concerns itself with questions about the love of God, the divine purpose of the natural world, the connection between faith and reason, and natural philosophy. Yet these were the topics that most interested these women. In addition to choice of content, there are also problems with their choice of style. Although some women published systematic treatises, a number of their philosophical contributions are in the form of letters. In *The Patriarch's Wife*, Margaret Ezell identifies a tendency for historians to ignore any method of intellectual exchange that does not conform to twentieth-century practices.[4] As a consequence, letters are often overlooked as a source of serious philosophical discussion. But in the seventeenth century, correspondences between philosophers were a formal and well-respected type of intellectual exchange. Women seemed to favour the epistolary form, and often initiated the exchanges themselves. Ruth Perry remarks that 'So common were these epistolary

---

[1] Astell to Norris, 21 September 1693; in Mary Astell and John Norris, *Letters Concerning the Love of God, Between the Author of the Proposal to the Ladies and Mr. John Norris: Wherein his late Discourse, shewing That it ought to be intire and exclusive of all other Loves, is further cleared and justified* (London: J. Norris, 1695), pp. 1–2.

[2] Judith Drake, *An Essay In Defence of the Female Sex. In which are inserted the Characters Of A Pedant, A Squire, A Beau, A Vertuoso, A Poetaster, A City-Critick, and c. In a Letter to a Lady. Written by a Lady*, unabridged republication of 1696 edition (New York: Source Book Press, 1970), p. 82.

[3] On the exclusion of women from the history of philosophy, see Eileen O'Neill, 'Disappearing Ink: Early Modern Women Philosophers and their Fate in History', in *Philosophy in a Feminist Voice: Critiques and Reconstructions*, edited by Janet A. Kourany (Princeton: Princeton University Press, 1998), pp. 32–9.

[4] Margaret J. M. Ezell, *The Patriarch's Wife: Literary Evidence and the History of the Family* (Chapel Hill and London: The University of North Carolina Press, 1987), p. 64.

relationships between intellectual women and philosophers or divines that they may be said to constitute a minor genre in late seventeenth-century letters.'[5]

While early women's philosophy might appear to be 'out of date' in various ways, we must remember that little has been done to make their thought accessible, or to re-assess it in light of recent scholarship. In the late twentieth century, the growing influence of feminist theory, and the call for a more inclusive type of historical scholarship, has led to a renewal of interest in early modern women. From a feminist perspective, these women might be considered daring or 'impertinent' in the more modern sense of the word. As Mary Astell remarks in her *Reflections upon Marriage* (1700), not even the most liberal thinkers of her time 'wou'd cry up Liberty to poor Female Slaves, or plead for the Lawfulness of Resisting a Private Tyranny'.[6] Yet these women often embrace the philosophies of their male peers to raise the concerns of women. In this sense, their contributions to early philosophical discourse are strikingly original and modern. They reveal not only that women were intellectually active during this time, but that the current feminist movement had an historical precedent long before the twentieth century.

More recently, the process of interpreting the writings of past women thinkers has begun in earnest. While once there was the popular mis-conception that their philosophy is fragmentary, obscure, and irrelevant to current debate, there are now concerted efforts to re-visit their views in light of modern scholarship. Historians of philosophy regard the early modern period as absolutely crucial for our understanding of philoso-phy as we now think about it. The ideas of women philosophers pro-vide us with a richer historical background to that significant period. In so far as these women actively engaged in the philosophical enterprise of their time, they also contributed to the development of our current concerns.

In this study, I focus on the changing fortunes of Cartesian philosophy in the writings of seventeenth-century women. I trace the development of women's thought from Elisabeth of Bohemia's letters in the 1640s, to the works of Anne Conway and Margaret Cavendish in the 1660s and 1670s, and the writings of Mary Astell, Damaris Masham, and Catharine Cockburn in the 1690s and early eighteenth century. My particular claim

[5] Ruth Perry, 'Radical Doubt and the Liberation of Women', *Eighteenth-Century Studies* 18:4 (1985), 482.
[6] Mary Astell, *Reflections upon Marriage*, in *Astell: Political Writings*, edited by Patricia Springborg (Cambridge: Cambridge University Press, 1996), pp. 46–7.

is that these women philosophers – like some recent feminist theorists –
are highly critical of dualists of their time.

At first glance, this assertion may appear to be at odds with a common belief that Cartesian philosophy had a profound impact on women
writers of the early modern period. Cavendish, Conway, Astell, and
Masham were writing during the mid to late-seventeenth century, a
period that Sterling Lamprecht calls 'the Cartesian period in English
philosophy'.[7] During this time, no English intellectual escaped the influence of Descartes' writings, and recent scholarship has shown that
women philosophers were no exception. Ruth Perry, Margaret Atherton,
Hilda L. Smith, and others claim that the advocacy of a Cartesian
conception of reason is distinctive of seventeenth-century women's
thought.[8] In 'Radical Doubt and the Liberation of Women', Perry says
that 'Cartesian assumptions and Cartesian method, ironic as it may seem,
liberated women intellectually and thus psychically, by making it possible
for numbers of them to participate in serious mainstream philosophical
discourse'.[9] Similarly, in her 1993 essay 'Cartesian Reason and Gendered Reason', Atherton says of seventeenth-century feminist authors
that 'what encouraged them to write in support of women's intellectual capacities was precisely the concept of reason that could be found
in Descartes';[10] and this same point is supported by Hilda L. Smith in
her pioneering work, *Reason's Disciples*. Along the same lines, Catherine
Gallagher believes that Cartesian metaphysics played a significant role.
'Many seventeenth century women writers,' she says, 'were inspired by
Descartes' dualism to assert their intellectual equality with men; for if, as
Descartes argued, mind has no extension, then it also has no gender.'[11]

---

[7] Sterling P. Lamprecht, 'The Role of Descartes in Seventeenth-Century England', *Studies in the
History of Ideas* 3 (1935), 188. See also Marjorie Nicolson, 'The Early Stage of Cartesianism in
England', *Studies in Philology* 26 (1929), 356–74.

[8] See Margaret Atherton, 'Cartesian Reason and Gendered Reason', in *A Mind of One's Own:
Feminist Essays on Reason and Objectivity*, edited by Louise M. Antony and Charlotte Witt (Boulder
and Oxford: Westview Press, 1993), pp. 19–34; Perry, 'Radical Doubt and the Liberation of
Women', 472–93; Hilda L. Smith, *Reason's Disciples: Seventeenth Century English Feminists* (Urbana:
University of Illinois Press, 1982); and Hilda L. Smith, 'Intellectual Bases for Feminist Analyses:
The Seventeenth and Eighteenth Centuries', in *Women and Reason*, edited by Elizabeth D. Harvey
and Kathleen Okruhlik (Ann Arbor: University of Michigan Press, 1992), pp. 19–38. See also
Katharine M. Rogers, *Feminism in Eighteenth-Century England* (Urbana: University of Illinois Press,
1982), chapter 2.

[9] Perry, 'Radical Doubt and the Liberation of Women', p. 475.

[10] Atherton, 'Cartesian Reason and Gendered Reason', p. 20.

[11] Catherine Gallagher, 'Embracing the Absolute: the Politics of the Female Subject in Seventeenth-
Century England', *Genders* 1:1 (1988), 34.

In short, much of the interpretive literature on early modern women credits Cartesianism with providing both the inspiration and the subject matter for their intellectual writings.

I do not dismiss or debunk the 'Cartesian interpretation' of early modern women's writings. But it is important to distinguish between different aspects of Descartes' philosophy, such as his concept of reason, his method of doubt, his rationalism, his soul–body dualism, and his mechanistic theory of matter. It is undeniable that *some* aspects of Cartesian thought were inspirational for seventeenth-century women. In particular, Descartes' style of writing is accessible to those individuals who have received no institutional education in philosophy. Not only is his prose conversational and anecdotal rather than weighty and abstract, but his new method could be practised without books, language skills, or a classical training. This made his works highly appealing to upper-class women who had received no education beyond the feminine accomplishments of singing, dancing, and sewing. His *Discourse on the Method of rightly conducting one's reason* (1637) taught women that all human beings possess reason or 'common sense', a natural ability to distinguish between truth and error. From this basis, feminist writers such as Cavendish, Astell, Masham, and Cockburn were able to point out that if women were intellectually slow, it was only because society had prevented them from sharpening their minds by denying them a proper education.

Cavendish remarks that 'through the carelesse neglects, and despisements of the masculine sex to the effeminate' women had become 'like worms that onely live in the dull earth of ignorance, winding our selves sometimes out, by the help of some refreshing rain of good education which seldom is given us'.[12] Cockburn likewise ascribes women's ignorance to their disadvantages in a society that discourages women intellectuals. Masham suggests that women be raised by their mothers to use their reason rather than trust the opinions of others; and Mary Astell goes so far as to suggest that a formal academic training and the study of Cartesian method could improve women's natural reason. Furthermore, while Elisabeth and Anne Conway cannot really be called feminists, their intellectual careers are proof that women could practise the new method. Elisabeth is well known for her philosophical exchange with Descartes, and Conway began her studies by taking what Sarah Hutton calls 'the

---

[12] Margaret Cavendish, *The Philosophical and Physical Opinions, Written by her Excellency, the Lady Marchionesse of Newcastle* (London: J. Martin and J. Allestrye, 1655), 'To the Two Universities', sig. B2ᵛ.

earliest correspondence course in Cartesian philosophy'.[13] In a general sense, Cartesian method also encouraged the challenging of preconceived opinions, and welcomed doubts and criticisms of former beliefs. This enabled women to criticise their male contemporaries without fear of being considered too daring or bold.

The problem with the 'Cartesian' interpretation, however, is that it threatens to render early women's philosophy 'irrelevant' in another sense. Modern feminist writers such as Genevieve Lloyd, Susan Bordo, Freya Mathews, Val Plumwood, and others[14] have criticised the radical split between mind and body, the reduction of matter to mere extension (with no inherent motion or life), and belief in the soul as a self-sufficient entity. Dualist theories of the mind and body are said to have had negative consequences for women because femaleness is typically associated with the body and the non-rational, whereas men have associated themselves with the superior categories of mind and reason. Perhaps most famously, in *The Man of Reason*, Genevieve Lloyd presents a feminist critique of the sex-specific characteristics of matter and reason. According to Lloyd, 'Rational knowledge has been construed as a transcending, transformation or control of natural forces; and the feminine has been associated with what rational knowledge transcends, dominates or simply leaves behind.'[15] With regard to Cartesian method, Lloyd reminds us that this procedure involves putting aside or transcending the senses and the body. She believes that as a consequence of Cartesianism, a distinction arose between a highly abstract mode of thought and our everyday, ordinary thought processes. This difference, according to Lloyd, has been exploited to mark a gender distinction: women have become associated with the lesser type of reason, men with the superior.

Lloyd also claims that Descartes' method must be seen in the context of his dualism, the theory that the soul and body are distinct substances. In particular, she identifies an alignment in Cartesian method between the body and untrained reason. A true philosopher, Descartes

---

[13] Sarah Hutton, 'Ancient Wisdom and Modern Philosophy: Anne Conway, F. M. van Helmont and the Seventeenth-Century Dutch Interchange of Ideas', in *Quaestiones Infinitae* (Utrecht: Department of Philosophy, Utrecht University, 1994), p. 3.

[14] See Susan Bordo, 'The Cartesian Masculinization of Thought', *Signs: Journal of Women in Culture and Society* 11:3 (1986), 439–56; Susan Bordo (ed.), *Feminist Interpretations of René Descartes* (University Park, Pennsylvania: Pennsylvania State University Press, 1999); Genevieve Lloyd, *The Man of Reason: 'Male' and 'Female' in Western Philosophy* (London: Methuen, 1984), chapter 3; Freya Mathews, *The Ecological Self* (London: Routledge, 1994); Val Plumwood *Feminism and the Mastery of Nature* (London and New York: Routledge, 1993); and Janna Thompson, 'Women and the High Priests of Reason', *Radical Philosophy* 34 (1983), 10–14.

[15] Lloyd, *The Man of Reason*, p. 2.

says, must avoid entanglement with the senses because they will not yield certainty; clear and distinct thought can be attained only by dis-associating the mind from the material body. Thus, according to Lloyd, the 'foundations of [Descartes'] enquiry into truth demanded that the mind rigorously enact the metaphysical truth of its separation from the body'.[16] This theory of mind, she says, paved the way for a powerful version of the sexual division of mental labour in which women are assigned responsibility for 'that realm of the sensuous which the Carte-sian Man of Reason must transcend, if he is to have true knowledge of things'.[17]

For the modern feminist philosopher, seventeenth-century women's thought thus presents something of a paradox. On the one hand, histori-ans highlight the fact that an egalitarian conception of reason formulated and promoted by Descartes and his followers was the catalyst for a fe-male intellectual awakening in the seventeenth century. Yet, on the other hand, recent feminists identify a male bias in the dominant philosophies of the early modern period, particularly in Cartesianism. This bias, they say, reinforced and facilitated the exclusion of women from philosophy, and fostered a common perception that women have a lesser capacity for reason than men. How, then, are we to deal with this difficulty?

Two scholars explicitly address the disparity between modern femi-nists and their seventeenth-century counterparts: Margaret Atherton in her 'Cartesian Reason and Gendered Reason', and Hilda Smith in her 'Intellectual Bases for Feminist Analyses: The Seventeenth and Eigh-teenth Centuries'. Atherton asks how Descartes' texts could lead 'both to a decline in the status of women and to arguments for improving their status? How can Descartes' concept of reason be seen both as having deprived women of a mind of their own and as having encouraged them to take control of their own minds'?[18] Atherton's solution is to point out that Lloyd's interpretation of Cartesian reason is flawed. She claims that Lloyd faces difficulties in trying to make Descartes' trained and untrained reason fit with our stereotypes of masculinity and femininity. Atherton believes that Astell and Masham, on the other hand, remind us that there is another conception of Cartesian reason, one in which the general characteristics underlying all human thought processes are emphasised without distinguishing between the trained and untrained mind.

---

[16] *Ibid.*, p. 47.   [17] *Ibid.*, p. 50.
[18] Atherton, 'Cartesian Reason and Gendered Reason', p. 20.

Hilda Smith also challenges Lloyd's interpretation of early modern philosophy and its implications for women. Smith denies that there is any conflict between reason and femininity. She says that to argue that reason is a masculine concept, as Lloyd does, is to fall into 'the mother earth understanding of female nature', to accept 'the Cartesian mind–body split', and that it 'simply glorifies what philosophy has traditionally portrayed as subordinate emotions and natural functions'.[19] She also says that Lloyd's critique does a disservice to seventeenth-century feminists, since it leads to further marginalisation of their work. Smith says that

Partly because of their limited access to serious learning, early feminists glorified women's rational abilities. Surely, they would not have appreciated the irony that later scholars and feminists have fully sided with their male and conservative critics at the time in maintaining that reason and learning were traps, catching would-be feminists in the structures, principles, and practices that were, indeed, a male preserve.[20]

Nevertheless, there are problems with Atherton and Smith's critiques. First, it is undoubtedly a misrepresentation of Lloyd's position to claim that she 'accepts the mind–body split' and 'falls into the mother earth understanding of femininity'. Lloyd simply *describes* the role of Cartesian dualism in the 'sexual division of mental labour'; she does not condone the historical and cultural associations between maleness and reason. Nowhere does Lloyd endorse the claim that 'women have their own truth, or that there are distinctively female criteria for reasonable belief'.[21] It is simply that in Lloyd's view masculinity has come to be associated with Descartes' highly abstract mode of reasoning, and, on the reverse side, the feminine has been symbolically associated with a lack of rigorous thought. But these associations are historical and contingent rather than necessary.

Furthermore, it is difficult to deny the basic empirical claim that women were associated with a lesser form of reason following the rise of Cartesianism. A number of seventeenth-century texts support this view both literally and metaphorically. The exclusion of women from the search for knowledge is explicit in the work of Nicolas Malebranche (1638–1715), one of Descartes' immediate successors. In *The Search After Truth* (1674–5), Malebranche devotes half a chapter to 'the imaginations of women', whom he claims are 'incapable of penetrating to truths that are slightly difficult to discover'. He says that 'everything abstract is

---

[19] Smith, 'Intellectual Bases for Feminist Analyses', p. 35.   [20] *Ibid.*, p. 22.
[21] Lloyd, *The Man of Reason*, p. ix.

incomprehensible to them', and the reason for this is the 'delicacy of the brain fibers', which are best suited to understanding the senses rather than seeking truth.[22] Malebranche believes that women cannot use their imaginations for deciphering 'complex and tangled questions', they are easily distracted, and they are usually only concerned with surface details. He says that 'the style and not the reality of things suffices to occupy their minds to capacity; because insignificant things produce great motions in the delicate fibers of their brains, these things necessarily excite great and vivid feelings in their souls, completely occupying it'.[23] Malebranche generalises that 'there is no Woman that has not some traces in her Brain, and motion in her Spirits, which carry her to something Sensible'.[24] In sum, Malebranche argues that women cannot practise Cartesian method because they can neither avoid the prejudices of their senses nor conduct their thought in a rigorous manner.

Women themselves also promote negative conceptions of female intellectual capabilities. Indeed, they often appeal to this inferiority as an excuse for any perceived deficiencies in their work. In *The Worlds Olio* (1655), Margaret Cavendish writes that the softness of the female brain is the reason why women are not mathematicians or logicians. She says that

Men have great Reason not let us in to their Governments, for there is great difference betwixt the Masculine Brain and the Feminine, the Masculine Strength and the Feminine; For could we choose out of the World two of the ablest Brain and strongest Body of each Sex, there would be great difference in the Understanding and Strength; for Nature hath made Mans Body more able to endure Labour, and Mans Brain more clear to understand and contrive than Womans; and as great a difference there is between them, as there is between the longest and strongest Willow, compared to the strongest an[d] largest Oak.[25]

Here again, men are perceived as capable of attaining clear ideas, while the female intellect is regarded as weak and lacking in rigour. Likewise, Mary Chudleigh (1656–1710), the author of the feminist polemic *The Ladies Defense* (1701), uses both Cartesian and Lockean terminology to criticise women's reasoning skills:

[22] Nicolas Malebranche, *The Search After Truth*, translated by Thomas M. Lennon and Paul J. Olscamp (Cambridge: Cambridge University Press, 1997), pp. 130–1.
[23] *Ibid.*, p. 130.
[24] Quoted in Damaris Masham, *A Discourse Concerning the Love of God* (London: Awnsham and John Churchil, 1696), p. 75.
[25] Margaret Cavendish, *The Worlds Olio. Written By the Right Honorable, the Lady Margaret Newcastle* (London: J. Martin and J. Allestrye, 1655), 'The Preface to the Reader', sig. A4ʳ.

I know most People have false Idea's of Things; they think too superficially to think truly; they find it painful to carry on a Train of Thoughts; with this my own Sex are principally chargeable: We are apt to be misled by Appearances, to be govern'd by Fancy, and the impetuous Sallies of a sprightly Imagination, and we find it too laborious to fix them; we are too easily impos'd on, too credulous, too ready to hearken to every soothing Flatterer, every Pretender to Sincerity.[26]

These common attitudes toward women's intellectual capacity provide some support for Lloyd's claims. The ideals of Cartesian reason (specialised, rigorous thought) are celebrated as ideal character traits for men, whereas the denigrated aspects (the disorderly progression of ideas and an unquestioning reliance on the senses and the imagination) are associated with women and femininity.

In my approach to the paradoxical relationship between recent feminist philosophy and the writings of early modern women, I do not challenge Lloyd's analysis. Instead, there is another way to dispel the tensions. In addition to highlighting each woman's indebtedness to reason and rational method, I examine their metaphysical views – particularly their anti-Cartesian and anti-dualist views, and their representations of the stereotypically 'feminine' categories of matter, nature, and the body.

In assuming that matter, nature, and the body are culturally coded as 'feminine', I follow the practice of modern feminists, such as Lloyd and Bordo.[27] I allow, however, that the cultural and symbolic associations between femaleness and materiality might have been over-exaggerated or simplified. There are, to be sure, a number of metaphorical connections between *maleness* and materiality (in terms of brute strength, lasciviousness, and so on). But I do not delve into these issues here. Regardless of whether one accepts the modern feminist analysis, it cannot be denied that early modern women *themselves* have a much more complex approach to femaleness and materiality. They do not perceive women as purely bodily creatures, and nor do they regard matter and the body as entirely separate from the soul and the spiritual realm in general. If one does support the modern feminist stance, however, then these responses to dualism are further illustrative of a metaphysical outlook that avoids reinforcing male values to the exclusion of women.

Elisabeth of Bohemia is the first woman to express anti-Cartesian sentiments, in her letters to Descartes on the soul–body union. In this

---

[26] Mary Chudleigh, *Essays Upon Several Subjects in Prose and Verse* (1710), in *The Poems and Prose of Mary, Lady Chudleigh*, edited by Margaret J. M. Ezell (New York and Oxford: Oxford University Press, 1993), pp. 348–9.
[27] See Bordo, 'Introduction' to *Feminist Interpretations of René Descartes*, p. 2.

exchange, Elisabeth anticipates many of the concerns of her female successors in England, including the problem of explaining soul–body interaction within a dualist framework. Although the English women philosophers do not form a homogeneous group, their educational backgrounds and intellectual influences are sufficiently similar to produce parallels between their ideas. Their limited access to formal education has significant implications for their writings: without great proficiency in Latin and French, their critiques are usually confined to works written or translated into English. As a consequence, their understanding of Cartesianism often comes from reading other English philosophers, particularly the Cambridge Platonists, who are highly critical of a number of Descartes' doctrines.

The Cambridge Platonists were a group of philosopher–theologians associated with Emmanuel College, and then later Christ's College, at the University of Cambridge in the mid-seventeenth century. The central figures in this group are Ralph Cudworth (1617–88), Henry More (1614–87), John Smith (1618–52), Nathanael Culverwell (*c.* 1618 – *c.* 1651), and Benjamin Whichcote (1609–83). Although there is no single, orthodox 'Cambridge Platonist' position, the Cambridge thinkers share a common theological outlook. In their moral theology, they advocate a liberal 'tolerationist' approach, grounded in both reason and faith. In terms of their metaphysics, they are united in their theological purpose: the Cambridge philosophers tend to accept or dismiss a philosophical viewpoint solely in order to affirm the existence of a providential God, the spiritual world, and immaterial souls. Toward this anti-atheistic end, they are receptive to both ancient and modern writings. The theory of nature espoused by Cudworth and More, for example, draws on Plato, Plotinus, and Aristotle, as well as the views of Descartes and the new mechanical science. Cudworth and More, the most influential members of the group, are extremely suspicious of any philosophy that places a radical divide between spirit and matter. Although they are inspired by Descartes' arguments for God and the immateriality of the soul, they are critical of other aspects of his views, such as his rejection of final causality in nature, the belief that animals have no souls, and his purely mechanistic account of nature.

I show that the women who are influenced by the Cambridge School share this ambivalence toward Cartesian philosophy and its intellectual legacy in their own time, such as Spinozism, Malebranchean occasionalism, and Leibniz's theory of pre-established harmony. In his study of the general English reception of Descartes, Lamprecht points out that his admirers 'carried on intense controversy over his ideas, accepting some, rejecting others, and above all, gradually modifying Descartes' own meaning'.[28] This same pattern of 'accepting some, rejecting others' emerges when one examines women's philosophy of the time. The common 'Cartesian' interpretation of early modern women's writings obscures these anti-Cartesian and anti-dualist themes in their thought. It is far from the case that these female *virtuosi* – Cavendish, Conway, Astell, Masham, and Cockburn – are the devoted, unquestioning disciples of their dualist contemporaries. Like their continental predecessor, Princess Elisabeth, they find inspiration in the new Cartesian conception of reason, but they are also critical of other aspects of Cartesian philosophy – particularly its metaphysical doctrines. For this reason, early modern women often challenge those aspects of Cartesianism now under scrutiny by feminist philosophers in the late twentieth century.

[28] Lamprecht, 'The Role of Descartes in Seventeenth-Century England', 182.

Elisabeth of Bohemia

Recent commentators have raised methodological questions about how women philosophers of the past can be incorporated into the philosophical canon.[1] One common and useful method of inclusion is to show that these women participated in the great intellectual debates of their time, and that they were perceptive critics of their famous male contemporaries. This is the usual approach taken to the philosophical writings of Princess Elisabeth of Bohemia, the friend and correspondent of René Descartes. On the basis of her famous exchange of letters with Descartes (from 1643 to 1649), Elisabeth is celebrated as one of the first writers to raise the problem of mind–body interaction for Cartesian dualism. She is also remembered as the intellectual inspiration behind Descartes' final treatise, *The Passions of the Soul* (1649), a work that developed out of their correspondence. In the preface to another text, Descartes commends Elisabeth for 'the outstanding and incomparable sharpness' of her intellect.[2] He describes her as 'the only person I have so far found who has completely understood all my previously published works'.[3] Today she is one of the best-known early modern women philosophers – despite the fact that she left no systematic philosophical writings of her own, and that her key philosophical contributions are in the form of letters. Other than her correspondence with Descartes, there are only a handful of letters from Elisabeth to other male thinkers, such as Nicolas

---

[1] Here I am thinking of Sarah Hutton, 'Damaris Cudworth, Lady Masham: Between Platonism and Enlightenment', *British Journal for the History of Philosophy* 1:1 (1993), 29–54; Sarah Hutton, 'Like Father Like Daughter? The Moral Philosophy of Damaris Cudworth, Lady Masham', presented at the South Eastern meeting of the American Philosophical Association in Atlanta, 28–30 December 1996; and O'Neill, 'Disappearing Ink', pp. 39–43.

[2] René Descartes, *Principles of Philosophy*, in *The Philosophical Writings of Descartes*, translated by John Cottingham, Robert Stoothoff, and Dugald Murdoch, 3 vols. (Cambridge: Cambridge University Press, 1985–91), vol. 1, p. 192.

[3] *Ibid.*

Malebranche,[4] Gottfried Wilhelm Leibniz,[5] and the Quaker Robert Barclay (1648–90).[6]

Nevertheless, historians of philosophy agree that there is also something limiting about the 'add women and stir' approach to women philosophers of the past. In the case of Elisabeth, this 'assimilation' method has meant that until recently the study of her own philosophical themes remained incomplete. Commentators examined the philosophical import of Elisabeth's objections to Descartes, and acknowledged the impact that her queries had on Descartes' subsequent writings;[7] but their studies did not really proceed beyond the first year of the correspondence. As a consequence, there is the perception that Elisabeth's sole philosophical contribution is a particularly astute re-phrasing of the mind–body problem.

More recently, scholars have started to draw out the implicit arguments, themes, and lines of development in the bulk of Elisabeth's letters.[8] In 'Princess Elizabeth and Descartes: The Union of Soul and Body and

---

[4] Nicolas Malebranche, *Oeuvres complètes de Malebranche*, edited by A. Robinet (Paris: J. Vrin, 1958–84), vols. 18–19. Elisabeth made contact with Malebranche through her sister, Louise, Abbess of Maubisson.

[5] E. J. Aiton, *Leibniz: A Biography* (Bristol: Adam Hilger, 1985), pp. 90–1; and Robert Merrihew Adams, *Leibniz: Determinist, Theist, Idealist* (New York and Oxford: Oxford University Press, 1994), pp. 192–3. Elisabeth met Leibniz at her sister Sophie's court in Hanover in Winter 1678. He wrote to Elisabeth in the same year on the subject of the Cartesian ontological argument for the existence of God. He then visited Elisabeth on her sick bed at the Herford Abbey in 1680.

[6] Colonel D. Barclay, *Reliquiae Barclaianae: Correspondence of Colonel D. Barclay and Robert Barclay of Urie and his son Robert, including Letters from Princess Elisabeth of the Rhine, the Earl of Perth, the Countess of Sutherland, William Penn, George Fox and others* (London: Winter and Bailey, 1870).

[7] Daniel Garber, 'Understanding Interaction: What Descartes Should Have Told Elisabeth', *Southern Journal of Philosophy* 21, Supplement (1983), 15–32; Ruth Mattern, 'Descartes's Correspondence with Elizabeth: Concerning Both the Union and Distinction of Mind and Body', in *Descartes: Critical and Interpretive Essays*, edited by Michael Hooker (Baltimore and London: John Hopkins University Press, 1978); R. C. Richardson, 'The "Scandal" of Cartesian Interactionism', *Mind* 91 (1982), 20–37; and Beatrice H. Zedler, 'The Three Princesses', *Hypatia* 4:1 (1989), 28–63.

[8] Erica Harth, *Cartesian Women: Versions and Subversions of Rational Discourse in the Old Regime* (Ithaca and London: Cornell University Press, 1992), pp. 67–78; Albert A. Johnstone, 'The Bodily Nature of the Self or What Descartes Should have Conceded Princess Elizabeth of Bohemia', in *Giving the Body Its Due*, edited by Maxine Sheets-Johnstone (Albany: State University of New York Press, 1992), pp. 16–47; Andrea Nye, 'Polity and Prudence: The Ethics of Elisabeth, Princess Palatine', in *Hypatia's Daughters: Fifteen Hundred Years of Women Philosophers*, edited by Linda Lopez McAlister (Bloomington and Indianapolis: Indiana University Press, 1996); Andrea Nye, *The Princess and the Philosopher: Letters of Elisabeth of the Palatine to René Descartes* (Lanham: Rowman and Littlefield, 1999); Lisa Shapiro, 'Princess Elizabeth and Descartes: The Union of Soul and Body and the Practice of Philosophy', *British Journal for the History of Philosophy* 7:3 (1999), 503–20; Deborah Tollefsen, 'Princess Elisabeth and the Problem of Mind–Body Interaction', *Hypatia* 14:3 (1999), 59–77; and

the Practice of Philosophy', Lisa Shapiro traces the development of Elisabeth's thought throughout the correspondence, interpreting Elisabeth's letters to Descartes in light of Elisabeth's own independent position on the relationship between the soul and body. Shapiro's point is that Elisabeth takes a unique approach to substances, one that lies somewhere in between dualism and a strict monistic-materialism. Similarly, in her 'Polity and Prudence: The Ethics of Elisabeth, Princess Palatine', Andrea Nye argues that Elisabeth adopts an original *moral* position of her own. Then in her book, *The Princess and the Philosopher*, Nye claims that this moral outlook stems from Elisabeth's 'nondualist metaphysics of thinking body and material mind'.[9] Both writers suggest that Elisabeth's famous objection can be seen as a symptom of her broader dissatisfaction with Descartes' dualist metaphysics.

In this chapter, I examine Elisabeth's criticisms of soul–body dualism in her correspondence with Descartes, also with the aim of highlighting Elisabeth's independent concerns. First, I emphasise that Elisabeth is a Cartesian in terms of her philosophical method and her application of Descartes' criterion of truth and certainty (clear and distinct ideas). In this sense, Elisabeth can be regarded as one of the earliest female disciples of Cartesian reason, and a precursor to feminists in her own time. I further demonstrate that this sympathy for Cartesianism extends to her broader metaphysics, and that many of Elisabeth's suggestions are *not* as anti-dualist, or as incompatible with Cartesian metaphysics, as Shapiro and Nye suggest. Nevertheless, I agree with these writers that women thinkers such as Elisabeth should be regarded as more than mere handmaidens to the great philosophical masters. If we are to examine their philosophical contributions, and see these women as more than surrogate men or 'men in petticoats',[10] we must not lose sight of what is distinctive about *women's* thought. For this reason, I highlight the critical content of Elisabeth's letters, and especially those queries and objections she raises from a woman's point of view. On the basis of these letters, Elisabeth can be regarded as a precursor to modern feminist philosophers who give an equal role to the body and the emotions in their moral and metaphysical

---

Thomas E. Wartenberg, 'Descartes's Mood: The Question of Feminism in the Correspondence with Elisabeth', in Bordo (ed.), *Feminist Interpretations of René Descartes*, pp. 190–212. See also Eileen O'Neill, 'Elisabeth of Bohemia (1618–80)', in *Routledge Encyclopedia of Philosophy*, edited by Edward Craig (London and New York: Routledge, 1998), vol. III, pp. 267–9.

9 Nye, *Princess and the Philosopher*, p. xii.

10 Mary Astell, *The Christian Religion, As Profess'd by a Daughter Of The Church of England. In a Letter to the Right Honourable, T.L. C.I.* (London: R. Wilkin, 1705), p. 293.

writings. She also anticipates many of the metaphysical concerns of later seventeenth-century women philosophers in England.

I

Elisabeth was born at Heidelberg Castle on 26 December 1618, the eldest daughter of Elisabeth Stuart (the only daughter of James I of England), and Frederick V of Palatine, the exiled 'Winter King' of Bohemia. In 1620, Elisabeth's family lost their fortunes and land, and was forced to live in exile in the Netherlands. Elisabeth was educated by Royal tutors at the Prinsenhof in Leiden where her family resided from 1623 to 1641. She also received some of her training from professors at the University of Leiden. Elisabeth had an extremely good education in Latin, logic, and mathematics, and demonstrated such an aptitude for languages that her family nickname was 'La Grecque'. Her youngest sister, Sophie (1630–1714), later the Electress of Hanover, also expressed an interest in philosophy: she was the patron and correspondent of Leibniz, and her daughter, Sophie-Charlotte (1668–1705), was also philosophically minded. In their early life, Elisabeth and Sophie were fortunate to be part of a courtly circle that included several leading intellectuals of the day, such as Constantijn Huygens (1596–1648), Henri Regius (1598–1679), Francis Mercury van Helmont (1614–98), and Descartes. But the Palatine family was also beset with misfortune, and tragedies such as the 1649 beheading of Elisabeth's uncle, King Charles I of England. As a consequence of these family troubles, Elisabeth seems to have suffered from depression – a common theme in her letters to Descartes. She remained single all her life, and once refused an offer of marriage because she would not convert to Catholicism. She was appointed coadjutrix of the Protestant Herford Abbey in 1661, and then abbess in 1667, remaining so until her death on 8 February 1680. In her final years, she offered asylum to members of the persecuted religious sects, the Labadists and the Quakers.

Elisabeth expressed admiration for Descartes' writings shortly after their first meeting at The Hague in about 1642. She visited Descartes at his home in Endegeest near Leiden, and from 1643 they wrote to one another for a period of seven years until Descartes' death in 1650. Claude Clerselier first published Descartes' letters to Elisabeth in 1657, but Elisabeth refused the publication of her letters to Descartes (she also refused to have them shown to Queen Christina of Sweden). In the nineteenth century, her letters were discovered in a library near Arnheim, the Netherlands, and published by Foucher de Careil in 1879. Among the surviving correspondence, there are 26 letters from Elisabeth to Descartes, and 33 from Descartes to Elisabeth. He dedicated his *Principles of Philosophy* to her in 1644, praising her great expertise in both metaphysics and mathematics. He says that 'the outstanding and incomparable sharpness of your intelligence is obvious from the penetrating examination you have made of all the secrets of these sciences, and from the fact that you have acquired an exact knowledge of them in so short a time'.[11] In a letter to Alphonse Pollot, dated 6 October 1642, Descartes says of Elisabeth that 'I attach much more weight to her judgment than to those messieurs the Doctors, who take for a rule of truth the opinions of Aristotle rather than the evidence of reason.'[12]

Although Elisabeth is chiefly remembered as a critic of Descartes, there are in fact strong Cartesian elements in her thinking. Her general approach to philosophy is in stark contrast to that of her scholastic friend, Anna Maria van Schurman (1607–78).[13] The early relationship between these women can be seen as a microcosm of the 'ancient *versus* modern' debate that flourished in the seventeenth century. Elisabeth apparently first met Schurman at the University of Leiden.[14] At the time, Schurman was known as one of the most learned women in seventeenth-century Europe. She was the first woman to study at the University of Utrecht, and the protégé of Descartes' adversary, the Aristotelian philosopher Gisbertus Voetius (1589–1676). Schurman and Elisabeth engaged in a brief correspondence from around 1639, shortly after the publication in Latin of Schurman's *Dissertatio* (1638).[15] In this work, Schurman appeals

---

[11] Descartes, *Principles of Philosophy*, in *Philosophical Writings*, vol. 1, p. 192.

[12] Descartes to Pollot, 6 October 1642; in *Descartes: His Moral Philosophy and Psychology*, translated with an introduction by John J. Blom (New York: New York University Press, 1978), p. 105; and René Descartes, *Oeuvres de Descartes*, edited by Charles Adam and Paul Tannery, new edition (Paris: Librairie Philosophique J. Vrin, 1996), vol. III, p. 577.

[13] On Schurman's feminism and philosophy, see Joyce Irwin, 'Learned Woman of Utrecht: Anna-Maria van Schurman', in *Women Writers of the Seventeenth Century*, edited by Katharina Wilson and Frank Warnke (Athens and London: University of Georgia Press, 1989), pp. 164–85; Caroline van Eck, 'The First Dutch Feminist Tract? Anna Maria van Schurman's Discussion of Women's Aptitude for the Study of Arts and Sciences', and Angela Roothaan, 'Anna Maria van Schurman's "Reformation" of Philosophy', both in *Choosing the Better Part: Anna Maria van Schurman (1607–1678)*, edited by Mirjam de Baar, et al., and translated by Lynne Richards (Dordrecht and London: Kluwer, 1996), pp. 43–54, 103–16; and Eileen O'Neill, 'Schurman, Anna Maria Van (1607–78)', in Craig (ed.), *Routledge Encyclopedia of Philosophy*, vol. VIII, pp. 556–9.

[14] Elizabeth Godfrey, *A Sister of Prince Rupert: Elizabeth Princess Palatine and Abbess of Herford* (London and New York: John Lane, 1909), p. 58.

[15] This work was translated into English as *The Learned Maid or, Whether a Maid may be a Scholar* (1659).

to Aristotelian principles in defence of the view that 'the study of letters is fitting for a Christian woman'. Like Voetius, Schurman follows the path of scholasticism.

Elisabeth, on the other hand, shares Descartes' mistrust of ancient authority and book learning. In one letter to Descartes, Elisabeth emphasises that she does not follow his views 'out of prejudice or indolent imitation', but because his way of reasoning 'is the most natural I have encountered and seems to teach me nothing new, save that I can extract from my mind knowledge I have not yet noticed'.[16] This attitude is distinctively Cartesian in its respect for the self-reliance of the individual, and faith in the natural abilities of the mind to attain truth. In his *Discourse on the Method*, Descartes asserts that all human beings, however dull or slow, possess a natural capacity for reasoning. He emphasises that those individuals who are uneducated in traditional scholastic philosophy are the best fitted for the apprehension of truth, since their minds are the least clouded by prejudices. He claims that anybody can attain knowledge, so long as he or she begins with self-evident ideas in the mind, and proceeds from simple to complex ideas in an orderly, rigorous manner.

Schurman, however, appreciates the value of studying historical texts and the methods of the ancients. In one letter to Elisabeth (7 September 1639), Schurman eulogises 'the livelier way the examples [of Tacitus] strike the senses and the imagination than do the precepts of philosophy'.[17] Elisabeth, on the other hand, believes that human knowledge is limited because 'the greater part use their thought only with reference to the senses': 'Even among those who apply themselves to study, few use anything but their memory, and few take truth as the goal of their labour.'[18] Like Descartes, Elisabeth believes that only the overthrow of preconceived opinions and detachment from the senses can lead to certainty. Perhaps in an effort to convert Elisabeth, in another letter, dated 26 January 1644, Schurman says 'It is true that I have high regard for the Scholastic Doctors':[19]

---

[16] Elisabeth to Descartes, 16 August 1645; in Blom (tr.), *Descartes*, p. 135; and Descartes, *Oeuvres*, vol. IV, p. 269. There is no unabridged edition of the Descartes–Elisabeth correspondence in English. As a rule, I give references to the English translation first, and then to the original language.

[17] Anna Maria van Schurman, *Whether a Christian Woman Should be Educated and Other Writings from Her Intellectual Circle*, edited and translated by Joyce L. Irwin (Chicago and London: The University of Chicago Press, 1998), p. 58.

[18] Elisabeth to Descartes, 28 October 1645; in Blom (tr.), *Descartes*, p. 165; and Descartes, *Oeuvres*, vol. IV, p. 321.

[19] Schurman, *Whether a Christian Woman*, pp. 66–7.

I do not wish to deny that they sometimes go astray through vain and dangerous speculations, which have brought upon them the censure of a number of learned people of our time. Nevertheless that ought not to prejudice either the solidity or the excellence of their ideas, which we are accustomed to admire in their works, when it is a question either of clarifying the secrets of philosophy or of sustaining the highest points of the Christian religion against secular skeptics and atheists. It would be hard to tell whether they have been more ingenious in conjuring up doubts and objections or more adept in resolving them; whether they have been more rash in undertaking lofty and difficult matters or more fortunate and capable in clearing them up... it is not strange that they have arrived at such a high degree of perfection, inasmuch as they have not scorned the legacy of their predecessors or the heritage of all past centuries.[20]

Schurman's remarks are obviously directed against Cartesianism, a philosophy that *does* scorn the legacy of its predecessors. While Descartes' method of doubt is specifically designed to overthrow Aristotelian metaphysics, Schurman criticises those who set 'chaotic muddles of errors' against 'the brilliant light' of Aristotle.[21] Her remarks about 'secular skeptics and atheists' also echo Voetius's claim that Descartes' writings controvert traditional theology.[22] Schurman herself had a difficult personal relationship with Descartes, whom she first met in Utrecht in 1635. Descartes suspected that Schurman was too much under the influence of Voetius;[23] he once referred to her as 'the greatest pedant in the world';[24] and she was apparently insulted by Descartes' remark that reading the Bible in Hebrew was a waste of time. Possibly because of these differences, Elisabeth and Schurman lost touch after their brief correspondence. But in their later years, the two women shared a common interest in religious mysticism, and were reconciled in around 1670, when Elisabeth offered asylum to Schurman and her Labadist friends at the Herford Abbey.

Elisabeth's attitude toward Cartesian reason and the Cartesian approach to philosophy is not unusual for a woman of her time − it is Schurman who is the exception. Descartes' works taught women that a poor formal education need not prevent them from engaging in philosophy: his new method can be practised without an extensive library and a scholastic training; the only prerequisite is one's natural reasoning ability. From 1640 to 1660, this aspect of Cartesian philosophy had a notable impact on the celebrated French 'salons', those informal, female-led

---

[20] *Ibid.*, p. 67.   [21] *Ibid.*
[22] Around this time (1643 to 1644), Voetius publicly accused Descartes of slander.
[23] Descartes to Marin Mersenne, 11 November 1640; in Descartes, *Oeuvres*, vol. VIII, p. 388.
[24] Godfrey, *A Sister of Prince Rupert*, p. 116.

circles of intellectual discussion. In their day, the salon women – including Anne de la Vigne (1634–84), Marie Dupré (dates unknown), and Catherine Descartes (1637–1706), the philosopher's niece – were known as 'Cartésiennes', or followers of Descartes. Today, however, scholars emphasise that the salon women are also highly critical of Descartes' doctrines. In *Cartesian Women*, Erica Harth observes that their admiration of Descartes is always qualified: 'their writings display a critical attitude toward those features of Descartes's philosophy that were to have the greatest impact on the development of modern rational discourse: his dualism, mechanism, and objectivity'.[25] But while they might be critical of 'broad trends of the new rationality', they do not raise specific or detailed philosophical objections to Cartesian metaphysics.[26] Their writings are often in the form of poems, and their criticisms are couched in the language of metaphor, analogy, and allusion.

Elisabeth, on the other hand, raises precise queries from a distinctive philosophical position. In this respect, she is much closer to her English counterparts, Margaret Cavendish, Anne Conway, Mary Astell, Damaris Masham, and Catharine Trotter Cockburn.

II

Elisabeth's letters raise queries about two principal claims in Descartes' *Meditations*: the claim that the soul and body are distinct substances, and the claim that nevertheless the soul and body are 'intermingled' in human beings. In the Sixth Meditation, Descartes argues that we can clearly and distinctly conceive of the unextended soul existing apart from the extended body, and therefore the soul and body are distinct. Nevertheless, he also emphasises that 'I am not merely present in my body as a sailor is present in a ship',[27] but I am closely joined and connected to this body such that I feel pain when it is hurt, thirst when it is dehydrated, and so on. In the Descartes–Elisabeth correspondence, we are reminded that Descartes is also concerned with explaining the nature of the soul–body union in light of their real distinction. In her early

---

[25] Harth, *Cartesian Women*, p. 66. See also Erica Harth, 'Cartesian Women', and Eileen O'Neill, 'Women Cartesians, "Feminine Philosophy", and Historical Exclusion', both in Bordo (ed.), *Feminist Interpretations of René Descartes*, pp. 213–31, and 232–57.

[26] Harth, *Cartesian Women*, p. 66. More recently, Eileen O'Neill argues that these women do not have even a 'critical attitude' toward Cartesian dualism. For her argument, see O'Neill, 'Women Cartesians', pp. 239–45.

[27] Descartes, *Meditations*, in *Philosophical Writings*, vol. II, p. 56.

letters, Elisabeth highlights perceived inadequacies in his explanations of this union.

'I beseech you,' Elisabeth writes to Descartes on 6/16 May 1643, 'tell me how the soul of man (since it is but a thinking substance) can determine the spirits of the body to produce voluntary actions'.[28] How can an essentially thinking thing move or have an impact on an extended substance? If every movement involves an impact between the mover and the moved, then it seems impossible for the mind to have any effect on the body: 'For it seems every determination of movement happens from an impulsion of the thing moved, according to the manner in which it is pushed by that which moves it, or else, depends on the qualification and figure of the superficies of this latter.'[29] Because the soul is neither extended nor capable of contact, it cannot meet the necessary conditions for impact. Elisabeth proposes that a solution might be found in a more precise definition of the soul, 'a definition of the substance separate from its action, thought'.[30] Anticipating Locke, she suggests that it is difficult to show that the 'soul' and 'thought' are always inseparable, especially in the case of 'infants in their mother's womb and deep faints'.[31]

In his first reply of 21 May 1643, Descartes appeals to certain 'primitive notions' that provide the foundations or the 'models' for all our other knowledge.[32] These three notions can be recognised by three different operations of the soul. Our notion of the soul is grasped only by the *pure intellect*, completely devoid of any sensory or imaginative input. The notion of the body as extension, figure, and movement, is understood through the *intellect* and the *imagination*; and those things that pertain to the soul–body union can be known clearly only by the *senses*. 'All human knowledge', Descartes says, 'consists only in carefully distinguishing these notions, and attributing each of them only to the things to which they pertain. For when we wish to explain some difficulty by means of a notion that does not pertain to it, we cannot fail to make a mistake.'[33] Elisabeth, according to Descartes, goes wrong in thinking of soul–body interaction in terms of the second primitive notion, rather than the third. The prejudices of our senses often lead us to think of soul–body interaction along the same lines as body–body interaction because 'the use of

[28] Elisabeth to Descartes, 6/16 May 1643; in Blom (tr.), *Descartes*, p. 106; and Descartes, *Oeuvres*, vol. III, p. 661.
[29] *Ibid.*   [30] *Ibid.*   [31] *Ibid.*
[32] Descartes to Elisabeth, 21 May 1643; in Blom (tr.), *Descartes*, p. 108; and Descartes, *Oeuvres*, vol. III, p. 665.
[33] Descartes to Elisabeth, 21 May 1643; in Blom (tr.), *Descartes*, p. 108; and Descartes, *Oeuvres*, vol. III, pp. 665–6.

the senses has rendered the notions of extension, figures, and movements very much more familiar to us than the others'.[34] People get confused about the soul–body relationship, according to Descartes, because they think of causal interaction on the mechanical model of impact and resistance.

Instead Descartes demonstrates how the soul might move the body, without extension or contact, through the illustrative analogy of gravity. When we think of gravity, he says, we have no difficulty in conceiving how it moves the body or is united to it – even though there is no impact between extended surfaces. When weight or heaviness moves a corporeal being – for example, by pulling it to the ground – this action does not involve touching. Gravity causes the body to move in a non-mechanical way, it is extended or diffused throughout the whole body, and yet it is a quality distinct from the body (capable of being separated from it). In this way, as Ruth Mattern observes, the gravity analogy gives us some way of conceiving how the soul and body are united, and how the soul can have a causal influence on the body, while still allowing that the two substances are distinct.[35]

In her 10/20 June 1643 response, Elisabeth says that Descartes' gravity analogy does not solve the problem of soul–body interaction. Even if the old scholastic conception of gravity were correct, she says, this does not explain *exactly how* an immaterial thing moves a material thing. Four years later, Descartes sent Elisabeth a work by his friend, the Dutch physician Cornelis van Hogelande (1590–1662). In reply, Elisabeth says that she cannot support Hogelande's analogy for the soul–body relationship either. While Descartes uses the gravity analogy to explain the soul's influence on the body (*soul–body* causation), Hogelande attempts to account for the body acting on the soul (*body-soul* causation). He draws on a comparison of 'gross matter' enveloping a more subtle kind of matter by 'fire or fermentation', to explain the fact that the soul is constrained to suffer along with the body. Elisabeth says that this theory still does not solve the difficulty: the 'subtle matter' is corporeal, and is therefore moved in the same way that any material thing is moved – by the pressure of parts on parts.[36]

[34] Descartes to Elisabeth, 21 May 1643; in Blom (tr.), *Descartes*, p. 108; and Descartes, *Oeuvres*, vol. III, p. 666.

[35] Mattern, 'Descartes's Correspondence with Elizabeth', p. 215. While Descartes does not uphold this conception of gravity, Mattern believes that Descartes' gravity analogy is useful because it enables him to maintain that the soul is both distinct from and united with the body.

[36] Elisabeth to Descartes, May 1647; in Nye, *The Princess and the Philosopher*, p. 122; and Descartes, *Oeuvres*, vol. V, p. 48.

The intuition behind Elisabeth's rejection of these two analogies is the same: she adheres to the old scholastic concept of 'causal likeness', or the notion that the cause must be essentially similar to the effect (and vice versa).[37] This notion, that 'like causes like' or that 'like can only be caused by like', has its origin in the intuition that 'something cannot come from nothing'.[38] In challenging Descartes thus, Elisabeth probably believes that Descartes holds this principle himself.[39] For Elisabeth, the problem is that if the unextended mind bears no *essential similarity* to the extended body (as Descartes claims), then it seems impossible for there to be causal interaction between them. Descartes' gravity analogy is unhelpful because Elisabeth can conceive of the immaterial only as 'the negation of matter', and therefore incapable of engaging with the body. Likewise, the Hogelande analogy is unhelpful because the soul–body problem is about explaining how two utterly *dissimilar* entities can interact, not two like substances.

Hence Elisabeth goes from questioning soul–body interaction, to challenging Descartes' dualism. She says that

I admit it would be easier for me to concede matter and extension to the soul, than the capacity of moving a body, and being moved, to an immaterial being. If the soul's moving the body occurred through 'information', the spirits that perform the movement would have to be intelligent, which you accord to nothing corporeal. And although in your metaphysical meditations you show the possibility of the second, it is, however, very difficult to comprehend that a soul, as you have described it, after having had the faculty and habit of reasoning well, can lose all of it on account of some vapors, and that, although it can subsist without the body and has nothing in common with it, is yet so ruled by it.[40]

Elisabeth's point about the vapours is regarded as crucial for understanding the development of her own independent position on the soul–body relationship.[41] Two years later, the 'vapours' re-emerge in Elisabeth's

---

37 On the causal likeness principle, see Richard Watson, *The Breakdown of Cartesian Metaphysics* (Atlantic Highlands, NJ: Humanities Press International, 1987), especially pp. 50–2; Lois Frankel, 'The Value of Harmony', in *Causation in Early Modern Philosophy: Cartesianism, Occasionalism and Preestablished Harmony*, edited by Steven Nadler (University Park, Pennsylvania: Pennsylvania State University Press, 1993), pp. 197–216; and Eileen O'Neill, 'Mind–Body Interaction and Metaphysical Consistency: A Defence of Descartes', *Journal of the History of Philosophy* 25 (1987), 227–45.

38 Watson, *Breakdown of Cartesian Metaphysics*, pp. 50–1.

39 A few modern commentators maintain that Descartes does in fact hold the causal likeness principle. But recently this view has been challenged by O'Neill, 'Mind–Body Interaction'.

40 Elisabeth to Descartes, 10/20 June 1643; in Blom (tr.), *Descartes*, p. 112; and Descartes, *Oeuvres*, vol. III, p. 685.

41 Shapiro 'Princess Elizabeth and Descartes', 505.

rejection of Descartes' neo-Stoic advice about overcoming depression. In the seventeenth century, the vapours were a medical condition where 'exhalations' in the stomach or spleen were supposed to rise up into the brain and produce a mental imbalance. More generally, the vapours are a 'depression of spirits, hypochondria, hysteria, or other nervous disorder' (*OED*). Those who are afflicted 'struggle, cry out, make odd and inarticulate Sounds or Mutterings, they perceive a Swimming in their Heads, a Dimness come over their Eyes, they turn Pale, are scarce able to stand, their Pulse is weak, they shut their Eyes, cry, shriek out, groan, foam at the mouth, and remain senseless for some time'.[42] In the First Meditation, Descartes speaks of madmen whose brains 'are so damaged by the persistent vapours of melancholia that they firmly maintain that they are kings when they are paupers'.[43]

The vapours are also a typically *female* ailment. In the literature of the time, they are known as 'Fits of the Mother', or 'Hysterick fits'.[44] The condition was once connected with the phenomenon of the 'wandering womb',[45] a theory that derives from the ancient Platonic view that the uterus has the power of self-movement. This 'wandering' was meant to explain why women were prone to be hysterical (the word 'hysteria' has its origin in the Greek word for uterus).[46] Although the theory was in decline in the seventeenth century,[47] and *men* were also thought to suffer from the vapours, stereotypical associations between women and the vapours persisted. Margaret Cavendish, in her *Grounds of Natural Philosophy* (1668), writes that 'those Diseases that are named the *Fits of the Muther*, the *Spleen*, the *Scurvy*' are common 'especially amongst the Females'.[48] Then in 1728, in an ironic verse on sexual temperament, Edward Young writes that 'Sometimes, thro' pride, the Sexes change their airs, My lord *has vapours*, and my lady *swears*.'[49]

---

[42] Anonymous, *An Account of the causes of some particular rebellious distempers: viz. the scurvey, cancers in women's breasts, &c. vapours, and melancholy, &c. weaknesses in women, &c. . . . by an eminent practitioner in physick, surgery and chymistry* (London: 1670), p. 34.

[43] Descartes, *Meditations*, in *Philosophical Writings*, vol. II, p. 13.

[44] Anonymous, *Account of the causes*, p. 33.   [45] *Ibid.*, p. 34.

[46] On this topic and the ancient Aristotelian–Galenic theory of women's temperament, see Londa Schiebinger, *The Mind Has No Sex? Women in the Origins of Modern Science* (Cambridge, Mass.: Harvard University Press, 1989), pp. 160–88; and Merry E. Wiesner, *Women and Gender in Early Modern Europe* (Cambridge: Cambridge University Press, 1993), pp. 26–7.

[47] See John P. Wright, 'Hysteria and Mechanical Man', *Journal of the History of Ideas* 42 (1980), 233–47.

[48] Margaret Cavendish, *Grounds of Natural Philosophy: Divided into Thirteen Parts: With an Appendix containing Five Parts*, with an introduction by Colette V. Michael, facsimile reprint of 1668 edition (West Cornwall, CT: Locust Hill Press, 1996), p. 151.

[49] Edward Young, 'Satire III' in *Love of Fame, The Universal Passion. In Seven Characteristical Satires*, third edition (London: J. Jonson, 1730), p. 51.

In her 10/20 June 1643 letter, Elisabeth points out that the vapours prevent the soul from engaging in *purely intellectual thought*. She highlights the fact that when the soul and body intermingle, this is not just a disinterested exercise on the part of the soul: the soul can be so affected by the body that the soul radically changes its character – it can become *incapable* of pure intellection. This phenomenon is seemingly difficult to square with Descartes' real distinction between the unextended soul and the extended body. Why *is* the soul so enslaved by the body, when it could subsist separately and 'has nothing in common with it'?

Here, at first glance, Elisabeth appears to challenge what Margaret Wilson calls Descartes' 'robust' form of dualism, according to which there are no corporeal correlates of the operations of the pure intellect.[50] For the robust dualist, the understanding can operate independently of the brain, and the brain 'cannot in anyway be employed in pure understanding, but only in imagining or perceiving by the senses'.[51] Presumably, if this type of dualism is plausible, then we ought to be able to detach ourselves from the senses and the imagination, even when we are hysterical or deluded; yet we cannot. Hence some scholars interpret Elisabeth as tentatively suggesting that the intellect is *contingent*, or *somehow depends upon*, the body. Lisa Shapiro notes that, throughout her letters, Elisabeth 'defends neither a reductionist materialism nor a substance dualism, but rather wants to find a way of respecting the autonomy of thought without denying that *this faculty of reason is in some essential way dependent on our bodily condition*'.[52] Shapiro interprets Elisabeth as saying that 'in order to be autonomous...the mind depends upon the good health of the body'.[53]

It is not obvious, however, that this 'dependence' that Elisabeth identifies between the intellect and body is incompatible with, or 'an alternative to', Descartes' own conception of the soul–body relationship. Here we must distinguish between different senses of the word 'dependence'.[54] On the one hand, there might be a *metaphysical* dependence between the soul and body, such that the existence of the pure intellect *absolutely requires* the existence of the body; and the soul could not exist unless the body does.[55] On the other hand, there might be a *causal* dependence,

[50] On Descartes' 'robust dualism', see Margaret Dauler Wilson, *Descartes* (London and New York: Routledge, 1993), p. 181.
[51] Descartes, 'Fifth Set of Replies', in *Philosophical Writings*, vol. 11, p. 248.
[52] Shapiro, 'Princess Elizabeth and Descartes', 505; my italics.   [53] *Ibid.*, 516.
[54] I am indebted to Rae Langton for raising this point about 'dependence'.
[55] On the distinction between metaphysical and causal dependence, see John Heil, *Philosophy of Mind: A Contemporary Introduction* (London and New York: Routledge, 1998), p. 42.

where in order to have clear and distinct ideas, the soul depends upon the proper functioning of the body. But in the second case, my clear and distinct ideas do not depend *for their existence* on something distinct from me; I could still have them even if I had no body at all. Elisabeth, I believe, points to a causal dependence between the soul and body, rather than a metaphysical one. In that case, her remarks are entirely consistent with Descartes' own view in the *Meditations* that the soul is susceptible to the causal influence of the body. 'If this were not so,' he says, 'I, who am nothing but a thinking thing, would not feel pain when the body was hurt, but would perceive the damage purely by the intellect, just as a sailor perceives by sight if anything is broken in his ship.'[56] But the soul's being susceptible to bodily distempers is very different to being 'in some *essential* way dependent on the body'.

In keeping with this interpretation, Descartes regards Elisabeth's comments as perfectly compatible with the soul–body distinction. In his reply to Elisabeth, dated 28 June 1643, he suggests that Elisabeth go ahead and attribute matter and extension to the soul, 'for that is nothing but to conceive it united to the body'.[57] When affected by the vapours, the soul is incapable of pure intellection. But this does not show that the soul is incapable of attaining pure understanding *full stop*; only that when the soul is so affected by the body, it is difficult to have access to the intellect.

Nevertheless, Elisabeth *does* diverge from Descartes in expanding on her suggestion that 'it is easier' to ascribe extension and materiality to the soul. In her third letter, dated 1 July 1643, Elisabeth points out that we can doubt the 'inextension' of the soul according to Descartes' own rule about truth and falsity in the Fourth Meditation: 'namely that all our errors occur from forming judgments about what we do not sufficiently perceive'.[58] Descartes believes that errors arise when my intellect has a confused rather than *clear and distinct idea* about something, and my will jumps to a hasty conclusion about it. But if 'I simply refrain from making a judgement in cases where I do not perceive the truth with sufficient clarity and distinctness, then it is clear that I am behaving correctly and avoiding error.'[59] Elisabeth points out that by the light

---

[56] Descartes, *Meditations*, in *Philosophical Writings*, vol. 11, p. 56.
[57] Descartes to Elisabeth, 28 June 1643; in Blom (tr.), *Descartes*, p. 115; and Descartes, *Oeuvres*, vol. 111, p. 694.
[58] Elisabeth to Descartes, 1 July 1643; in Blom (tr.), *Descartes*, p. 117; and Descartes, *Oeuvres*, vol. IV, p. 2.
[59] Descartes, *Meditations*, in *Philosophical Writings*, vol. 11, p. 41.

of this theory, and the difficulty in explaining how two utterly distinct entities can interact, Descartes ought to have refrained from affirming that the soul is unextended. He should have allowed that there might be certain 'unknown properties' in the soul. Elisabeth says that 'Although extension is not necessary to thought, yet not being contradictory to it, it will be able to belong to some other function of the soul.'[60] She accepts that the soul could exist without the body. But for her, that does not imply that extension is contrary to, or incompatible with, thought; it is possible that extension is a property of the soul.

In this respect, Elisabeth anticipates the views of the English Platonist, Henry More. Elisabeth later developed an interest in More's writings through her associate, Francis Mercury van Helmont, son of the chemist and physician Jan Baptiste.[61] Some time between 1644 and 1648, van Helmont the younger entered the circle surrounding the Palatine family, and became particularly close to Elisabeth and Sophie. He was instrumental in helping Elisabeth to become the abbess at Herford, and went to England in 1670 on her behalf, to petition the English government for a promised pension. During this visit, van Helmont brought commendations to Henry More from Elisabeth.[62] Earlier, in a letter to Descartes, More writes that 'the first moment I read your works, I at once decided in my own mind that your illustrious disciple, the Princess Elizabeth, must – in order to have entered so perfectly into the comprehension of your philosophy – be infinitely wiser than all the sages and philosophers of Europe put together'.[63] In 1671, More's friend Anne Conway sent Elisabeth a copy of his most anti-Cartesian work, *Enchiridion Metaphysicum* (1671).[64]

---

[60] Elisabeth to Descartes, 1 July 1643; in Blom (tr.), *Descartes*, p. 117; and Descartes, *Oeuvres*, vol. IV, p. 2.

[61] For details on Francis Mercury van Helmont, one of the most widely travelled and best-known characters of the seventeenth century, see Allison P. Coudert, *The Impact of the Kabbalah in the Seventeenth Century: The Life and Thought of Francis Mercury van Helmont (1614–1698)* (Leiden: Brill, 1999).

[62] Henry More to William Penn, 22 May 1675; in William Penn, *The Papers of William Penn*, edited by Mary and Richard Dunn (Philadelphia: University of Pennsylvania Press, 1981), vol. 1, p. 323. Elisabeth shared a correspondence with More's close friend, Anne Conway in the 1670s. Their exchange was probably initiated (or mediated) by van Helmont, who was physician to both Conway and Elisabeth. Elisabeth discusses Conway's conversion to Quakerism with her English correspondent, Robert Barclay.

[63] Quoted in Marie Blaze de Bury, *Memoirs of the Princess Palatine, Princess of Bohemia* (London: Richard Bentley, 1853), p. 202.

[64] Marjorie Hope Nicolson, *The Conway Letters: The Correspondence of Anne, Viscountess Conway, Henry More and Their Friends, 1642–1684*, revised with an introduction and new material, edited by Sarah Hutton (Oxford: Clarendon Press, 1992), p. 337.

In his correspondence with Descartes (from 1648 to 1649), More – like Elisabeth – suggests that extension is a property of both material and spiritual substances. The notion of extended spirits, according to More, provides a better explanation of how God acts on the created world, and of how souls influence bodies (and vice versa). This notion also has greater religious merit than the concept of unextended souls; to affirm that souls and spirits are *nowhere* is dangerously close to atheism. In the *Immortality of the Soul* (1659), More claims that 'it is plain that if a thing be at all it must be extended' because 'to take away all Extension is to reduce a thing onely to a Mathematical point, which is nothing else but pure Negation or Non-entity'.[65] For More, the distinction between spirit and matter is that spirit is essentially active, indivisible (or 'indiscerpible') and penetrable, whereas matter is passive, divisible and impenetrable.[66] Despite rejecting the Cartesian viewpoint, More is still very much a dualist.

Likewise, despite her claim that the soul is extended, it is not obvious that Elisabeth advocates a completely *non-dualist* philosophy, in which the soul is dependent on the body for its existence. Her later objections to the philosophy of another Englishman, Kenelm Digby (1603–65), confirm this picture. In 1645, Elisabeth read Digby's book on the immortality of the soul: *Two Treatises: in the one of which, the nature of bodies, in the other, the nature of mans soule is looked into, in way of discovery of the immortality of reasonable souls* (1644).[67] In a letter to Descartes on 28 October 1645, Elisabeth challenges Digby's claim that the soul is 'tormented' by passions after the body's death. She believes that the soul will be much happier following its separation from the body, given that the body is the cause of all human suffering. Digby, on the other hand, believes that the passions 'leave some traces in the soul', even after the soul and body are separated. In purgatory, the soul is tortured by vestiges of repressed passions, and frustrated by its inability to satisfy them. These views, according to Elisabeth, are inconsistent with the soul's *immateriality*. If the immortal soul is a purely incorporeal substance, completely disconnected from the body, then the body cannot continue to exert its confusing influence.

---

[65] Henry More, *The Immortality of the Soul; So farre forth as it is demonstrable from the Knowledge of Nature and the Light of Reason*, facsimile reprint of 1659 edition (Bristol: Thoemmes Press, 1997), 'The Preface', sig. a5ᵛ.

[66] To complicate matters further, More holds that matter is made up of parts 'indiscerpible', or 'of particles that have indeed real extension but so little, that they cannot have less and be anything at all, and therefore cannot actually be divided' (*Ibid.*, 'The Preface', sig. a4ᵛ)

[67] As befitting the granddaughter of James I of England, Elisabeth was proficient in both written and spoken English.

Once the self is no longer part of the soul–body hybrid, presumably it is capable of overcoming the passions and attaining a *purely* intellectual state.

Most of Elisabeth's suggestions, then, are consistent with the basic tenets of Cartesian dualism, especially the notion that the soul is capable of existing in separation from the body. But for Elisabeth, to explain how the two substances interact, we cannot rule out the possibility that the soul has certain affinities with the body, such as extension. According to her, this view is more plausible, because if the soul is an essentially unextended, thinking thing, then soul–body interaction is unintelligible; but it is absurd to suggest that the soul and body do not interact. In this sense, at least, Shapiro is right to regard Elisabeth as offering a distinctive alternative to Cartesian dualism. This alternative, moreover (or something approaching it), is one that later women philosophers in England, such as Cavendish and Conway, would regard as a first step toward a monistic theory of substance.

III

Descartes' response to Elisabeth's suggestion about extended souls is now lost. The subject of soul–body relations is not raised in their letters again until two years later, in the context of a discussion on Elisabeth's depression and Seneca's *De Vita Beata* ('The Happy Life'). One of Elisabeth's early objections to Cartesian dualism hinges on the striking and disturbing effects that bodily distempers have on clear thought in the soul. The feminine significance of 'the vapours' is confirmed in a 24 May 1645 letter from Elisabeth to Descartes.

In this letter, Elisabeth confesses that she herself suffers from the vagaries of her sexual temperament. 'Know then,' she says, 'that I have a body filled with a great many of the weaknesses of my sex; it very easily feels the afflictions of the soul and does not have the force to bring itself into harmony with the soul.'[68] The natural condition of her female body, and a general lack of exercise, according to Elisabeth, mean that 'it is not necessary for sadness to oppress the heart for a long time before the spleen becomes obstructed and infects the rest of the body by its vapors'.[69]

---

[68] Elisabeth to Descartes, 24 May 1645; in Blom (tr.), *Descartes*, p. 121; and Descartes, *Oeuvres*, vol. IV, p. 208.
[69] *Ibid.*

In his response, dated May/June 1645, Descartes suggests a remedy for Elisabeth's malady: diverting one's imagination and senses from subjects of displeasure, and using the understanding alone (more accurately, the intellect *and* the will) to focus on subjects of contentment and joy. In the seventeenth century, the imagination was believed to play a vital causal role in cases of hysteria.[70] In keeping with this, Descartes tells Elisabeth that the imagination and the senses tend to make us melancholy; they occupy the mind with objects of sadness and pity; they 'accustom [the] heart to contract and send out sighs; and in a consequence of this, the circulation of the blood being retarded and slowed, and the largest parts of the blood attaching themselves to one another, they would easily obstruct [the] spleen'.[71] Descartes ignores Elisabeth's claim that her body 'does not have the force to bring itself into harmony with the soul'. He prescribes detachment from the senses and the imagination, in favour of the pure understanding.

Descartes' advice on this topic is in direct contrast to that of Malebranche, who says that the 'delicacy of the brain fibers' make women best suited to understanding the senses rather than seeking truth.[72] Malebranche believes that women are incapable of overcoming their sexual temperament, and pursuing clear and distinct ideas. Descartes' attitude is more faithfully represented in the feminist views of François Poulain de la Barre (1647–1723), the author of *De l'Égalité des Deux Sexes* (1673). Poulain de la Barre recommends to women that 'there is nothing more proper to depress the Vapours' than the learning of true knowledge.[73] He points out that 'what temperament soever *Women* have, they are no less capable than we, of truth and studies';[74] they *are* capable of overcoming their bodily distempers and attaining knowledge.[75] Descartes accords with this viewpoint; but Elisabeth, surprisingly, has difficulty in accepting it.

[70] Wright, 'Hysteria and Mechanical Man', 244.
[71] Descartes to Elisabeth, May/June 1645; in Blom (tr.), *Descartes*, p. 124; and Descartes, *Oeuvres*, vol. IV, p. 219.
[72] Malebranche, *The Search After Truth*, pp. 130–1.
[73] François Poulain de la Barre, *The Woman as Good as the Man; Or, the Equality of Both Sexes*, edited with an introduction by Gerald M. MacLean (Detroit: Wayne State University Press, 1988), p. 117.
[74] *Ibid.*, p. 137.
[75] In a twist on this theme, in 1660 the courtier Samuel Sorbière tells Elisabeth that women are well suited to the search for truth because 'the softness of their constitution . . . is much more suitable to the actions of the mind than the dryness and hardness of ours' (quoted in Schiebinger, *The Mind Has No Sex?*, p. 167).

According to Elisabeth, there is something obstinate about the body that makes it impervious to the influence of the soul, and vice versa. In reply to Descartes (22 June 1645), Elisabeth says that 'I find difficulty in separating from my senses and imagination the topics continually represented there by the conversation and the letters I could not avoid without sinning against my obligations.'[76] She says that 'there is something that overtakes one in the passions', such that one is incapable of thinking clearly till the passions have subsided.[77] Instead, the friendship expressed in his letters is a far better 'antidote to melancholy'.[78]

The same themes are elaborated in Descartes and Elisabeth's letters on Seneca's *De Vita Beata*. Descartes recommends this work in the hope that it will provide Elisabeth with a further means of attaining happiness. But he is disappointed with Seneca's lack of philosophical rigour, and decides to modify the Stoic viewpoint with his own precepts.[79] In his 'modernising' of Seneca (4 August 1645), Descartes suggests that beatitude or 'the happy life' can be attained by (i) using the intellect to determine what it is best to do; (ii) overcoming the passions by regulating the will according to reason; and (iii) ridding oneself of insatiable desires and pointless regrets. For Descartes, the happy life is ideally one of detachment from those functions of the soul associated with the soul–body composite, rather than the soul alone. He admits that there are pleasures that depend upon the body, but true and lasting contentment comes from the mind alone.

In response (16 August 1645), Elisabeth doubts that Descartes' precepts are a practical means for attaining the happy life. This is because 'there are maladies that completely deprive one of the power of reasoning, and consequently of enjoying a reasonable satisfaction; others diminish the force of reasoning and prevent one from following those maxims that good sense would institute'.[80] Here, as in her earlier letters on soul–body interaction, Elisabeth's point is that bodily indispositions can 'render the most moderate man subject to allowing himself to be

---

[76] Elisabeth to Descartes, 22 June 1645; in Blom (tr.), *Descartes*, p. 127; and Descartes, *Oeuvres*, vol. IV, p. 233.
[77] Elisabeth to Descartes, 22 June 1645; in Blom (tr.), *Descartes*, p. 127; and Descartes, *Oeuvres*, vol. IV, p. 234.
[78] *Ibid.*
[79] For a recent analysis of Descartes' account of the passions, see Susan James, *Passion and Action: The Emotions in Seventeenth-Century Philosophy* (Oxford: Clarendon Press, 1997).
[80] Elisabeth to Descartes, 16 August 1645; in Blom (tr.), *Descartes*, p. 135; and Descartes, *Oeuvres*, vol. IV, p. 269.

carried away by his passions'.[81] The will alone cannot help such a man achieve happiness: attaining the blessed life also depends upon the body and its fortunes. In the context of a discussion on the soul–body relationship, Elisabeth's point about the vapours does not constitute a formidable objection to Descartes' philosophy. But in the context of a discussion on moral theory, or 'how we should live', she offers a much stronger criticism.

For Elisabeth, the body cannot be ignored when discussing the conduct of *human beings*. To live amongst others, she suggests (30 September 1645), we must follow the dictates of the society in which we live, unreasonable though they might be.[82] She also says (28 October 1645) that avoiding repentance for our faults, and suppressing the emotions, are not viable methods for achieving a balance between our own interests and those of others. Instead, it is much wiser to learn from our faults, and to be aware of our emotions, so that we can improve the moral character accordingly. This 'moral balancing', as Nye calls it, is an ongoing project throughout life, developed through trial and experience, not just by exercising one's reason.[83] In moral dilemmas in everyday life, prompt decisions must be made based on relationships between yourself and others; this, in turn, requires an honest perspective on yourself as an embodied, social creature – *a substantial union of both soul and body*. While disassociation from the senses and the imagination is necessary for attaining clear and certain knowledge, it is just not practical in our lives with others.

Elisabeth's views on the happy life are, moreover, consistent with Descartes' threefold theory of the 'primitive notions'. Two years earlier, Descartes tells Elisabeth that the way in which we understand the soul–body union is very different to the way in which we understand things that involve the soul and the body taken in isolation. He says that one learns to conceive of the soul–body union, not through the intellect, but 'by availing oneself only of life and ordinary conversations, and by abstaining from meditating and studying things that exercise the imagination'.[84] In his neo-Stoic advice on how to live in accordance with one's human nature, Descartes ought to have advised Elisabeth, as he did before, to look to common sense.

[81] *Ibid.*
[82] For this exegesis on Elisabeth's 'ethics of polity', I am indebted to Nye, 'Polity and Prudence', pp. 81–7. Elisabeth's moral views are also explored in Wartenberg, 'Descartes's Mood'; and Johnstone, 'The Bodily Nature of the Self'.
[83] Nye, 'Polity and Prudence', p. 84.
[84] Descartes to Elisabeth, 28 June 1643; in Blom (tr.), *Descartes*, pp. 113–4; and Descartes, *Oeuvres*, vol. III, p. 692.

Queen Christina of Sweden (1626–89) also criticises the neo-Stoic viewpoint in her *Maxims* (*c*. 1670–80). Christina was first introduced to Descartes as someone with 'a disposition marvellously detached from servitude toward popular opinions'.[85] Elisabeth says of Christina that she is pleased to have an idea that 'acquits our sex of the imputation of imbecility and weakness pressed on it by Messieurs the pedants'.[86] Most famous for her association with Descartes (he moved to Sweden in 1650 at her invitation, and died there soon afterwards), Christina was never in fact a Cartesian.[87] In her youth, Christina was trained in the Stoic writings of Tacitus, Epictetus, and Seneca; and in her later years, she seems to have held a Stoic conception of the soul and body. In 1647, Christina corresponded with Descartes (*via* Hector-Pierre Chanut) on the subject of the passions and the sovereign good. But like Elisabeth, she regards the neo-Stoic moral approach as inapplicable in everyday life. One of Christina's maxims is that 'The passions are the salt of life; which without them would be insipid. That undisturbable tranquillity, so much boasted by philosophers, is dull and insipid; it is a fine chimera.'[88] With the same realism, she says 'Passions are only triumphed over when they are weak.'[89]

Descartes' neo-Stoicism seems to be particularly unpalatable for women thinkers. On the one hand, Descartes' rational philosophy is extremely liberating for women. If we can all reason clearly by training ourselves to overcome the confusing influence of the body, then women can also participate in the search for truth; if they learn to follow their reason, they can also endeavour to attain the blessed life. But, at the same time, prevalent social attitudes about 'the weakness of the female sex', and the natural temperament of the female body, impose certain limitations on the philosophical enterprise for women. These attitudes are reflected in Elisabeth's remarks about the clouding and distorting effects that the body has on clear thought. A plausible and practical

---

[85] Chanut to Descartes, 1 December 1646; in Blom (tr.), *Descartes*, p. 200; Descartes, *Oeuvres*, vol. IV, p. 582.

[86] Elisabeth to Descartes, 4 December 1649; in Nye, *Princess and the Philosopher*, p. 167; Descartes, *Oeuvres*, vol. V, pp. 451–2.

[87] See O'Neill, 'Women Cartesians', pp. 235–6.

[88] Christina, Queen of Sweden, *The Works of Christina Queen of Sweden. Containing Maxims and Sentences, In Twelve Centuries; and Reflections on the Life and Actions of Alexander the Great* (London: Wilson and Durham, 1753), p. 35. On Christina's philosophy, see Susanna Åkerman, *Queen Christina of Sweden and Her Circle: The Transformation of a Seventeenth-Century Philosophical Libertine* (Leiden: E. J. Brill); and Susanna Åkerman, 'Kristina Wasa, Queen of Sweden', in *A History of Women Philosophers*, edited by Mary Ellen Waithe (Dordrecht: Kluwer Academic Publishers, 1991), vol. III, pp. 21–40.

[89] Christina, *The Works of Christina*, p. 39.

philosophy, she suggests, whether it be a method of thought or a way of attaining happiness, must take into account the soul–body union, or *human embodiment*, and not just the soul taken separately.

Recent feminist theorists, most notably Carol Gilligan, also stress the usefulness of a 'different' moral outlook, one that is based primarily on relationships with others, rather than an impartial and detached viewpoint. Gilligan's empirical research suggests that this moral orientation is distinctive of women's reasoning in moral situations.[90] They take a contextualist approach that recognises the needs of others, and the individual's responsibility to meet those needs. Their focus is not on isolated individuals, but on *relations between individuals*, governed by care and concern. In constructing a moral outlook that emphasises human embodiment, Elisabeth's ideas both reflect and anticipate such modern-day theories.

Princess Elisabeth is remembered as one of Descartes' favourite students, and as someone whose criticisms prompted him to give serious and considered responses. She is a faithful disciple to Descartes to the extent that she embraces his egalitarian concept of reason, and extols the virtues of a natural logic, free from the shackles of a scholastic education. She also embraces his criterion of truth and certainty, and is a dualist to the extent that she affirms that the soul and body are distinct. But in other respects, her reputation as a critic of Descartes is well deserved. First, Elisabeth maintains that interaction between extended and non-extended substances is inconceivable, and, as a solution to this problem, she suggests that extension is an attribute of the soul. Second, in her discussion of Descartes' moral theory in their letters, she emphasises the impracticality of recommending that the soul must strive to be detached from the body. Many of Elisabeth's objections are, moreover, developed from a woman's point of view. The vapours, a stereotypical female complaint, figure in one of her earliest objections to Cartesian dualism, and also provide the basis for her later rejection of Descartes' neo-Stoic advice. Today's feminist theorists share Elisabeth's concerns about the soul–body dichotomy, and the practicality of a moral outlook based on impartiality and detachment. I now show that Elisabeth's English female contemporaries also raise these concerns in their critiques of dualism.

---

[90] Carol Gilligan, *In A Different Voice: Psychological Theory and Women's Development* (Cambridge, Mass.: Harvard University Press, 1982).

2

Margaret Cavendish

Margaret Cavendish, the Duchess of Newcastle, was one of the most prolific and outspoken female philosophers of the early modern period. While Elisabeth's philosophy is confined to her correspondence, Cavendish published no less than six philosophical treatises in defence of her own distinctive form of monistic materialism.[1] In these lengthy works, Cavendish deliberately and self-consciously defines her position alongside those of the leading philosophers of her day. Like Elisabeth, Cavendish is inspired by the rise of the new 'egalitarian' style of philosophy in seventeenth-century Europe; she is a champion of reason above the senses in natural philosophy; and she too addresses the problem of how two entirely distinct substances, the soul and the body, can causally interact. But unlike Elisabeth, Cavendish's mature philosophy was conceived in England in the 1660s, a period of growing mistrust and opposition to Cartesianism – particularly from the Cambridge Platonists, who, after an initial period of acceptance, were rather dissatisfied with the 'atheistic' overtones of Cartesian mechanism.

In this chapter, I examine Cavendish's responses to three key philosophical figures of her time: Descartes,[2] Thomas Hobbes, and Henry More. Recent scholars emphasise that Cavendish has many views in common with Hobbes.[3] Like the materialist philosopher, Cavendish

---

[1] These are *Poems, and Fancies* (1653; second edition, 1664; third edition, 1668), *Philosophical Fancies* (1653), *The Philosophical and Physical Opinions* (1655; second edition, 1663), *Philosophical Letters* (1664), *Observations Upon Experimental Philosophy* (1666; second edition, 1668), and a much-revised edition of the *Opinions* titled *Grounds of Natural Philosophy* (1668).

[2] Cavendish is the only English woman who met Descartes in person – but it seems that she did not form a very favourable opinion. In her *Philosophical and Physical Opinions*, she says that 'I never spake to monsieur *De Cartes* in my life, nor ever understood what he said, for he spake no English, and I understand no other language, and those times I saw him, which was twice at dinner with my Lord at *Paris*, he did appear to me a man of the fewest words I ever heard' (Cavendish, *Philosophical and Physical Opinions*, 'An Epilogue to My Philosophical Opinions', sig. B3ᵛ).

[3] Anna Battigelli, 'Political Thought/Political Action: Margaret Cavendish's Hobbesian Dilemma', in *Women Writers and the Early Modern British Political Tradition*, edited by Hilda L. Smith (Cambridge:

believes that the only substance in the created world is matter; she rejects Cartesian dualism on the grounds that the idea of immaterial substance is inconceivable; and she supports Hobbes's separation of theology and philosophy. But here I emphasise that Cavendish's position is also shaped in response to the Cambridge Platonists, and especially Henry More. In the 1660s, Cavendish actively courted the attention of this circle of thinkers. She dedicated prefaces to 'The Most Famous University of Cambridge'; she sent lavishly bound copies of her books to More and the university libraries; and from around 1666–7, Cavendish engaged in a correspondence with Joseph Glanvill (1636–80), an admirer of the Cambridge circle and a fellow of the Royal Society.[4] Glanvill once told Cavendish that she had 'convinced the World, by a great instance, that Women may be Philosophers, and, to a Degree fit for the Ambitious emulation of the most improved Masculine Spirits'.[5] Yet Cavendish has an ambivalent attitude to the theories of the Cambridge men. In so far as Cavendish supports materialism, her position radically differs from the Cambridge school; but where she diverges from Hobbes, Cavendish holds a surprising number of the Platonist's views. Like the Cambridge men, Cavendish explicitly rejects Hobbes's mechanistic conception of nature, and she defends the view that animals have the capacity for sense and reason. She also employs a method of argument that is distinctive of Henry More's explanatory approach to the natural world. Cavendish takes More's method to its logical extreme, to develop a full-bodied monist theory in which the entire natural world possesses intelligence, and the soul is material and extended.

I

Cavendish was born in 1623 as Margaret Lucas, the youngest daughter of Sir Thomas Lucas, a wealthy gentleman of Colchester. Her father died when Margaret was only an infant, and she and her siblings were brought up by their mother Elizabeth. Margaret was given a typical female

Cambridge University Press, 1998), pp. 40–55; and Sarah Hutton, 'In Dialogue with Thomas Hobbes: Margaret Cavendish's Natural Philosophy', *Women's Writing* 4:3 (1997), 421–32.

[4] Glanvill's letters to Cavendish are in *A Collection of Letters And Poems: Written by several Persons of Honour and Learning, Upon divers Important subjects, to the Late Duke and Dutchess of Newcastle* (London: Langly Curtis, 1678). In their correspondence, Glanvill and Cavendish discuss a number of issues that Cavendish brings up in her published works: the origins of the immaterial soul, the existence of witches, the Platonist doctrine of plastic nature, and questions concerning God's role in his creation.

[5] Glanvill to Cavendish, 22 April 16 – [?]; in Cavendish, *Collection of Letters And Poems*, p. 136.

education in singing, dancing, music, reading, and writing. She was given no tuition in the learned languages, and nor did she receive any formal education in philosophy or science. But in 1643 she became a maid of honour to Queen Henrietta Maria, and followed her into exile in 1644. In Paris, Margaret met William Cavendish (later the Duke of Newcastle), whom she married in 1645 following a brief courtship. The couple remained abroad in exile for fifteen years, returning to England upon the Restoration in 1660.[6] Thirty years her senior, the Duke (1593–1676) introduced his young wife to a circle of intellectuals that has been described as an 'unofficial "university"' of the mechanical philosophy' in Paris.[7] The members of this group, known as the 'Cavendish' or 'Newcastle Circle', included the Duke's brother, Charles Cavendish, as well as Thomas Hobbes, Kenelm Digby, and Walter Charleton. At one stage the network also extended to Descartes, Pierre Gassendi (1592–1655), and Marin Mersenne (1588–1648). It has been claimed that the Newcastle Circle was responsible for the re-introduction of atomic philosophy into England in the mid-seventeenth century.[8] They promulgated the view that all natural phenomena can be explained by the action of atoms in motion, and they adapted the mechanistic explanations of Gassendi toward this end.[9]

Shortly after her marriage, Margaret Cavendish became an active and enthusiastic participant in this group, and eventually developed her own ideas on natural philosophy. In a preface to *The Philosophical and Physical Opinions* (1655), she says that just as some women go from house to house for dancing, dining, and gossip, she would accompany her husband and 'dance a measure with the muses, feast with the Sciences, or

---

[6] Margaret Cavendish did spend an extended period in England with her brother-in-law Charles, from 1651 to 1654, in an attempt to raise money for her husband. For biographical details on Cavendish see George Ballard, *Memoirs of Several Ladies of Great Britain (who have been celebrated for their writings or skill in the learned languages, arts and sciences)*, with an introduction by Ruth Perry (Detroit: Wayne State University Press, 1985), pp. 277–82, 415, 455–7; Douglas Grant, *Margaret the First: A Biography of Margaret Cavendish, Duchess of Newcastle 1623–1675* (London: Rupert Hart-Davis, 1957; Toronto: University of Toronto Press, 1957); Kathleen Jones, *A Glorious Fame: The Life of Margaret, Duchess of Newcastle, 1623–1673* (London: Bloomsbury, 1990); and H. Ten Eyck Perry, *The First Duchess of Newcastle and her Husband As Figures in Literary History* (Boston and London: Ginn and Company, 1918).

[7] Robert Hugh Kargon, *Atomism in England from Hariot to Newton* (Oxford: Clarendon Press, 1966), p. 68.

[8] *Ibid.*, pp. 63–76.

[9] More recently, however, Stephen Clucas argues that Pierre Gassendi was not the principal influence on the Cavendish circle as a whole, and that there is a persuasive case 'for an independent English atomistic milieu' (see Clucas, 'The Atomism of the Cavendish Circle: A Reappraisal', *The Seventeenth Century* 9:2 (1994), 256).

sit and discourse with the arts'.[10] Cavendish was not the first woman to take an interest in the Newcastle Circle. Elisabeth of Bohemia was acquainted with the scientific innovations of Charles Cavendish, a frequent visitor to her home; and in her letters to Descartes, Elisabeth comments on Kenelm Digby's views about the immortality of the soul. Queen Christina of Sweden was also interested in the Epicureanism of Gassendi, a key influence on the Newcastle Circle;[11] and Anna Maria van Schurman communicated with both Gassendi and Mersenne. It is possible that the reputations of these women boosted Margaret Cavendish's confidence as a philosopher, and legitimised her intellectual endeavours. By 1668, Cavendish had published thirteen original works ranging in style from philosophy and biography to poetry and drama.

Upon her return to England, Cavendish's reputation for eccentricity made her something of a celebrity. Her visit to London in 1667 aroused so much interest that crowds thronged the streets to catch a glimpse of her carriage; and her admission to a session of the Royal Society in May that year was the talk of the town.[12] But the contemporary judgements made on her intellect are stark reminders of seventeenth-century prejudices about women thinkers – the general consensus was that she was 'mad'. Upon meeting her, Mary Evelyn remarked that Cavendish's conversation was as whimsical and rambling 'as her books'.[13] Dorothy Osborne wrote that there were 'many soberer People in Bedlam';[14] Samuel Pepys said that she was mad, conceited, and ridiculous; and Katherine Jones, Lady Ranelagh, claimed that 'she [e]scapes Bedlam onely by being too rich to be sent theather'.[15] In this century, Cavendish's

---

[10] Cavendish, *Philosophical and Physical Opinions*, 'To the Reader', sig. A4[r].
[11] Åkerman *Queen Christina*, pp. 73–4.
[12] Cavendish was the first woman to be invited to a meeting of the Royal Society. For details, see Samuel Pepys, *The Diary of Samuel Pepys*, edited by Robert Latham and William Matthews (London: Bell, 1974), vol. IX; and Samuel Mintz, 'The Duchess of Newcastle's Visit to the Royal Society', *The Journal of English and Germanic Philology* 51 (1952), 168–76.
[13] Mary Evelyn to Ralph Bohun, April 1667; in the British Library, London, the 'Evelyn Papers' (uncatalogued). I am grateful to Dr Frances Harris in the MSS Department for referring me to these letters and those of Katherine Jones (below).
[14] Dorothy Osborne to William Temple, 8 May 1653; in Dorothy Osborne, *Letters to Sir William Temple* (Harmondsworth: Penguin, 1987), p. 79.
[15] Katherine Jones, Lady Ranelagh, to Richard Boyle, 13 April 1667; in the British Library, Althorp B4 (item 30):

and to shew y[u] w[t] things we are most taken up wth I assure y[u] y[e] Dutchess of NewCastle is more discoursed of y[n] y[e] Treatie, and by al y[e] Caracters I heare given her I am resolved she scapes Bedlam onely by being too rich to be sent theather. but she is madd enough to convay y[t] title to y[e] place of her Residence, whose boldnes and profannes is allowed to pass for wit because soe many others can put in noe other claymes to y[t] qualety y[n] those very same. (*Ibid*.)

works have received more critical attention than any other woman's writings of the early modern period.[16] But belief in her irrationality still persists. Joseph Knight in the *Dictionary of National Biography* writes that 'Her philosophy is the dead weight which drags her to the ground. In these deliveries an occasional piece of common sense is buried in avalanches of ignorance and extravagance.'[17] Virginia Woolf remarks that 'order, continuity, the logical development of her argument are all unknown to her';[18] Sylvia Bowerbank says that 'her writing is muddled and indecisive';[19] and Carolyn Merchant claims that her theories are 'often inconsistent, contradictory, and eclectic'.[20]

It must be acknowledged that these criticisms have some justification. Cavendish presents her ideas in a non-systematic, repetitive, and tortuous style; and she often simply asserts her views, rather than articulating

Katherine Jones, the sister of Robert Boyle, was also a woman of science, and her house a meeting place for the London intellectual community of the 1640s. Being an experimental philosopher herself, Jones may not have looked favourably on Cavendish's critique of the new science in her *Observations*. See Lynette Hunter, 'Sisters of the Royal Society: The Circle of Katherine Jones, Lady Ranelagh', in *Women, Science and Medicine 1500–1700*, edited by Lynette Hunter and Sarah Hutton (Stroud: Sutton, 1997), pp. 178–97.

[16] For discussions on Cavendish's philosophy, see Battigelli, 'Political Thought/Political Action'; Sophia B. Blaydes, 'Nature is a Woman: The Duchess of Newcastle and Seventeenth Century Philosophy', in *Man, God, and Nature in the Enlightenment*, edited by Donald C. Mell, Theodore E. D. Braun and Lucia M. Palmer (East Lansing, MI: Colleagues Press, 1988), pp. 51–64; Sylvia Bowerbank, 'The Spider's Delight: Margaret Cavendish and the "Female" Imagination', *English Literary Renaissance* 14 (1984), 392–408; Clucas, 'The Atomism of the Cavendish Circle', pp. 247–73; Stephen Clucas, 'The Duchess and Viscountess: Negotiations between Mechanism and Vitalism in the Natural Philosophies of Margaret Cavendish and Anne Conway', *In-Between: Essays and Studies in Literary Criticism* 9:1 (2000), 125–36; Gallagher, 'Embracing the Absolute', 24–39; Sarah Hutton, 'Anne Conway, Margaret Cavendish and Seventeenth-Century Scientific Thought', in Hunter and Hutton (eds.), *Women, Science and Medicine*, pp. 218–34; Hutton, 'In Dialogue with Thomas Hobbes'; Susan James, 'The Philosophical Innovations of Margaret Cavendish', *British Journal for the History of Philosophy* 7:2 (1999), 219–44; Kargon, *Atomism in England*, pp. 73–6; Eve Keller, 'Producing Petty Gods: Margaret Cavendish's Critique of Experimental Science', *English Literary History* 64 (1997), 447–71; Rebecca Merrens, 'A Nature of "Infinite Sense and Reason": Margaret Cavendish's Natural Philosophy and the "Noise" of a Feminized Nature', *Women's Studies* 25 (1996), 421–38; Eileen O'Neill, 'Cavendish, Margaret Lucas (1623–73)', in Craig (ed.), *Routledge Encyclopedia of Philosophy*, vol. 1, pp. 260–4; John Rogers, *The Matter of Revolution: Science, Poetry and Politics in the Age of Milton* (Ithaca and London: Cornell University Press, 1996), pp. 177–211; Lisa T. Sarasohn, 'A Science Turned Upside Down: Feminism and the Natural Philosophy of Margaret Cavendish', *Huntington Library Quarterly* 47 (1984), 289–307; Londa Schiebinger, 'Margaret Cavendish', in Waithe (ed.), *A History of Women Philosophers*, vol. III, pp. 1–20; Smith, *Reason's Disciples*, chapter 3; and Jay Stevenson, 'The Mechanist–Vitalist Soul of Margaret Cavendish', *Studies in English Literature* 36 (1996), 527–43.

[17] Joseph Knight, 'Cavendish, Margaret', in *The Dictionary of National Biography*, edited by Leslie Stephen and Sidney Lee (Oxford: Oxford University Press, 1917–), vol. III, p. 1266.

[18] Virginia Woolf, *The Common Reader* (London: Hogarth Press, 1968), p. 103.

[19] Bowerbank, 'The Spider's Delight', 406.

[20] Carolyn Merchant, *The Death of Nature: Women, Ecology and the Scientific Revolution* (San Francisco: Harper and Row Publishers, 1980), p. 270.

her reasons for holding them. Nevertheless, to be fair to Cavendish, her philosophy must be understood in light of its gradual development and in the context of seventeenth-century debate surrounding soul–body dualism and the new mechanical science. Viewed from this perspective, Cavendish's thought can be seen as a rational contribution to the philosophical enterprise of her time.

II

First, Cavendish is undoubtedly inspired by the 'popular Cartesianism' that took hold on the English mind in the mid to late-seventeenth century, a Cartesianism characterised by opposition to ancient authority, and an emphasis on the thinking self as the source of knowledge.[21] The shunning of tradition, and the emphasis on 'starting anew', inspires Cavendish to develop her own highly original and radical hypotheses. Like Elisabeth of Bohemia, Cavendish says that her own natural rationality is 'a better tutor than education'.[22] She claims her theories 'did meerly issue from the Fountain of my own Brain, without any other help or assistance'.[23] This highly individualist approach is also promoted by Hobbes, a regular visitor to the Cavendish household in Paris. Cavendish seems to be influenced by Hobbes's claim that true science depends on reason and rational deduction rather than sensory experience.[24] In 'The Preface' to *Observations Upon Experimental Philosophy* (1666), she expresses a mistrust of sensory experience, saying that 'sense deludes more than it gives true Information... Wherefore Regular Reason is the best guide to all Arts'.[25] She also says that 'the best judg is Reason, and the best study is Rational Contemplation joyned with the observations of regular sense, but not deluding Arts';[26] and in her correspondence with Joseph Glanvill,

---

[21] Nicolson, 'The Early Stage of Cartesianism', 369, 372.
[22] Cavendish, *Philosophical and Physical Opinions*, 'To the Reader', sig. B2ʳ.
[23] Margaret Cavendish, *Philosophical Letters: Or, Modest Reflections Upon some Opinions in Natural Philosophy, Maintained By several Famous and Learned Authors of this Age, Expressed by way of Letters: By the Thrice Noble, Illustrious, and Excellent Princess, The Lady Marchioness of Newcastle* (London: privately published, 1664), p. 3.
[24] On this topic, see Hutton, 'In Dialogue with Thomas Hobbes', 424; and Battigelli, 'Political Thought/Political Action', p. 44.
[25] Margaret Cavendish, *Observations Upon Experimental Philosophy. To which is added, The Description of A New Blazing World. Written By the Thrice Noble, Illustrious, and Excellent Princesse, The Duchess of Newcastle* (London: A. Maxwell, 1666), sig. d1ʳ.
[26] *Ibid.*, p. 12. Cavendish's preference for reason over the senses also informs her critique of the experimental method of Robert Boyle, Henry Power, and Robert Hooke. In her 'Further Observations upon Experimental Philosophy', she scorns the microscopists for trusting 'more to the deceiving sights of their eyes, and deluding glasses, then to the perception of clear and regular Reason' (*ibid.*, p. 4).

she objects to his setting 'the perfection of the sense higher than that of Ratiocination'.[27] Cavendish is, however, non-dogmatic and open-minded about this approach: 'I love Reason so well,' she says, 'that whosoever can bring most rational and probable arguments, shall have my vote, although against my own opinion.'[28]

Cavendish's reverence for reason is also evident in her occasional feminist remarks. In *Poems, and Fancies* (1653), she appeals to all 'Writing Ladies' to 'show our selves a degree above Beasts; and not eate, and drink, and sleep away our time as they doe; and live only to the sense, not to the reason'.[29] In the *Philosophical and Physical Opinions*, she calls on the universities of Cambridge and Oxford to encourage her sex, 'lest in time we should grow irrational as idiots, by the dejectedness of our spirits, through the carelesse neglects, and despisements of the masculine sex to the effeminate'.[30] She challenges those who think 'it impossible we should have either learning or understanding, wit or judgement, as if we had not rational souls as well as men'.[31] She regrets that women adopt the same negative view, and are led to 'quit all Industry towards profitable knowledge' and engage in 'lowe and pettie imployments'.[32] She believes that by neglecting their intellectual capacities women 'are become like worms that onely live in the dull earth of ignorance',

for we are kept like birds in cages, to hop up and down in our houses, not sufferd to fly abroad to see the several changes of fortune, and the various humors, ordained and created by nature; thus wanting the experiences of nature, we must needs want the understanding and knowledge and so consequently prudence, and invention of men.[33]

Women are intellectually deficient not because they are without reason or a rational soul, but because they are prevented from improving their natural reasoning abilities. 'Our counsels are despised, and laught at, the best of our actions are troden down with scorn, by the over-weaning conceit men have of themselves and through a dispisement of us.'[34]

At first glance, Cavendish's uncritical acceptance of reason places her at odds with recent feminist philosophers who believe that the Cartesian conception of rationality has negative implications for women. Genevieve Lloyd identifies a distinction between two types of reason

---

[27] Glanvill to Cavendish, [undated]; in Cavendish, *Collection of Letters And Poems*, p. 99.
[28] Cavendish, *Philosophical Letters*, 'A Preface to the Reader', sigs. B1^{r-v}.
[29] Margaret Cavendish, *Poems, and Fancies: Written By the Right Honourable, The Lady Newcastle*, facsimile reprint of 1653 edition (Menston: Scolar Press, 1972), sig. A a1^{v}.
[30] Cavendish, *Philosophical and Physical Opinions*, 'To the Two Universities', sig. B2^{r}.
[31] *Ibid.*   [32] *Ibid.*   [33] *Ibid.*   [34] *Ibid.*

in Cartesianism: the untrained reason that relies on the senses, subsequently associated with femininity; and a highly abstract, specialised
kind of thought, aligned with masculinity.[35] In eschewing the senses,
Cavendish appears to support the 'masculine' side of the dichotomy.
Nevertheless, Lloyd also argues that Descartes' concept of reason must
be seen in the context of his *dualism*. She believes that in Cartesian method
there is an association between untrained reason and the body. A true
philosopher, according to Descartes, must avoid immersion in the senses;
clear and distinct thought can be attained only by distancing the soul
from the material body. In Cavendish's writings, however, we are shown
that a reverence for rationality need not imply an acceptance of dualism.
Cavendish explicitly rejects Cartesian dualism by using the very 'natural
reason' Descartes so revered. The reasons for this rejection can be traced
to the materialist influences on her thought.

The first obvious influence is the natural philosophy of the Newcastle
Circle. Robert Kargon believes that, as part of this group, Cavendish
played 'an interesting role in the establishment of atomism in England
which has been largely overlooked'.[36] In her first published work, the
Poems, and Fancies, she maintains that the world is composed of atoms and
that all change in nature can be attributed to the motion of differently
shaped atoms. In one poem, 'A World Made by Atomes', she says that
these atoms 'by chance, may a New *World* create'.[37] They bring about
changes through forced impulsion: by cutting and piercing, taking hold
and pulling, or by beating each other. This philosophy contains one
key feature of Cavendish's later philosophy – the view that the natural
world is entirely composed of matter in motion, without any dependence
upon God or spiritual substances. But Cavendish explicitly renounces her
atomistic views a few years later in her *Philosophical and Physical Opinions*,
a revised version of the *Philosophical Fancies* (1653).

In a prefatory piece titled 'A Condemning Treatise of Atomes',
Cavendish says that she cannot believe that there is no solidity in the
world except the solidity made up of atoms; and nor can she believe that
there is 'no change or variety, but as they move, onely by fleeing about
as dust and ashes, that are blown about with winde, which me thinks
should make such uncertainties, such disproportioned figures, and confused creations, as there would be an infinite and eternal disorder'.[38]
Such 'wandering and confused figures' could never produce those 'rare

35 Lloyd, *The Man of Reason*.   36 Kargon, *Atomism in England*, p. 73.
37 Cavendish, *Poems, and Fancies*, pp. 5–6.
38 Cavendish, *Philosophical and Physical Opinions*,' A Condemning Treatise of Atomes'.

compositions' that we see in nature; they cannot account for nature's constancy, or the exact rules and laws that govern the natural world; and nor can they explain why there is evidence of life and intelligence in nature. Moreover, if nature were really made up of 'dull and immoving' atoms, she says, then it is difficult to see how material things can move. Atoms must be 'of a living substance, that is innate matter, otherwise they could not move'.[39]

Stephen Clucas claims that Cavendish's later works espouse a form of neo-atomism, 'in which the basic premises of atomism are augmented and enhanced'.[40] But the neo-atomistic label seems inappropriate when rather than expand on her former views Cavendish is at pains to deny or condemn them.[41] Cavendish presents further arguments against atomism in *The Philosophical and Physical Opinions* (1663), the *Philosophical Letters* (1664),[42] her *Observations Upon Experimental Philosophy* (1666, with a second edition in 1668), and a revised edition of the *Opinions*, titled the *Grounds of Natural Philosophy* (1668). In the *Observations*, Cavendish says that colours are not made by 'dusty Atomes, flying about as Flies in Sun-shine'. For if this were true, 'all colours, and other Creatures would be composed or made by chance, rather then by reason, and chance being so ignorantly inconstant, not any two parts would be of the like colour, nor any kind or species would be preserved'.[43] From this, it is clear that Cavendish rejects atomism because it fails to provide a satisfactory explanation for the appearance of order and harmony in the natural world. Susan James suggests that this teleological approach against atomism may be indebted to More's *Antidote Against Atheism* (1653).[44] It might also be the case that Cavendish adopts this method of argument independently of More, and then later develops it in light of her reading of the *Antidote* and More's *Immortality of the Soul* (1659). In any case, the attempt to explain the

---

[39] *Ibid.*   [40] Clucas, 'The Atomism of the Cavendish Circle', 249, 259–64.
[41] Eileen O'Neill argues that there is more reason to think that Cavendish's mature philosophy is consciously developed in opposition to atomism, in O'Neill's paper 'Philosophical Ambition: The System of Nature in Margaret Cavendish's Corpus', presented at the 'Seventeenth-Century Women Philosophers' conference at the University of Massachusetts, Amherst, November 1997.
[42] In this work, Cavendish argues against the atomistic views of her colleague Walter Charleton (see *Philosophical Letters*, p. 455). It is not surprising that Charleton wrote to Cavendish (7 May 1667), saying of her natural philosophy that 'I have not yet been so happy, as to discover much therein that is *Apodictical*, or wherein I think my self much obliged to acquiesce' (Cavendish, *Collection of Letters And Poems*, p. 111).
[43] Cavendish, *Observations*, 'Observations upon Experimental Philosophy', pp. 63–4. See also 'Observations upon Experimental Philosophy', pp. 135, 141–2, 209; and 'Observations upon the Opinions of Some Ancient Philosophers', p. 16.
[44] James, 'The Innovations of Margaret Cavendish', 222–3.

order and regularity of nature is a persistent theme in both Cavendish and More's writings.

In the *Philosophical Letters: Or, Modest Reflections Upon some Opinions in Natural Philosophy* (1664), teleological reasoning re-emerges in Cavendish's arguments against soul–body dualism and mechanism. Cavendish's letters are addressed to an anonymous female correspondent who has requested the duchess's opinions about Descartes, Hobbes, More, and the chemist Jan Baptiste van Helmont. In the process of rejecting their views, Cavendish spells out her own beliefs. The soul and body are not two distinct substances, she says, but both are made from the same matter, which is infinite throughout the universe in bulk and quantity. We can distinguish – in theory, at least – between three different kinds of matter: rational, sensitive, and inanimate. The rational and sensitive kinds are animated and self-moving; they constitute 'the life and knowledg of nature'. The inanimate or 'grosser part of matter', on the other hand, is incapable of moving itself. The sensitive can be distinguished from the rational in that the sensitive alone acts on the inanimate part of nature, helping it to move, while rational matter remains 'subtil and pure'. This materialism has affinities with the Stoic theory of blending.[45] Every particular creature, Cavendish says, contains a thorough *intermixture* of the three different kinds of matter: 'all matter is partly animate, and partly inanimate, and all matter is moving and moved, and there is no part of Nature that hath not life and knowledg, for there is no Part that has not a comixture of animate and inanimate matter'.[46] Every human being, animal, vegetable, and mineral is endued with 'Life and Soul, Sense and Reason'. Although created things are 'discerned from each other by their several Figures', every particular body is still made of the same material substance.[47]

A vitalist–materialist philosophy, according to Cavendish, avoids explanatory problems associated with soul–body dualism. Like Elisabeth, Cavendish says that she cannot understand how an immaterial substance can make an imprint upon a material substance, 'for Printing is a corporeal action, and belongs onely to bodies'.[48] Nor can she imagine how an immaterial substance, being without body, can have an impact on 'gross, heavy, dull, and dead matter'.[49] 'I ask you,' Cavendish says, 'how a bodiless motion can have force and strength to carve and cut?'[50]

---

[45] On this topic, see Eileen O'Neill's 'Introduction' to Margaret Cavendish, *Observations upon Experimental Philosophy*, edited by O'Neill (Cambridge: Cambridge University Press, 2001), pp. x–xxxvi. This modern edition of Cavendish's work has only recently come to my attention.
[46] Cavendish, *Philosophical Letters*, pp. 98–9.   [47] *Ibid.*, p. 7.   [48] *Ibid.*, p. 330.
[49] *Ibid.*, p. 196.   [50] *Ibid.*, p. 77.   [51] *Ibid.*, p. 197.

Appealing to the principle of causal similarity, she claims: 'I cannot conceive how a Spirit should fill up a place or space, having no body, nor how it can have the effects of a body, being none itself; for the effects flow from the cause; and as the cause is, so are its effects.'[51] She also rejects the 'transfer' model of causation, which she sees as part and parcel of the mechanist picture.[52] Transference is the process whereby the cause gives or imparts something of itself to the effect. The immaterial soul cannot act by transference, Cavendish says, because 'being individable, [it] cannot be diminished nor increased in its substance or Nature'.[53] As a consequence, Cavendish believes that soul–body interaction does not make sense within a dualist framework.

These views lead Cavendish to challenge Descartes' 'pineal gland' theory. In *The Passions of the Soul*, a work that developed out of his correspondence with Elisabeth, Descartes says that the soul is conjoined with the entire body, but that there is a particular bodily part in which the soul exercises its functions more specifically.[54] This is the pineal gland, located in the innermost part of the brain. Here the soul has its principal seat, a place from where 'it radiates through the rest of the body by means of the animal spirits, the nerves, and even the blood, which can take on the impressions of the spirits and carry them through the arteries to all the limbs'.[55] When I wish to kick my leg, my volition is so intimately united with this gland that my desire causes it to send the animal spirits to my leg-muscles, which then cause movement. The problem with Descartes' pineal gland 'solution' is that it still fails to provide an intelligible account of soul–body interaction. By positing a physical location for soul–body interaction, he does not solve the basic metaphysical problem. If it is impossible for an unextended thing to influence an extended thing, then it must be equally impossible for the soul to influence the pineal gland. Hence, in the *Philosophical Letters*, Cavendish rejects the idea that

the Mind's or Soul's seat should be in the *Glandula* or kernel of the Brain, and there sit like a Spider in a Cobweb, to whom the least motion of the Cobweb gives intelligence of a Flye, which he is ready to assault, and that the Brain should get intelligence by the animal spirits as his servants, which run to and fro like Ants to inform it.[56]

In the *Observations*, Cavendish says that this theory is absurd because it is inconceivable that unintelligent sensitive spirits 'can inform the mind

---

[52] On Cavendish and the transfer model, see O'Neill, 'Cavendish, Margaret Lucas (1623–73)', p. 261.

[53] Cavendish, *Philosophical Letters*, p. 330.

[54] Descartes, *The Passions of the Soul*, in *Philosophical Writings*, vol. 1, p. 340.   [55] *Ibid.*, p. 341.

[56] Cavendish, *Philosophical Letters*, p. 111.

of what they do not know themselves'; if they have no knowledge, then they are incapable of imparting information.[57]

Cavendish overcomes the soul–body problem by making the soul and body sufficiently similar to allow them to interact. In Cavendish's theory, all substances are alike to the extent that they have some degree of sense and reason. Against Descartes, Cavendish denies that the soul is a distinct entity that can be separated from the body and subsist without it. What Descartes calls the soul, she says, is really only rational and sensitive matter: that is, 'the purest and subtilest parts of Nature, as the active parts, the knowing, understanding and prudent parts, the designing, architectonical and working parts'.[58] For Cavendish, there is no specific 'seat' of the rational such as the pineal gland: every particle of matter has sense and reason. 'I do not absolutely confine the sensitive perception to the Organs,' she says, 'nor the rational to the Brain, but as they are both in the whole body, so they may work in the whole body according to their own motions.'[59] Furthermore, the soul can never be separated from inanimate matter, since it is 'a part of one and the same matter the inanimate is of…onely it is the self-moving part'.[60] She writes that although 'there is but one Soul in infinite Nature, yet that soul being dividable into parts, every part is a soul in every single creature, were the parts no bigger in quantity then an atome'.[61]

III

Cavendish's arguments against dualism are partly indebted to the natural philosophy of Thomas Hobbes – especially his arguments against the conceivability of incorporeal or immaterial substances.[62] Hobbes was a tutor in the Devonshire branch of the Cavendish family from 1608 onwards. During his exile in Paris from 1640–51, he occasionally dined with Margaret and William Cavendish at their salon. The period of Hobbes's exile was one of the most intellectually productive times of his career,[63] and the time in which he wrote *Leviathan, or The Matter, Forme, & Power of a Common-wealth Ecclesiasticall and Civill* (1651). In France, Hobbes found a sympathetic audience for his new ideas, something he did not

---

[57] Cavendish, *Observations*, 'Observations upon Experimental Philosophy', p. 183.
[58] Cavendish, *Philosophical Letters*, 'Preface', sig. b2ᵛ.
[59] *Ibid.*, p. 19.   [60] *Ibid.*, p. 111.   [61] *Ibid.*, p. 433.
[62] For a full discussion of the similarities between Cavendish and Hobbes, see Hutton, 'In Dialogue with Thomas Hobbes', 421–32.
[63] See Quentin Skinner, 'Thomas Hobbes and his Disciples in France and England', *Comparative Studies in Society and History* 8 (1965), 153–67.

receive in England following the publication of his book.[64] Although
Cavendish says that she never discussed philosophy with Hobbes, she
reports overhearing his conversations with her husband about subjects
in *Leviathan*.[65] In this work, Hobbes claims that the joining together of
contradictory names, such as 'round quadrangle' or 'incorporeal body',
produce unintelligible and senseless terms. He believes that the words
'incorporeal substance' are equally meaningless.[66] No one can conceive
of incorporeal substances through natural cogitation; 'though men may
put together words of contradictory signification, as *Spirit*, and *Incorporeall*;
yet they can never have the imagination of any thing answering to
them'.[67] For Hobbes, the terms signify nothing. Similarly, according
to Cavendish, it is impossible to conceive of immaterial substance. We
cannot have an idea of anything that is beyond our own finite, natural intellects; yet the supernatural, immaterial soul is, by definition,
a thing that surpasses our natural understanding. As such, she says, it
is a meaningless concept, like 'so many Hobgoblins to fright Children
withal'.[68] On the other hand, it is possible to conceive of a material
soul:

As for the Natural Soul, humane sense and reason may perceive, that it consists
of Matter, as being Material; but as for the Divine Soul, being not material,
no humane sense and reason is able naturally to conceive it; for there cannot
possibly be so much as an Idea of a natural nothing, or an immaterial being,
neither can sense and reason naturally conceive the Creation of an Immaterial
Substance; . . . The truth is, what is Immaterial, belongs not to a Natural knowledg or understanding, but is Supernatural, and goes beyond a natural reach or
capacity.[69]

The terms 'immaterial soul', according to Cavendish, are purely
metaphorical.

For Hobbes, the rejection of incorporeal substances also goes hand
in hand with the exclusion of theological concerns from philosophy. He
says that

The *subject* of Philosophy, or the matter it treats of, is every body of which we
can conceive any generation, and which we may, by any consideration thereof,

---

[64] On the critical response to *Leviathan*, see Samuel I. Mintz, *The Hunting of Leviathan: Seventeenth
Century Reactions to the Materialism and Moral Philosophy of Thomas Hobbes* (Cambridge: Cambridge
University Press, 1970).
[65] Margaret Cavendish, *The Life of the Thrice Noble, High and Puissant Prince William Cavendishe* (London:
A. Maxwell, 1667), p. 144.
[66] Thomas Hobbes, *Leviathan, Or The Matter, Forme, and Power of a Common-wealth Ecclesiasticall and
Civil*, reprint from the 1651 edition (Oxford: Clarendon Press, 1929), p. 30.
[67] *Ibid.*, p. 84.   [68] Cavendish, *Philosophical Letters*, p. 187.   [69] *Ibid.*, pp. 230–1.

compare with other bodies, or which is capable of composition and resolution; that is to say, every body of whose generation or properties we can have any knowledge . . . Therefore it excludes *Theology*, I mean the doctrine of God, eternal, ingenerable, incomprehensible, and in whom there is nothing neither to divide nor compound, nor any generation to be conceived.[70]

The philosophical study of God's nature is pointless because 'the nature of God is incomprehensible; that is to say, we understand nothing of *what he is*, only *that he is*'.[71] Cavendish also emphasises God's incomprehensibility: 'Gods attributes,' she says, 'are not Communicable to any Creature.'[72] On this topic, she accords with Hobbes's view that 'the knowledge of what is infinite can never be attained by a finite inquirer'.[73] We cannot know the essence of God, according to Cavendish, because we have only a finite knowledge, whereas God's attributes are infinite; and 'how can there be a finite idea of an Infinite God'?[74] She agrees that the subject matter of philosophy should be kept apart from theological concerns. 'Faith and Reason,' she says, 'are two contrary things, and cannot consist together'.[75] She still holds the orthodox religious view that there are immaterial spirits and divine souls, but she does so through faith, not reason. Her arguments refer to divine matters only

in those places, where I am forced by the Authors Arguments to reflect upon it, which yet shall be rather with an expression of my ignorance, then a positive declaration of my opinion or judgment thereof; for I think it not onely an absurdity, but an injury to the holy Profession of Divinity to draw her into the Proofs in *Natural Philosophy*.[76]

Like Hobbes, Cavendish shuns any appeal to God as an explanation for natural occurrences.[77]

Nevertheless, Cavendish is also extremely critical of Hobbes's mechanical model of causation, according to which 'there is no cause of motion in any body, except it be contiguous and moved'.[78] Cavendish offers

[70] Thomas Hobbes, *Elements of Philosophy. The First Section, Concerning Body*, in *The English Works of Thomas Hobbes of Malmesbury*, edited by William Molesworth, reprint of 1839 edition, 11 vols. (London: Scientia Aalen, 1962), vol. 1, p. 10.
[71] Hobbes, *Leviathan*, p. 304.   [72] Cavendish, *Philosophical Letters*, p. 14.
[73] Hobbes, *Elements of Philosophy*, p. 411.
[74] Cavendish, *Philosophical Letters*, p. 139.   [75] *Ibid.*, p. 210.   [76] *Ibid.*, p. 3.
[77] In Cavendish's later works, there are exceptions to this rule. In the *Observations*, Cavendish uses God's attributes as an explanatory principle, arguing that there cannot be a vacuum, because God is the 'fulness and perfection of all things', and he would not allow a 'pure Nothing' to exist (Cavendish, *Observations*, 'Observations upon Experimental Philosophy', p. 57). Cavendish also appeals to God's attributes in her arguments against ancient philosophers in the same work.
[78] Hobbes, *Elements of Philosophy*, p. 125.

three main reasons for denying the mechanical view that the pressure of parts upon parts causes sensation. First, she says that if our sensations were caused by pressures, then the information we receive from the senses would be obscured and confused. This would be so, because the impression would remain ('or at least not so soon be dissolved'), and there would become a 'horrid confusion of Figures, for not any figure would be distinct'.[79] If several external objects should press upon the eye, 'the eye would no more see the exterior objects then the nose, being stopt, could smell a presented perfume'.[80] Second, if our sensations were caused by imprints, then we would be able to detect indentations and worn patches in our sensory organs.[81] If light did press upon the eye, 'it might put the Eye into as much pain as Fire doth';[82] and if loud music should impress upon the ear 'it would soundly be beaten, and grow sore and bruised'.[83] Moreover, if the mechanical theory were true, then the organs would eventually be moved; the eye, for example, 'would in time be pressed into the centre of the brain'.[84] Third, Cavendish notes that if our sensations were caused by impact and resistance (or 'reaction'), then there would be a continual warring between our senses and the objects, or else a cessation of all motion: 'if there were any Resistance, Reaction or Indeavour in the organ, opposite to the Endeavour of the object, there would, in my opinion, be always a war between the animal senses and the objects... and if equal in their strengths, they would make a stop'.[85]

For Cavendish, the transfer model also poses a difficulty because it is impossible to conceive of motion without a body. She objects to the view that one body can give or transfer motion to another body: 'For how can motion, being no substance... quit one Body, and pass into another.'[86] On this point, Cavendish anticipates Leibniz's claim in the *Monadology* (1714), that 'Accidents cannot separate themselves from substances nor go about outside of them, as the "sensible species" of the Scholastics used to do.'[87] 'Perception, in my opinion,' Cavendish says, 'is not made by Pressure, nor by Species, nor by matter going either from the Organ to the Object, or from the Object to the Organ.'[88] If motion is always united to some portion of matter, then in the act of transference 'all bodies that receive motion from other bodies, must needs increase in their substance

---

[79] Cavendish, *Philosophical Letters*, p. 22.   [80] *Ibid.*, p. 68.   [81] *Ibid.*, p. 22.
[82] *Ibid.*, p. 63.   [83] *Ibid.*, p. 72.   [84] *Ibid.*, p. 60.   [85] *Ibid.*   [86] *Ibid.*, p. 98.
[87] Gottfried Wilhelm Leibniz, *The Monadology and Other Philosophical Writings*, translated and edited by Robert Latta (London: Oxford University Press, 1951), p. 219.
[88] Cavendish, *Philosophical Letters*, p. 20.

and quantity, and those which impact or transferr motion must decrease as much as they increase'.[89]

Finally, in the *Observations*, Cavendish echoes a common theme in the Cambridge–Platonist literature of the time: the view that it is entirely implausible that 'such a curious variety and contrivance of natural works should be produced by a senseless and irrational motion'.[90] Cavendish points out that one part moving another part through pressure could not produce all things 'so orderly and wisely as they are in nature'.[91] Her own theory (in her view) provides a more intelligible account of natural phenomena.

To explain how sensations are produced, Cavendish distinguishes between *principal* and *occasional* causes.[92] In one sense, we might say that the sensation of heat is 'caused' by the presence of fire. This fire, however, is not the true cause of our sensation, but merely the occasion for the internal self-motion of matter. The *internal motion*, according to Cavendish, is the true or principal cause. Every particle of matter, at every moment, has a 'natural and inherent power to move' that can be triggered by external causes.[93] No material body is able to lose this power, or transfer it to another object: matter and motion are united as one. Instead, we gain sensations of external objects by a process of 'patterning'. The sensitive and rational corporeal motions in an object 'pattern out' the figure of another object, without that object actually applying pressure or transferring part of itself. 'The sensitive perception of forreign objects,' she says, 'is by making or taking copies from these objects.'[94] Such 'patterning' is made possible by a system of mutual agreement and sympathy between parts.

IV

Cavendish's rejection of Cartesian dualism and the mechanistic theory of nature also leads her to reject the view that animals are mere machines, devoid of reason, and incapable of experiencing pain.[95] In the fifth part of his *Discourse on the Method*, Descartes argues that an important

[89] *Ibid.*, p. 98.
[90] Cavendish, *Observations*, 'Observations upon Experimental Philosophy', p. 44.
[91] *Ibid.*, p. 47.
[92] Eileen O'Neill provides a useful definition of the terms 'occasional cause' and 'principal cause' in 'Cavendish, Margaret Lucas (1623–1673)', p. 261.
[93] Cavendish, *Philosophical Letters*, p. 24.   [94] *Ibid.*, p. 127.
[95] On the reception of Descartes' views on animals, see Leonora Cohen Rosenfield, *From Beast-Machine to Man-Machine: Animal Soul in French Letters from Descartes to La Mettrie*, new and enlarged edition (New York: Octagon Books, 1968).

distinction between humans and brutes is that animals can conceivably be mistaken for mindless automata, whereas it is always possible to distinguish humans from machines. This is primarily because all human beings are capable of using a language, even those that must use sign language. Although magpies and parrots may have organs which enable them to utter words, they cannot show that they *understand* what they say, or declare their own thoughts, or give impromptu replies in a diversity of circumstances. The perfect uniformity and regularity of animal behaviour in some situations, and its complete absence in new circumstances, also indicates that animals function without the guidance of thought. From this basis – the idea that animals can give no linguistic or behavioural evidence that they think – Descartes argues that animals have no consciousness and are incapable of experiencing pain. Thomas Hobbes also maintains that animals lack reason, even though he believes that they are sentient.[96] Humans are superior to animals, he says, because they can inquire into the consequences of their conceptions, and because a man 'can by words reduce the consequences he finds to general Rules, called *Theoremes*, or *Aphorismes*'.[97]

Against these writers, Cavendish claims that the ability to use a language is irrelevant as an indication of whether or not an animal has consciousness. Descartes' mistake is that he assumes that animals will exhibit the outward signs of human intelligence, when intelligence can have various manifestations in nature. If animals do not express their rational capacity in the same manner, she says, this 'doth not prove that there is no intelligence at all betwixt them, no more then the want of humane Knowledg doth prove the want of Reason; for reason is the rational part of matter, and makes perception, observation, and intelligence different in every creature'.[98] In simple terms, Cavendish believes that the mind is a particular sort of thing (the 'rational part of matter') that enables creatures to behave in a diverse number of ways; the external behaviour patterns themselves are not constitutive of the mind. Descartes' behavioural tests are inadequate because different parts of nature manifest different dispositions, depending on the degree of rational and sensitive matter they possess.

Here Cavendish's remarks resemble a set of more famous criticisms – those of the Epicurean atomist Gassendi in his *Fifth Objections* to Descartes' *Meditations*. Gassendi says that although animals are 'without human

[96] In this respect, Hobbes follows the traditional scholastic view.
[97] Hobbes, *Leviathan*, p. 35.   [98] Cavendish, *Philosophical Letters*, p. 114.

reason, they do have a reason of their own'. They cannot be called irrational 'except in comparison with us, or relatively to our species of
reason'. And 'though they do not reason so perfectly and about so many
things as man, they still do reason; and the difference seems to be one
of more or less'.[99] Cavendish agrees with Gassendi that animals have
'a reason of their own'. But where Gassendi fails to provide independent support for his claims,[100] Cavendish offers a plausible 'argument
by analogy' against Descartes' tests. Cavendish directs this argument
against Hobbes, but the criticism applies equally well to Descartes. In
the *Philosophical Letters*, she considers Hobbes's view that animals lack
reason alongside his claim that '*Children are not endued with Reason at all,
till they they have attained to the use of Speech.*'[101] In response, Cavendish says
that

it might as well be said that a Child when new born hath not flesh and blood,
because by taking in nourishment or food, the Child grows to have more flesh
and blood...For though Reason doth not move in a Child as in a Man, in
Infancy as in Youth, in Youth as in Age, yet that doth not prove that Children
are without Reason.[102]

In her 1995 paper on 'Animal Ideas', Margaret Wilson observes that
pre-lingual human infants pose a problem for Descartes' tests because
they inevitably fail both the linguistic and the behavioural criteria for
thought. Yet, in his correspondence with Henry More, Descartes explicitly ascribes thought to human foetuses and newborn infants. Infants,
he says, can be seen as rational because they are 'of the same nature
as adults; but animals never grow up enough for any certain sign of
thought to be detected in them'.[103] Descartes' claims about children
significantly undermine his tests for rationality: as Wilson notes, pre-
lingual children demonstrate that there is no strict correlation between
the possession of a mind (or a 'rational soul') and the ability to express
thoughts in a language.[104] This is the same point that Cavendish makes
against Hobbes. To say that *animals* lack rationality because they cannot
express their thoughts in words, is like saying that human infants have no

[99] Pierre Gassendi, 'Fifth Set of Objections', in Descartes, *Philosophical Writings*, vol. II, p. 189.
[100] On Gassendi's criticisms, see Margaret Dauler Wilson, 'Animal Ideas', *Proceedings and Addresses of the American Philosophical Association* 69:2 (1995), 11.
[101] Cavendish, *Philosophical Letters*, p. 41.   [102] *Ibid.*, p. 42.
[103] Descartes to Henry More, 15 April 1649; in *Descartes: Philosophical Letters*, translated and edited by Anthony Kenny (Oxford: Clarendon Press, 1970), p. 251; and Descartes, *Oeuvres*, vol. V, p. 345.
[104] Wilson, 'Animal Ideas', 10.

reason because they cannot talk; yet the latter obviously have some form of rationality.

The Cambridge Platonists also maintain that animals have souls. Ralph Cudworth dismisses the Cartesian theory of animal mechanism as atheistic in tendency. Likewise, in his correspondence with Descartes, Henry More speaks in defence of animal souls against Descartes' 'murderous and cutthroat view'.[105] Despite this, however, in his *Antidote Against Atheism* (1653), More emphasises that animals are evidently designed to be useful to human beings, and he writes enthusiastically about the joys of hunting.[106] Cavendish does not support this theory of human supremacy. Against this view, she says that 'Man cannot well be judged of himself, because he is a Party, and so may be Partial; But if we observe well, we shall find that the Elemental Creatures are as excellent as Man.'[107] As finite creatures, humans can have no vantage point from which to judge that their perspective is best. Cavendish insists that human beings and animals share a common materiality; there is nothing distinctive about *Homo sapiens* to make them superior to the brute creation; in terms of their basic constituent substance, they are on an equal footing. It is ignorance that leads humans to think of themselves as 'flower and chief of all the products of nature',[108] when in reality the sharp distinction they make between species is untenable.

There are, however, close parallels between Cavendish's views and those of Cudworth in his *True Intellectual System of the Universe* (1678). Although Cudworth dismisses Cavendish's materialist philosophy as 'atheistic',[109] he appears to have been influenced by her claim that animals were not created solely in order to serve human beings. In the *Observations*, Cavendish says that 'Man, out of self-love, and conceited pride, because he thinks himself the chief of all Creatures, and that all the World is made for his sake; doth also imagine that all other Creatures are ignorant, dull, stupid, senseless, and irrational.'[110] In similar terms, Cudworth criticises those writers (such as More) who believe that

[105] More to Descartes, 11 December 1648; Wilson, 'Animal Ideas', 7; and Descartes, *Oeuvres*, vol. v, p. 243.
[106] Henry More, *An Antidote Against Atheism, Or, An Appeal to the Naturall Faculties of the Minde of Man, whether there be not a God*, with a new introduction by G. A. J. Rogers, facsimile of 1655 second edition (Bristol: Thoemmes Press, 1997), pp. 114–15.
[107] Cavendish, *Philosophical Letters*, p. 147.   [108] *Ibid.*
[109] Ralph Cudworth, *The True Intellectual System of the Universe: The First Part; Wherein, All the Reason and Philosophy Of Atheism is Confuted; And Its Impossibility Demonstrated*, facsimile reprint of 1678 edition (Stuttgart-Bad Cannstatt: Friedrich Frommann Verlag, 1964), p. 137.
[110] Cavendish, *Observations*, 'Further Observations', p. 41.

'the world and all things therein, were Created only for the Sake of Man...by their own Self-love, their Over-Weaning, and Puffy Conceit of themselves'.[111] He suggests that if fleas and lice had understanding they 'might Conclude the Bodies of other greater Animals and Men also, to have been made only for them'. But, he says, 'the Whole was not properly made for any Part, but the Parts for the Whole'.[112] Likewise, Cavendish says that 'the Ignorance of Man concerning other Creatures is the cause of despising other Creatures, imagining themselves as petty Gods in Nature'.[113]

Cavendish's opinions are also echoed in the writings of other seventeenth-century women. Queen Christina of Sweden questions Descartes' doctrine of the beast-machine, saying that 'If animals had the use of speech, they would convince men, that they were little more beasts than they.'[114] Following her, Catherine Descartes and the French writer Madeleine de Scudéry (1607–1701) both reject the theory that animals are mindless automata.[115] Then in 1696, Judith Drake belittles the credulity of those writers who hold 'Brutes to be no more than meer Machines, a sort of Divine Clock-Work, that Act only by the force of unseen Springs without Sensation, and cry without feeling Pain'.[116] Elizabeth Thomas, the poet also known as 'Corinna' (1675–1731), initiated a correspondence with John Norris in early 1699.[117] In one letter (30 March 1700), Thomas tells John Norris that the 'Generality of Readers' cannot accept his view that 'Brutes are *Mere Machines*'.[118] In her essay 'Of Anger', Mary Chudleigh observes that animals 'sure are more than Machines' and 'sensible of Pain':

I cannot, without a sort of Horrour, without some Sentiments of Pity, see them tortur'd; they are part of thy Creation, and may claim the Good adapted to their Nature, and ought not to be treated cruelly to gratify a savage inclination, or divert a sanguinary Temper; I could with pleasure let them live, and satisfy

---

[111] Cudworth, *True Intellectual System*, p. 875.   [112] *Ibid.*
[113] Cavendish, *Philosophical Letters*, p. 41.   [114] Christina, *The Works of Christina*, p. 95.
[115] See Harth, *Cartesian Women*, pp. 98–9.   [116] Drake, *Essay In Defence of the Female Sex*, p. 34.
[117] Thomas sent Norris a laudatory poem, 'Ode to the Reverend Mr. John Norris'. He wrote back
    on 25 April 1699 to tell her that her time would be better spent upon more serious and useful
    studies, rather than poetry, and he offered her advice on the direction of her studies. The letters
    between Norris and Thomas are in Elizabeth Thomas and Richard Gwinnett, *The Honourable
    Lovers: Or, The Second and Last Volume of Pylades and Corinna* (London: [E. Curll], 1732). The original
    manuscripts are in the Bodleian Library, University of Oxford, titled 'Original Letters under the
    Hands of Mr John Dryden. [Mr] Charles Dryden. [Mr] Norris. [Mr] Pope. Lady Chudleigh.
    Lady Pakington. Mrs Thomas and Dr. Ed. Young' (MS Rawlinson Letters 90).
[118] Bodleian Library, University of Oxford, MS Rawlinson Letters 90, fol. 63.

myself with Roots and Herbs, and Fruits, the cheap and wholsome Viands Nature does provide.[119]

Finally, Catharine Trotter Cockburn also believes that 'to give pain unnecessarily, even to brutes, out of a cruel humour, or wantonly only for sport, is contrary to nature and reason, and morally *unfit*'.[120]

From these statements, it is apparent that early modern women have a special sympathy for animals. This affinity may stem from the recognition that animals and women are oppressed for the same reason: the belief that they were not fully rational or sentient beings. Three of these women – Drake, Chudleigh, and Cockburn – were outspoken defenders of women's education.

There are certainly connections between Cavendish's feminist remarks, her opposition to the Cartesian view of animal automata, and her broader metaphysical views. Cavendish's philosophy is founded on a conception of nature as diffused with 'sense and reason'. This leads Cavendish to reject those aspects of Cartesianism brought under scrutiny in Genevieve Lloyd's analysis. Cavendish does not uphold a hierarchical conception of reason or maintain a distinction between the trained and untrained mind. Instead she believes that reason is in 'every Creature more or less'. Just because animals cannot speak or learn sign language, this does not mean that they have no reasoning abilities *per se*. Similarly, even though women do not express their ideas in the language of the schools, this does not mean that they are devoid of reason either. Cavendish does not revere or glorify an ideal or specialised type of reason, nor does she make an alignment between untrained reason and the body. For Cavendish, the rational soul could never transcend or separate itself from the body, because it is made of the same material substance.

V

The anti-dualist aspects of Cavendish's thought are further apparent in her criticisms of Henry More's theory of the spirit of nature. More was once best known for introducing and popularising Cartesian philosophy in English universities and intellectual circles. Today, however, scholars tend to note that More's attitude toward Cartesianism

---

[119] Chudleigh, *Essays Upon Several Subjects*, p. 331.
[120] Catharine Trotter Cockburn, *Remarks upon the Principles and Reasonings of Dr Rutherforth's Essay*, in *The Works of Mrs. Catharine Cockburn, Theological, Moral, Dramatic, and Poetical*, edited by Thomas Birch, 2 vols. (London: J. and P. Knapton, 1751), vol. II, p. 58.

was one of ambivalence.[121] In particular, More suspected that, contrary to Descartes' intentions, Cartesian mechanism might be used to advance the atheist's cause: the construction of a thoroughgoing mechanistic–materialist world-picture, completely devoid of any reference to God or spiritual substances.

More's first major philosophical work, *An Antidote Against Atheism*, is an attempt to refute atheism by providing arguments for the existence of God and the immateriality of the human soul. His strategy is to use the ideas of materialists to convince them of his arguments, working on the principle that he who converses with a Barbarian, 'must discourse to him in his own language'.[122] More argues that if one accepts the tenets of mechanistic philosophy – that matter is passive, mindless, and incapable of self-motion – then one must concede that the chance motions of matter cannot account for the appearance of design and structural perfection in the natural world. 'Wherefore the ordinary Phaenomena of Nature being guided according to the most Exquisite Wisdom imaginable, it is plain that they are not the effects of the meer motion of *Matter*, but of some *Immateriall* Principle.'[123] There are some phenomena, More says, that can be explained only by the existence of spiritual substances, which, in turn, provide proof of God's providence in the created world.

More specifically, More claims that all life, motion, and perception must be attributed to immaterial substances that pervade the material world. Toward this end, in *The Immortality of the Soul* (1659), he revitalises the Platonic doctrine of the World Soul, or the 'spirit of nature', which is

A substance incorporeal, but without Sense and Animadversion, pervading the whole Matter of the Universe, and exercising a plastical power therein according to the sundry predispositions and occasions in the parts it works upon, raising such *Phaenomena* in the World, by directing the parts of the Matter and their Motion, as cannot be resolved into mere Mechanical powers.[124]

More also calls this substance the '*Inferiour Soul of the World*'.[125] The bodies of human beings are capable of movement only because they enjoy a

---

[121] See Alan Gabbey's two papers 'Philosophia Cartesiana Triumphata: Henry More (1646–1671)', in *Problems of Cartesianism*, edited by Thomas M. Lennon, John M. Nicholas, and John W. Davis (Kingston and Montreal: McGill-Queen's University, 1982), pp. 171–250, and 'Henry More and the Limits of Mechanism', in *Henry More (1614–1687) Tercentenary Studies*, edited by Sarah Hutton (Dordrecht: Kluwer Academic Publishers, 1990), pp. 19–35.

[122] More, *Antidote Against Atheism*, 'The Preface', sig. B8^{r-v}.

[123] More, *Immortality of the Soul*, p. 88.   [124] *Ibid.*, p. 450.

[125] More, *Immortality of the Soul*, p. 266.

'vital congruity' with this part of the soul. In an appendix to the second edition of the *Antidote*, More writes that

it is demanded, why the Soul of Man which we acknowledge a Spirit, does not contract itself or withdraw itself from those parts which are pained, or why she does not dilate herself beyond the bounds of the Body. To which is answered, that the *Plantal faculty* of the Soul whereby she is unitable to this terrestrial body is not arbitrarious, but fatal or natural; which union cannot be dissolved unless the bond of life be loosened, and that vital congruity (which is in the body, and does necessarily hold the Soul there) be either for a time hindred or utterly destroy'd.[126]

This 'congruity' ceases once the soul forsakes its terrestrial body at death; but then the soul is able to enjoy another kind of congruity with an 'aerial vehicle', and then with an 'aethereal' one.[127]

To explain how a spirit might pervade matter, More dissents from the typical Cartesian view that the essence of matter is extension and the essence of the soul is thought. He maintains that both spirit and matter have extension, but that spirit is essentially active, indivisible (or 'indiscerpible') and penetrable, whereas matter is passive, divisible, and impenetrable. To show that it is possible to conceive of something that is both indivisible and extended, More draws on a typical symbol for the spirit: 'a Point of light from which rays out a luminous Orb according to the known principles of Optiques'.[128] It is not possible, he says, to imagine the luminous rays as divisible from the shining centre, because 'there is no means imaginable to discerp or separate any one ray of this Orbe and keep it apart by it self disjoyned from the Center'.[129] Likewise, a spiritual substance has a central essence that spreads out or extends into space; yet although it may be extended, one part is not separable or 'discerpible' from another. Thus we might conceive of a spirit or soul as analogous to an orb of light that is both extended and indivisible.

Like More, Cavendish challenges Cartesian and Hobbesian mechanism, and formulates an alternative hypothesis to explain the appearance of orderliness and intelligent behaviour in nature. But Cavendish turns More's own argument against him, claiming that her theory of self-moving matter is the better available explanation for the appearance of design in the world. She offers an impressively thorough case for her own theory: a vitalist–materialist explanation, she says, does not go beyond the bounds of natural reason, it is much simpler than More's theory of

[126] More, *Antidote Against Atheism*, pp. 306–7. [127] More, *Immortality of the Soul*, p. 258.
[128] More, *Antidote Against Atheism*, p. 304. [129] *Ibid.*, p. 357.

the spirit of nature, it explains more, and (in her view) it conforms best with religious orthodoxy. Above all, Cavendish challenges More for upholding a dualist philosophy when his views lend greater support to a monist theory of substance.

First, Cavendish takes a Hobbesian approach against More's views: her arguments appeal not only to the inconceivability of immaterial substances, but to the separation of theology and philosophy. She claims that because our natural faculties are unable to conceive of immaterial substances, it is pointless to invent such substances when they are of no instrumental value: all the effects of nature can be explained by self-moving matter.[130] In the *Observations*, she says 'why should we puzzle ourselves with multiplicity of terms and distinctions when there's no need of them ... we need not introduce an incorporeal mind, or intellect'.[131] It is unnecessary to appeal to a *divine* executor of God's will when a *natural* explanation will do just as well. Since all parts of nature are knowing, they have the intelligence to order themselves wisely, and nature knows how 'to adapt and fit [her laws] ... to her designed ends'.[132] Every part of the human body, for example, knows 'its own office, what it ought to do'.[133] Subverting the traditional symbol of woman-as-nature, Cavendish says that it is

absurd to believe Immaterial substances or spirits in Nature, as also a spirit of Nature, which is the Vicarious power of God upon Matter; For why should it not be as probable, that God did give Matter a self-moving power to her self, as to have made another Creature to govern her? For Nature is not a Babe, or Child, to need such a Spiritual Nurse, to teach her to go, or to move; neither is she so young a Lady as to have need of a Governess; for surely she can govern herself; she needs not a Guardian for fear she should run away with a younger Brother, or one that cannot make her a Jointure.[134]

As part of this attack, Cavendish highlights the materialistic aspects of More's conception of the soul. In his 1986 article on More's materialism, John Henry notes that 'a close reading of his pneumatology reveals a number of confusions and inconsistencies which bedevil, and even

---

[130] Cavendish, *Philosophical Letters*, p. 195.
[131] Cavendish, *Observations*, 'Observations upon the Opinions of some Ancient Philosophers', p. 40.
[132] *Ibid.*, 'Observations upon Experimental Philosophy', p. 44.
[133] Cavendish, *Philosophical Letters*, p. 189.
[134] *Ibid.*, pp. 149–50. Cavendish often draws on this symbol to celebrate the autonomy of nature and the self-moving power of matter. In another passage in the *Philosophical Letters*, she says that 'though Nature is old, yet she is not a Witch, but a grave, wise, methodical Matron, ordering her infinite family, which are her several parts, with ease and facility, without needless troubles or difficulties' (pp. 302–3).

belie, More's vigorously dualistic rhetoric'.[135] In his attempt to 'discourse with the Barbarians', More's views end up acquiring distinctly materialist overtones. Recognising this weakness, Cavendish targets More's idea that the soul can be both extended and indivisible. In her opinion, there is nothing in nature that is indivisible, for every substance 'hath extension, and all extension hath parts, and what has parts, is divisible'.[136] To show this, Cavendish dissects More's concept of the spirit of nature. She questions how it could be possible for one indivisible spirit to be in so many dividable parts throughout nature.[137] For example:

When a Worm is cut into two or three parts, we see there is sensitive life and motion in every part, for every part will strive and endeavour to meet and joyn again to make up the whole body; now if there were but one indivisible Life, Spirit, and Motion, I would fain know, how these severed parts could move all by one Spirit.[138]

According to Cavendish, if More's spirit of nature moves every part individually, then there must be as many spirits as there are parts in nature. She also points out that More's orb-of-light analogy does not really work because we can easily conceive of a light split into parts. For example, 'when a dark body is interposed, or crosses the rays of the Sun; it cuts those rays asunder, which by reason they cannot joyn together again, because of the interposed body, the light cut off, suddenly goeth out'.[139] This criticism falls somewhat short of its mark because the light is not really disjoined or separated from its source when a dark body interposes – the remainder of the sunbeam could not subsist independently of the sun. But Cavendish is not mistaken in questioning the strength of More's analogy. It was well known that More himself regarded light as a material body, and hence according to his *own* theory of matter the light would have to be divisible.[140] So, as Cavendish suggests, More's one attempt to illustrate the idea of an extended yet indivisible entity does not work.

Cavendish also challenges More's claim that the immaterial soul is 'dilatable' and 'contractible'. She says that 'contraction and dilation belong onely to bodies, or material things'.[141] Her argument for this view draws on the idea that 'dilation and contraction cannot be without extension'.[142] (With these remarks, Cavendish bears out John Henry's

---

[135] John Henry, 'A Cambridge Platonist's Materialism: Henry More and the Concept of Soul', *Journal of the Warburg and Courtauld Institute* 49 (1986), 173.
[136] Cavendish, *Philosophical Letters*, p. 194. [137] *Ibid.*, p. 197. [138] *Ibid.*, p. 198.
[139] *Ibid.*, p. 201. [140] See Henry, 'A Cambridge Platonist's Materialism', 179.
[141] Cavendish, *Philosophical Letters*, p. 186. [142] *Ibid.*, p. 208.

claim that 'The seventeenth-century reader could only regard an amplitude of dilation or contraction as taking place through space or "corporeal dimensions".')[143] According to Cavendish, if one allows that the soul occupies spatial dimensions, then one must also concede that it is divisible. But if the soul is extended, divisible, and capable of contracting and dilating, then this is one and the same as saying that it is material.

As for the typically spiritual attribute of 'penetrability', Cavendish believes that this too may be an attribute of matter. In her view penetrability is 'nothing else but division; as when some parts pierce and enter through other parts, as Duellers run each other thorow, or as water runs through a sieve'.[144] On this interpretation, matter could be both penetrable *and* impenetrable depending on what is doing the penetrating.

In addition, Cavendish dismisses More's claim that the immaterial soul must always be united to a body of some sort, whether terrestrial, aerial, or aetherial. More believes that upon release from the earthly body, the soul 'transmigrates' into either an aerial or aetherial body. He believes that few souls attain an aetherial body straight away, because this body is made of more subtle parts of matter than aerial bodies. Against More, Cavendish says that

as for the Natural Soul, she being material, has no need of any Vehicles, neither is natural death any thing else but an alteration of the rational and sensitive motions, which from the dissolution of one figure go to the formation or production of another. Thus the natural soul is not like a Traveller, going out of one body into another, neither is air her lodging; for certainly, if the natural humane soul should travel through the airy regions, she would at last grow weary, it being so great a journey, except she did meet with the soul of a Horse, and so ease her self with riding on Horseback.[145]

Cavendish's tongue-in-cheek remarks illustrate the notion that although the soul may be 'translated' into a more subtle kind of body after death, in her view it is still undeniably material. She also says that 'Since Spirits cannot appear without bodies, the neerest way is to ascribe such unusual effects or apparitions, as happen sometimes, rather to matter that is already corporeal, and not to go so far as to draw Immaterial spirits to Natural actions, and to make Spirits take vehicles fit for their purposes.'[146] Here Cavendish highlights a central weakness in More's concept of an immaterial soul: if this soul is *always* united to some body or other, as he says, then how is this any different from saying the soul

---

[143] Henry, 'A Cambridge Platonist's Materialism', 178.
[144] Cavendish, *Philosophical Letters*, p. 204.   [145] *Ibid.*, p. 218.   [146] *Ibid.*, p. 228.

is material? In conclusion, she remarks that 'By this you may plainly see…that I am no Platonick; for this opinion is dangerous, especially for married Women, by reason the conversation of Souls may be a great temptation, and means to bring Platonick Lovers to a neerer acquaintance, not allowable by the Laws of Marriage, although by the sympathy of the Souls.'[147] Here again her emphasis is on the materiality of the soul, for she does not believe that 'the conversation of Souls' is a completely disembodied exercise, but must inevitably lead to a more carnal kind of relationship.

In sum, to show that More's spirit of nature is an unviable explanatory hypothesis, Cavendish collapses every one of More's distinctions between spirit and matter, soul and body. In particular, she expands on the implications of More's view that the soul is extended.[148] If a substance is extended, then it is capable of being divisible, contractible, and dilatable. And if the soul is capable of being extended and divisible, then it is also capable of being both penetrable and impenetrable. But if the soul is extended, divisible, contractible and dilatable, penetrable and impenetrable, then it is redundant to say that it is always 'united' to matter. Instead, it makes more sense to say that the soul *is* material.

Cavendish also recognises that More's 'vital congruity' theory faces difficulties in accounting for soul–body interaction. Typically, if two things have a 'congruity' then they have an agreement or correspondence in qualities that promotes their union. But More's theory fails to explain how two entirely different substances can have an agreement in qualities. 'He may say, perchance, There is such a close conjunction betwixt Body and Spirit, as I make betwixt rational, sensitive, and inanimate Matter',[149] but for Cavendish these are all degrees of one and the same substance, whereas body and spirit in More's view 'are things of contrary natures'.[150] Hence Cavendish's theory has an explanatory advantage: it is easier to account for soul–body interaction when the soul and body share an essential likeness, as her theory claims.

Cavendish completes her rejection of More's spirit of nature by retorting the charge of atheism against his views. First, she asks, why should an all-powerful God need an intermediary when he could just give sense

---

[147] *Ibid.*, p. 219.
[148] Sarah Hutton makes a similar point about Conway's critique of More in her paper 'Anne Conway Critique d'Henry More: L'Esprit et la Matiere', *Archives de Philosophie* 58:3 (1995), 371–84. I expand on the similarities between the views of Cavendish and Conway in the following chapter.
[149] Cavendish, *Philosophical Letters*, p. 196.   [150] *Ibid.*, p. 197.

and reason to nature itself? It is much more pious to say that self-moving nature 'proves and confirms' the 'omnipotency and Infinite wisdom of God'.[151] To say otherwise, is a prejudice to God's power.[152] Second, Cavendish believes that it is irreligious to make immaterial spirits in nature like so many deities or demi-gods, who govern nature 'by a dilating nod, and a contracting frown'.[153] In what way do they differ from God if they are spiritual substances capable of bestowing motion on natural things? In her own philosophy, Cavendish stops short of affirming that God is corporeal. God and nature are *not* coequal: 'God is a Spirit, and not a bodily substance';[154] he is an 'Infinite Immaterial Purity',[155] with a 'Supernatural and Incomprehensible Infinite Wisdom and Power'.[156] It is impossible for Nature to change into God, because God cannot 'admit of diminution or addition'.[157] Third, Cavendish suggests that according to More's dualist theory only a very small part of the natural world is able to worship God. Yet it is more reasonable to affirm that all of creation is capable of adoring the creator, because 'it is very improbable that God should be worshipped onely in part, and not in whole, and that all creatures were made to obey man, and not to worship God, onely for man's sake...for man's use...for man's spoil'.[158] It is also more consistent to say that God is able to bestow freedom and self-motion on nature as a whole, given that he is capable of bestowing this capacity on human beings.

Cavendish is clearly inspired by More's method of argument to the best explanation. Like More, she rejects the atomistic and mechanistic models because they cannot provide a satisfactory account of nature's orderliness and perfection.[159] This means that Cavendish's philosophy shares a central feature of Cambridge Platonism: the rejection of Hobbesian mechanism. But Cavendish challenges More's dualism with the very criticism he turns against his opponents: a failure to account for the teleological aspects of nature. Her sympathy for Hobbesian *materialism* leads her to claim that while nature is the executor of God's commands, it does not partake in God's essence, and is in no way spiritual or immaterial. For these reasons, Cavendish's final position on created substance is essentially anti-dualist.

Cavendish's stand against all supernatural or immaterial substances, apart from God, is further strengthened in her later works, the *Observations*

[151] *Ibid.*, p. 164.   [152] *Ibid.*, p. 199.   [153] *Ibid.*, p. 195.   [154] *Ibid.*, p. 8.
[155] *Ibid.*, p. 10.   [156] *Ibid.*, p. 9.   [157] *Ibid.*, p. 10.   [158] *Ibid.*, p. 138.
[159] Cavendish and More also share an opposition to Hobbesian determinism (see Cavendish, *Philosophical Letters*, p. 96), and a mistrust of Epicurus.

and the much-revised edition of the *Philosophical and Physical Opinions*, the *Grounds of Natural Philosophy*. In her 'Observations upon the Opinions of some Ancient Philosophers', Cavendish says that God cannot be the 'Soul of the World' because the body of nature is dividable, whereas God is essentially indivisible.[160] She emphasises that 'God is a Supernatural, Individable, and Incorporeal Being, void of all Parts and Divisions'.[161] In an appendix to the *Grounds of Natural Philosophy*, Cavendish includes a chapter on 'the Differences between God, and Nature'. She says that 'GOD is an Infinite and Eternal Immaterial Being: Nature, an Infinite Corporeal Being. GOD is Immovable, and Immutable: Nature, Moving, and Mutable, GOD is Eternal, Indivisible, and of an Incompoundable Being: Nature, Eternally Divisible and Compoundable. GOD, Eternally Perfect: Nature, Eternally Imperfect.'[162] In highlighting the differences between God and his creation, Cavendish is led to abandon her earlier religious belief that human beings have 'supernatural souls'. The idea of created immaterial beings, she suggests, is inconsistent with her faith:

I cannot conceive how an Immaterial can be in Nature: for, first, An Immaterial cannot, in my opinion, be naturally created; nor can I conceive how an Immaterial can produce particular Immaterial Souls, Spirits, or the like. Wherefore, an Immaterial, in my opinion, must be some uncreated Being; which can be no other than GOD alone. Wherefore, Created Spirits and Spiritual Souls, are some other thing than an Immaterial: for surely, if there were any other Immaterial Beings, besides the Omnipotent God, these would be so much near the Divine Essence of God, as to be petty gods; and numerous petty gods, would, almost, make the Power of an Infinite God. But God is Omnipotent, and only God.[163]

With these remarks, Cavendish takes her monistic philosophy to its logical extreme: the entire created world is material, the only wholly immaterial being is uncreated, and that is God. In Cavendish's view, Heaven and Hell are also material realms, and Christ too is 'partly Divine, and partly Natural'.[164] Although Cavendish does not fully abandon the separation between theology and philosophy, in this later work her concept of God plays a significant role in her final rejection of immaterial substances. In this respect in particular, Cavendish's philosophy is poles apart from that of More.

[160] Cavendish, *Observations*, 'Observations upon the Opinions of some Ancient Philosophers', p. 5. This part of the *Observations* provides a commentary on the views of Thales, Plato, Pythagoras, Epicurus, and Aristotle, the writers discussed in Thomas Stanley's *The History of Philosophy* (1655–62).
[161] Cavendish, *Observations*, 'An Argumental Discourse', sig. p2^v.
[162] Cavendish, *Grounds of Natural Philosophy*, p. 241. [163] *Ibid.*, p. 239. [164] *Ibid.*, pp. 247–8.

In sum, although Cavendish values reason above the senses, this 'rationalism' is not supported by the dualist metaphysics of Cartesian philosophy. Although she renounces her early atomistic views, she upholds a consistent monistic materialist position throughout her career. According to Cavendish, the soul cannot subsist apart from the body, the soul is really only 'rational and sensitive' matter, this matter is capable of self-motion and perception, and no single particle of the material world is dead or inert. Contrary to historical opinion, this theory of nature emerges out of a careful and thorough analysis of the philosophical literature of the time. Her criticisms focus on those aspects of Cartesian philosophy also attacked by her contemporaries, including the problem of soul–body interaction, the idea of unextended substance, the mechanical conception of nature, and the belief that animals are mindless automata. Like her respected contemporary, Elisabeth of Bohemia, Cavendish points out that the dualist cannot explain how two entirely distinct substances are capable of causal interaction. Like Thomas Hobbes, Cavendish maintains that the idea of immaterial substance is inconceivable, and for this reason she also dismisses the explanatory value of the Cambridge–Platonist theory of the 'spirit of nature'. But like Henry More and Ralph Cudworth, Cavendish rejects mechanistic conceptions of the natural world, and defends the view that animals have the capacity for sense and reason. Furthermore, from a modern feminist viewpoint, Cavendish does not advocate a 'male-biased' metaphysical outlook. It has been claimed that in the context of cultural associations between the 'feminine' and the body, Cartesian dualism has detrimental consequences for women. Recent feminists oppose hierarchical conceptions of reason in which the body, matter, and nature are devalued or denigrated. In Cavendish's writings, every part of nature possesses some kind of rational capacity; we are not encouraged to transcend or conquer our material natures; and matter and the body are co-equal with the spirit and the soul.

3

Anne Conway

The Viscountess Anne Conway enjoys a more distinguished reputation as a metaphysician than her contemporary Margaret Cavendish.[1] In her own time, Conway was praised as 'a woman learned beyond her sex';[2] in the nineteenth century, James Crossley regarded her as 'the profoundest and most learned of the female metaphysical writers of England';[3] and in a recent article, Sarah Hutton describes Conway as 'the most important' woman philosopher in seventeenth-century England.[4] These accolades are well deserved. Unlike Cavendish, Conway presents concise and systematic arguments for her metaphysical views, and her ideas

---

[1] The main philosophical studies of Conway's thought are: Stuart Brown, 'Leibniz and More's Cabbalistic Circle', in Hutton (ed.), *Henry More (1614–1687)*, pp. 77–96; Clucas, 'The Duchess and Viscountess', 125–36; Allison P. Coudert, 'A Cambridge Platonist's Kabbalist Nightmare', *Journal of the History of Ideas* 36 (1975), 633–52; Coudert, *The Impact of the Kabbalah*, pp. 177–219; Jane Duran, 'Anne Conway: A Seventeenth Century Rationalist', *Hypatia* 4:1 (1989), 64–79; Lois Frankel, 'Anne Finch, Viscountess Conway', in Waithe (ed.), *A History of Women Philosophers*, vol. III, pp. 41–58; Frankel, 'The Value of Harmony', pp. 197–216; Alan Gabbey, 'Anne Conway et Henry More', *Archives de Philosophie* 40 (1977), 379–404; Hutton, 'Anne Conway Critique d'Henry More', 371–84; Sarah Hutton, 'Of Physic and Philosophy: Anne Conway, F. M. van Helmont and Seventeenth-Century Medicine', in *Religio Medici: Medicine and Religion in Seventeenth-Century England*, edited by Ole Peter Grell and Andrew Cunningham (Aldershot, England: Scolar Press, 1996); Hutton, 'Ancient Wisdom and Modern Philosophy'; Hutton, 'Anne Conway, Margaret Cavendish'; Sarah Hutton, 'Conway, Anne (c. 1630–79)', in Craig (ed.), *Routledge Encyclopedia of Philosophy*, vol. II, pp. 669–71; Sarah Hutton, 'On an Early Letter by Anne Conway', in *Donne filosofia e cultura nel seicento*, edited by G. Totaro (Rome: Consiglio Nazionale delle Ricerche, 2000); Peter Loptson, 'Introduction' to Anne Conway, *The Principles of the Most Ancient and Modern Philosophy* (Amsterdam: Martinus Nijhoff, 1982); Peter Loptson, 'Anne Conway, Henry More, and their World', *Dialogue* 34 (1995), 139–46; Carolyn Merchant, 'The Vitalism of Anne Conway: Its Impact on Leibniz's Concept of the Monad', *Journal of the History of Philosophy* 17 (1979), 255–69; Richard H. Popkin, 'The Spiritualistic Cosmologies of Henry More and Anne Conway', in Hutton (ed.), *Henry More (1614–1687)*, pp. 97–114.
[2] Anne Conway, *The Principles of the Most Ancient and Modern Philosophy*, translated and edited by Allison P. Coudert and Taylor Corse (Cambridge: Cambridge University Press, 1996), 'Published Preface', p. 7.
[3] John Worthington, *The Diary and Correspondence of Dr. John Worthington*, edited by James Crossley (Manchester: The Chetham Society, 1847), vol. I, p. 142, n. 1.
[4] Hutton, 'Conway, Anne (née Finch: 1631–79)', p. 208.

are developed from clearly defined philosophical and theological principles. While Cavendish's works seem to have been ignored by her peers,[5] Conway's system was admired by no less a philosopher than Gottfried Wilhelm Leibniz.[6]

Yet, in outward appearances, there are strong parallels between the ontological theories of Conway and Cavendish. Conway undoubtedly knew about Cavendish's writings through her correspondence with Henry More. In fact, More encouraged Conway to write a response to the *Philosophical Letters*.[7] But as far as we know, Conway's only surviving work is *The Principles of the Most Ancient and Modern Philosophy* (first published in Latin in 1690). In this treatise, her principal target is Cartesianism, but like Cavendish, she also takes a critical attitude toward Henry More's concept of the soul and his dualist theory of soul–body relations. The other main targets of the *Principles* are Spinoza and Hobbes. Against these writers, Conway argues for a monistic theory of created things distinct from God, and dismisses the idea that bodies are constituted of dead matter.

Two recent scholars compare the philosophies of Conway and Cavendish: Sarah Hutton in her 1997 article 'Anne Conway, Margaret Cavendish and Seventeenth-Century Scientific Thought', and Stephen Clucas in his 'The Duchess and the Viscountess: Negotiations between Mechanism and Vitalism'.[8] Clucas and Hutton come to similar conclusions about the metaphysical views of these writers. They agree that while both women believe that there is only one substance in the created world, and that there is no such thing as dead matter of the Cartesian kind, their monist views sharply diverge in one crucial respect. Whereas Cavendish upholds that there is only one *material* substance, Conway believes there is only *spirit*.

Nevertheless, in this chapter I argue that although Conway is not a materialist, there are aspects of her monist theory of substance that closely resemble Cavendish's. The two women's responses to Henry More's concept of the soul in his *Antidote Against Atheism* show that the qualities

---

[5] Ralph Cudworth is a notable exception.
[6] In a 1697 letter to Thomas Burnet of Kemnay, Leibniz describes his own views as quite similar to those of the late 'Countess of Conway'; see Gottfried Wilhelm Leibniz, *Die Philosophischen Schriften von Gottfried Wilhelm Leibniz*, edited by C. I. Gerhardt (Berlin: Georg Olms Hildesheim, 1960), vol. III, p. 216. On Conway and Leibniz, see Merchant, 'The Vitalism of Anne Conway', 255–69; Duran, 'Anne Conway', 64–79; and Brown, 'Leibniz and More's Cabbalistic Circle', p. 84.
[7] More to Conway, [undated] 1665; in Nicolson, *The Conway Letters*, p. 237.
[8] I am grateful to both Sarah Hutton and Stephen Clucas for showing me earlier drafts of their papers.

accorded to 'spirit' in Conway's case, and 'matter' in Cavendish's, are remarkably similar – despite the fact that these writers develop their views from radically different philosophical and theological perspectives. Henry More characterises all substances as extended. He sees the body (and other material things) as essentially dead, passive, divisible, and impenetrable, and the soul (and other spiritual things) as active, indivisible, and penetrable. Cavendish breaks down More's opposition between spirit and body. Here I show that Conway likewise ascribes spiritual characteristics to body, and material attributes to the soul. Conway, like Cavendish, challenges the ontological status of matter, and rejects the type of soul–body relationship that has been seen to have pernicious consequences for stereotypes of femininity. I argue that the differences between the two women are a product of their views about the relationship between theology and philosophy, rather than their theories of substance.

I

Anne Conway was born in London on 14 December 1631, the youngest child of Elizabeth Cradock and Sir Heneage Finch, an eminent statesman. Although she never received a formal tertiary education, Anne was tutored at home and her half-brother John Finch encouraged her interest in philosophy and theology. She is reputed to have learned Latin, Greek, and Hebrew, and to have studied the works of Plato and Plotinus in Latin. In about 1650, John introduced Anne to Henry More, his tutor at Christ's College, Cambridge. More became her intellectual mentor and one of her closest lifelong friends. In 1651, Anne married Edward Conway (1623–83), who also encouraged her interest in philosophy.[9] Their home at Ragley Hall in Warwickshire became a meeting point for many notable figures of the period. The life of the Ragley intellectual circle, and the letters of Anne Conway, More, and their friends, are the subject of Marjorie Hope Nicolson's 1930 work, *The Conway Letters*. The Conway–More correspondence began in the early 1650s when Conway appealed to More for help in understanding Descartes. The content of their first letters is largely philosophical: More tutored Conway in Cartesian philosophy and encouraged her to be critical; her questions, in turn, enabled More to clarify certain ideas for his treatises. In 1653, More dedicated his *Antidote Against Atheism* to Conway, telling her that 'in

---

[9] Together the Conways had one child, Heneage Edward Conway, born 6 February 1658. He died of smallpox in 1660.

the knowledge of things as well Natural as Divine, you have not onely out-gone all of your own Sex, but even of that other also'.[10] In the *Antidote*, More brings up a number of familiar issues from their correspondence: namely, the argument for the necessary existence of God, and questions concerning the soul–body relationship.

In future years, however, Conway found her own feet as a philosopher and rejected many central aspects of More's metaphysics. This departure may have been (in part) due to the influence of Francis Mercury van Helmont.[11] He was a permanent guest at Ragley Hall from 1670, when he became Anne Conway's physician. Conway suffered excruciating headaches from the age of twelve until her death in 1679. Her search for a cure, and the various treatments by great figures of the time, such as William Harvey, are well known.[12] Although he could not cure her illness, van Helmont found an intellectual ally in his patient. They shared an interest in the doctrines of the Lurianic Kabbalah, and upheld monistic and vitalistic theories of substance. Van Helmont also played a crucial role in Conway's religious conversion during the last two years of her life – he introduced her to Quakerism.

Both van Helmont and Henry More influenced Conway's only published work, the *Principles*. Written some time in the 1670s,[13] this treatise was found soon after Conway's death in 1679, jotted into a notebook 'in a very small and faint handwriting'.[14] The original English manuscript, which is now lost, was never revised or corrected by Conway herself. Her notes were edited and translated into Latin by van Helmont. He published the work in Amsterdam in 1690 as *Principia Philosophiae antiquissimae et recentissimae de Deo, Christo et creatura, id est de spiritu et materia in genere* in a

[10] More, *Antidote Against Atheism*, 'The Epistle Dedicatory', sig. A4ʳ.
[11] On van Helmont and Conway, see Coudert, *The Impact of the Kabbalah*, pp. 177–219; Coudert, 'A Cambridge Platonist's Kabbalist Nightmare', 633–52; Hutton, 'Of Physic and Philosophy'; Hutton, 'Ancient Wisdom and Modern Philosophy'; and Nicolson, *Conway Letters*, pp. 309–77. In her paper 'On an Early Letter by Anne Conway', Sarah Hutton notes that Conway's anti-dualist tendencies cannot be entirely attributed to van Helmont because her critique of More's dualism antedates van Helmont's arrival at Ragley. There are subtle suggestions that Conway would deviate from More, for example, in a letter from their early correspondence. For a transcription of this letter, see Richard Ward, *The Life of The Learned and Pious Dr Henry More*, edited with an introduction by M. F. Howard, facsimile reprint of 1911 edition (Bristol: Thoemmes Press, 1997), pp. 23–4.
[12] See Hutton, 'Of Physic and Philosophy'; Gilbert Roy Owen, 'The Famous Case of Lady Anne Conway', *Annals of Medical History* 9 (1937), 567–71; and Sarah E. Skwire, 'Women, Writers, Sufferers: Anne Conway and An Collins', *Literature and Medicine* 18:1 (1999), 1–23.
[13] Peter Loptson dates the writing of the *Principles* between 1677–1679; Nicolson speculates that it was written between 1671 and 1674. In the 'Preface', More states only that it was written 'towards the latter end of her long and tedious Pains and Sickness'; see Conway, *Principles*, p. 3.
[14] *Ibid.*, 'Published Preface', p. 7.

three-part collection entitled *Opuscula philosophica.*[15] It is likely that More also had a hand in the preparation of the work for publication. More wrote a preface for the *Principles*,[16] paying tribute to Conway, whom he claimed had 'understood perfectly' all of his writings.[17] His approbation is surprising given that Conway not only opposes More's belief that there is an essential difference between spirit and matter, she also objects to his view that matter is dead and passive, and she attributes life, perception, and self-motion to bodies.

In these last respects, the similarities between Conway and Cavendish are immediately apparent. There is no evidence, however, that the two women ever met, a fact that highlights the intellectual isolation facing women in the mid-seventeenth century. In a preface to her *Philosophical Letters*, Cavendish expresses her dismay that no one would engage with her in a dispute. She had been told that 'no man dare or will set his name to the contradiction of a Lady', and that most men would assume a female pseudonym, rather than openly criticise a woman. Against this practice, she says that

I cannot conceive why it should be a disgrace to any man to maintain his own or others opinions against a woman, so it be done with respect and civility; but to become a cheat by dissembling, and quit the Breeches for a Petticoat, meerly out of spight and malice, is base, and not fit for the honour of a man, or the masculine sex.[18]

But no man took up Cavendish's implicit challenge. Upon receiving a presentation copy of *Philosophical Letters*, Henry More wrote to Cavendish before he had even read her criticisms. In that letter, dated 9 June 1665, he praises her for 'piercing into the greatest difficulties and the most dark and obstruce Recesses of Philosophy'.[19] He also says 'I humbly crave Pardon for my boldness, and impatience that I offer so hastily and return thanks for so eminent a Favour, before I have well computed the value thereof.'[20] In this way, More saves himself the trouble of ever

[15] Conway's text was then subsequently translated back into English by 'J. C.' and re-published in 1692. The translator is believed to be either Jodocus Crull or John Clark. A new translation from the Latin, by Allison P. Coudert and Taylor Corse, was published in 1996.
[16] The 'Preface' is signed 'Fr. Mer. Helmont', but it is thought that More wrote the original.
[17] Conway, *Principles*, 'Preface', p. 4. More's remarks are very similar to those of Descartes about Elisabeth in *The Principles of Philosophy*.
[18] Cavendish, *Philosophical Letters*, 'The Preface', sig. c1ᵛ.
[19] More to Cavendish, 9 June 1665; in Cavendish, *Collection of Letters And Poems*, p. 90; and Nicolson, *Conway Letters*, p. 241.
[20] *Ibid.*

engaging in further correspondence with Cavendish.[21] But More does encourage Conway to respond to Cavendish's objections in a letter, dated 15 May 1665. He writes:

I wish your Ladiship were rid of your headache and paines, though it were no exchange for those of answering this great Philosopher. She is affrayd some man should quit his breeches and putt on a petticoat to answer her in that disguize, which your Ladiship need not. She expresses this jealousie in her book, but I beleave she may be secure from any one giving her the trouble of a reply.[22]

More did not know that Conway's own criticisms of his dualist philosophy have a striking resemblance to Cavendish's objections.

In Conway's system, there are three distinct types of substances: God, Christ, and the other creatures. These can be distinguished from one another in terms of their capacity for change. God's essence is to be immutable and eternal, whereas his creatures are mutable and temporal; they have an intrinsic power to change themselves either for good or bad.[23] Christ, who is the first-born of all creatures, is both 'God and man';[24] he is capable of changing, but only for the good. Christ is a necessary intermediary between God and the created world 'because otherwise a gap would remain and one extreme would have been united with the other extreme without a mediator, which is impossible and against the nature of things'.[25] Together these three species – God, Christ, and the other creatures – make up 'that vast infinity of possible things'.[26]

At a superficial level, this theory appears to be similar to the Cambridge–Platonist doctrine of plastic nature or the spirit of nature. Just as More and Cudworth argue for the existence of a fluid intermediary between the material and spiritual worlds, Conway also maintains that there is a mediating substance between God and his creation – Christ. But Conway differs from the Cambridge school in advocating a *monistic* theory of created substances. In her view, there is no essential difference between spirit and body, they differ only modally: 'body is nothing but fixed and condensed spirit; and spirit is nothing but volatile body or body made subtle'.[27] There is no such thing as dead matter, and

---

[21] His only other recorded opinion on the work is in a letter to Anne Conway, where he says that Cavendish has been 'by farr a more civill Antagonist' than Joseph Beaumont, the man who wrote a series of objections against More's *An Explanation of the Grand Mystery of Godliness* (1660); see Nicolson, *Conway Letters*, p. 237.

[22] More to Conway, [undated] 1665; in Nicolson, *Conway Letters*, p. 237.

[23] Conway, *Principles*, ch. 5, sect. 3, pp. 24–5.   [24] *Ibid.*, ch. 4, sect. 2, p. 21.

[25] *Ibid.*, ch. 5, sect. 3, pp. 24–5.   [26] *Ibid.*, ch. 6, sect. 4, p. 30.   [27] *Ibid.*, ch. 8, sect. 4, p. 61.

all material things have self-motion, life, and perception. Although More is not mentioned by name,[28] Conway distinguishes her philosophy from all those who say that body and spirit are distinct:

Cartesian philosophy claims that body is merely dead mass, which not only lacks life and perception of any kind but is also utterly incapable of either for all eternity. This great error must be imputed to all those who say that body and spirit are contrary things and unable to change into one another, thereby denying bodies all life and perception. This is completely contrary to the fundamentals of our philosophy. On this account it is so far from being Cartesianism in a new guise that it can more truly be called anti-Cartesianism because of its fundamental principles... For truly in nature there are many operations which are far more than merely mechanical. Nature is not simply an organic body like a clock, which has no vital principle of motion in it; but it is a living body which has life and perception, which are much more exalted than a mere mechanism or a mechanical motion.[29]

Clucas and Hutton observe the strong parallels between this body of theory and that of Cavendish. The most obvious similarities are that Cavendish and Conway both oppose the mechanical concept of matter by ascribing life, perception, and a principle of self-movement to material things; and they overcome the soul–body problem by making soul and body one and the same substance.

There are several other notable parallels. The first is that both women believe that nature is infinite. Conway writes that 'an infinity of worlds and creatures was made by God'.[30] These creatures, she says, cannot be limited by number or measure. Moreover, the smallest particles of created substance can be divided in infinite ways into even smaller parts, and thus every creature has an infinity of parts.[31] Similarly, in her *Philosophical Letters*, Cavendish says that nature is infinite in bulk and quantity, and 'divisible into infinite Parts'.[32] Both authors agree that God is the only true or pure spirit, without any corporeality. Conway's very first statement is that 'God is spirit',[33] and later she says that 'God is infinitely spirit having no body.'[34] Likewise, in one of Cavendish's earliest letters, she affirms that 'God is a Spirit, and not a bodily substance.'[35] Both women also note that God is wholly one, and incapable of being divided

---

[28] In the *Principles*, Conway's references to More's concept of 'vital congruity', and notions such as the 'indiscerpibility' and 'discerpibility' of substances, make it obvious when she is referring to More in particular.

[29] *Ibid.*, ch. 9, sect. 2, pp. 63–4.   [30] *Ibid.*, ch. 3, sect. 4, p. 16.   [31] *Ibid.*, ch. 3, sect. 9, p. 18.

[32] Cavendish, *Philosophical Letters*, p. 6.   [33] Conway, *Principles*, ch. 1, sect. 1, p. 9.

[34] *Ibid.*, ch. 7, sect. 1, p. 42.   [35] Cavendish, *Philosophical Letters*, p. 8.

into parts;[36] and they believe that it is impossible for created substances to turn into God.[37] Finally, they maintain that there is no death or annihilation in the natural world. Conway writes that 'the death of things is not their annihilation but a change from one kind or degree of life to another';[38] and Cavendish says of nature's creatures that although they can be transformed, they 'cannot be annihilated, except Nature herself be annihilated'; and that 'to die is nothing else, but that the parts of that figure divide and unite into some other figures'.[39]

But Clucas and Hutton also emphasise that there is a crucial point of *difference* between the two women. For Cavendish everything is made up of *matter*, whereas for Conway body is nothing but condensed *spirit*. Hutton says that

[Conway] too was a monist: that is she postulated that there was only one substance in created nature, and that all things were composed of this single substance. She too was a vitalist, for she imputed life, motion, perception and thought to this substance. But in her case the substance in question was not body; rather it was a form of spirit.[40]

Hutton notes that on the surface this difference would appear to be a question of semantics: what Cavendish means by the word 'body' is what Conway means by the word 'spirit'. But 'underlying this apparently small distinction in terminology is an entirely different structure of thought that reveals that the divergence between the two is of fundamental proportions'.[41] This is because, for Conway, all creatures are composed of configurations of 'spiritual particles, which contain within them the properties any Platonist would expect of spirit: life, perception and the principle of self-movement'.[42] In the *Principles*, Conway writes that 'every body is a spirit' and 'every body is a certain life or spirit in nature'.[43] She says that all creatures are composed of many spirits that are guided by one 'central, ruling, principal spirit'.[44] From these statements, one might be led to believe that when Conway collapses the distinction between soul and body, she is more concerned to emphasise the spirituality of matter, rather than the other way around. Or in other words, it seems that Conway primarily attacks More's concept of matter as essentially passive and inert, but agrees with his conception of the soul.

[36] Conway, *Principles*, ch. 1, sect. 2, p. 9.
[37] Cavendish, *Philosophical Letters*, p. 10; Conway, *Principles*, ch. 1, sect. 3, p. 9.
[38] *Ibid.*, ch. 8, sect. 7, p. 62.   [39] Cavendish, *Philosophical Letters*, pp. 145, 460.
[40] Hutton, 'Anne Conway, Margaret Cavendish', p. 227.   [41] *Ibid.*   [42] *Ibid.*, p. 228.
[43] Conway, *Principles*, ch. 6, sect. 11, pp. 39–40; ch. 7, p. 41.   [44] *Ibid.*, ch. 7, sect. 4, p. 55.

This 'spiritualist' interpretation of Conway's monist theory gains support from the fact that Conway was thoroughly immersed in the doctrines of the Lurianic Kabbalah.[45] The term 'kabbalah', in this context, refers to the Jewish mystical tradition that originated toward the beginning of the thirteenth century. In the seventeenth century, one of the most eminent kabbalist scholars was Christian Knorr von Rosenroth (1636–89), a colleague of Francis Mercury van Helmont. Together these men edited the kabbalistic writings of the followers of Isaac Luria (1534–72), and published them in a collection titled the *Kabbala Denudata* (part 1, 1677; part 2, 1684). Luria considers spirit and matter to be extremes at opposite ends of a continuum; he believes that matter will eventually be restored to its essentially spiritual state. This vision, according to Allison Coudert and Taylor Corse, 'rested on his monistic philosophy, meaning that he believed the created universe was formed from one basically spiritual substance'.[46] Coudert and Corse maintain that Conway's 'spiritual monism' is largely derived from the Lurianic Kabbalah, and hence she too holds that 'matter is in essence spirit'.[47] Making reference to the *Kabbala Denudata* in the *Principles*, Conway says that 'every human being, indeed, every creature whatsoever, contains many spirits and bodies. (The many spirits which exist in men are called by the Jews Nizzuzuth, or sparks.)[48] Truly, every body is a spirit and nothing else, and it differs from a spirit only insofar as it is darker.'[49] Remarks such as these lend strong support to the view that Conway advocates a purely spiritualist philosophy.

Nevertheless, while Conway might be called a spiritualist, there are undeniably materialistic overtones in Conway's conception of 'spirits' and 'spiritual particles'. Conway's critique of More's pneumatology[50] reveals that her theory of substance has more affinities with Cavendish's than might first appear to be the case. More upholds the Cartesian view that all matter is inert and passive, and uses this to show that movement can occur only through the activity of an immaterial substance. He claims that 'only a fool would believe that matter is wise', and he denies that

---

[45] On this topic, see Coudert, *The Impact of the Kabbalah*; Coudert, 'A Cambridge Platonist's Kabbalist Nightmare'; and Brown, 'Leibniz and More's Cabbalistic Circle', pp. 77–96.
[46] Coudert and Corse, 'Introduction' to Conway, *Principles*, p. xx.   [47] *Ibid.*, p. xxx.
[48] The original reference says 'See *Kabbala Denudata*, ii, pt. 2, *De Revolutione Animarum*, pp. 255–68, etc' (Conway, *Principles*, ch. 6, sect. 11, p. 39).
[49] *Ibid.*, ch. 6, sect. 11, pp. 39–40.
[50] For my understanding of this topic, I am indebted to Hutton, 'Anne Conway Critique d'Henry More'.

'a Body is capable of either Sense or Reason'.[51] The bodies of human beings are capable of movement only because they enjoy a 'vital congruity' with the inferior part of the soul. Both spirit and matter have extension, but spirit is indivisible and penetrable, whereas matter is divisible and impenetrable.

Margaret Cavendish challenges More's view that the soul is extended yet indivisible. In her opinion, there is no substance in nature that is not divisible, for whatever has a body is extended, and if a thing has extension then it also has parts, and a thing with parts must be divisible.[52] She also claims that More's orb-of-light analogy fails to establish the conceivability of an extended yet indivisible entity; and she suggests that the attribute of penetrability can also be an attribute of matter, like divisibility. In short, Cavendish denies every one of More's distinctions between spirit and matter: both types of substances, she says, are extended and capable of being divisible and impenetrable. Conway breaks down the same distinctions in her own theory of substance, and ascribes extension, divisibility, and impenetrability to the soul and to spirits in general.

Conway maintains that all spirits have vehicles, or that every created spirit has a body 'whether it is terrestrial, aerial or ethereal'.[53] While her terminology echoes More's, it means something different for Conway to say that souls always have bodies, because she does not see the soul and the body as distinct substances. One of Conway's main objections is that if one considers bodies to be impenetrable and divisible things, and souls penetrable and indivisible, as More does, then it is difficult to see how the two substances can interact. In the *Principles*, she says

how can a spirit move its body or any of its members if the spirit (as they affirm) is of such a nature that no part of its body may resist in any way, as one body usually resists another, when as a result of its impenetrability, it is moved by it? For if spirit so easily penetrates every body, why, when it moves from place to place, does it not leave the body behind since it can so easily pass through it without any or the least resistance?[54]

Conway also appeals to the sensation of pain, asking 'why does the spirit or soul suffer so with bodily pain'?[55] If the soul completely lacks any corporeality, then it ought not to feel anything when the body is harmed, since the soul is entirely penetrable. Basically Conway points

---

[51] More, *Antidote Against Atheism*, pp. 314, 356.   [52] Cavendish, *Philosophical Letters*, p. 194.
[53] Conway, *Principles*, ch. 5, sect. 6, p. 27.   [54] *Ibid.*, ch. 8, sect. 1, pp. 56–7.
[55] *Ibid.*, ch. 8, sect. 2, p. 58.

out that More's 'vital congruity' theory fails to explain exactly *how* the soul and body interact:

> If one says that the vital affinity of the soul for the body is the cause of this union and that this vital affinity ceases with the corruption of the body, I answer that one must first ask in what this vital affinity consists? For if they cannot tell us in what this affinity consists, they are talking foolishly with inane words which have sound but not sense. For surely according to *the sense in which they take body and spirit*, there is no affinity whatsoever. For body is always dead matter lacking life and perception, no less when spirit is in it than when spirit leaves it.[56]

But if some affinity does exist, it ought to remain the same whether the body is whole or corrupt. Surely the spirit does not require an *organised* body to perform its vital actions. Why does the spirit require a corporeal eye 'so wonderfully formed and organized that I may see through it?'[57] In fact, Conway suggests, why should More's soul or spirit need a body at all to act?

Conway's solution to these difficulties is to maintain that the soul and body are one and the same substance. One of her main arguments for this view is drawn from 'that great love and desire which spirits or souls have for bodies'.[58] This is both an argument by analogy and an argument to the best explanation. The four bases of love and desire, Conway says, are (i) that two beings are of one nature and substance; (ii) that they are similar to one another; (iii) that one has its being from another; and (iv) that one recognises the goodness in the other. For example, 'we see in every species of animal that males and females love each other and that in all their matings (which are not monstrous and against nature) they care for each other'.[59] What, we may ask, is the best explanation for this love and desire? They cannot love each other because one has its being from another, since this kind of love must be reserved by creatures for God. Instead, we must conclude that their love 'comes not only from the unity of their nature but also because of their remarkable similarity to each other'.[60] By analogy, she says, we can ask why the soul loves the body and unites with it. Once again, it cannot be because the spirit gave a distinct being to the body, or the body to the spirit, 'because it is solely the function of God and Christ alone to give being to things'.[61] Instead, we must conclude that love occurs between the soul and body because of the 'similarity or affinity between their natures'.[62] Of course, an alternative explanation may be that the soul loves the body because of

---

[56] *Ibid.*, my italics.   [57] *Ibid.*, ch. 8, sect. 1, p. 57.   [58] *Ibid.*, ch. 7, sect. 3, p. 46.
[59] *Ibid.*, p. 47.   [60] *Ibid.*   [61] *Ibid.*, p. 48.   [62] *Ibid.*

its goodness. But according to Conway, this would be the same as saying that the soul and body are similar: 'the reason why we call, or think, something is good is that it does us good and we share its goodness. Consequently, similarity remains the first cause of love'.[63]

Using this argument as a point of departure, Conway notes that the soul could not love the body if the two were so dissimilar that one was extended, impenetrable, and divisible, and the other unextended, penetrable, and indivisible. She collapses these distinctions between the soul and body by expanding on the monistic implications of More's views that both material and immaterial substances are extended, and his opinion that spirit can be extended 'more or less'.[64] Conway agrees that all substances are extended, but she asks: 'Why can the body not be more or less impenetrable and spirit more or less penetrable, as can happen, and indeed does, with other attributes?'[65] She points out that a particular body can change from heavy to light, from solid to liquid, and from hot to cold.

If one says that we always see in these changes that the body remains impenetrable, just as iron when it is tempered remains impenetrable, I concede that it remains impenetrable by any other equally coarse body. But it can be penetrated and is penetrated by a more subtle body, namely by fire, which enters it and penetrates all its parts.[66]

This shows that impenetrability cannot be the essence of a material thing, a characteristic it has to have in order to be the thing it is. Although two bodies of equal coarseness cannot penetrate each other, a coarse body can be easily penetrated by a more subtle body. Then Conway says '*the same thing can be said about spirits*, which also have their own degrees of greater or lesser grossness and subtlety inasmuch as they have bodies';[67] spirits too can have the typical material attribute of impenetrability.

In addition to saying that the soul is extended and capable of being impenetrable, Conway also believes that it is divisible:

What we commonly mean by the divisibility of bodies is that we can divide one body from another by placing a third between them. In this sense, spirits are not less divisible than bodies. For although one single spirit cannot become two or more spirits, nevertheless, a number of spirits coexisting in one body can be separated from each other as easily as bodies can.[68]

On this view, although spiritual particles make up the world, they are extended and potentially impenetrable and divisible particles. Because

---

[63] *Ibid.*, p. 47.   [64] *Ibid.*, p. 49.   [65] *Ibid.*   [66] *Ibid.*, sect. 4, pp. 49–50.
[67] *Ibid.*, p. 51; my italics.   [68] *Ibid.*, p. 52.

we could keep placing particles in between particles to infinity, there is no one particle that is not in principle divisible. This means that, according to Conway, *even spirits are capable of being divided*. Like Cavendish again, she claims that 'although the spirit of man is commonly said to be one single thing, yet this spirit is composed of many spirits, indeed, countless ones'.[69]

In sum, Conway believes that 'impenetrability and indivisibility are no more essential attributes of body than of spirit, because in one sense they apply to both, and in another sense they apply to neither body nor spirit'.[70] The attributes of penetrability and indivisibility can be applied to spirits; but, at the same time, a grosser spirit may be impenetrable to a more subtle spirit; and a single spirit may be divisible in the sense that one particle may separate other particles within that single entity. This is so because, in Conway's system, the soul and body are just two opposite extremes in a continuum; they do not differ essentially. In this last respect, Conway's monism is most likely indebted to the kabbalistic theory of substance. But Conway's created substance also retains most of the attributes that More ascribes to bodies: extension, divisibility, and impenetrability. This theory enables Conway to give a theory of soul–body interaction that is more intelligible than More's:

if one admits that the soul is of one nature and substance with the body, although it surpasses the body by many degrees of life and spirituality, just as it does in swiftness and penetrability and various other perfections, then all the above mentioned difficulties vanish; and one may easily understand how the soul and body are united together and how the soul moves the body and suffers with and through it.[71]

Once one accepts that body and spirit are of the same nature, then one can easily comprehend how the soul affects the body (and *vice versa*), because 'the most subtle and spiritual body can be united with a very gross and dense body by means of certain mediating bodies, which share the subtlety and crassness in various degrees between the two extremes'.[72] The union is broken when these intermediaries are absent. Thus Conway's account of 'vital congruity' is more coherent than the one More offers. Because 'the body itself is sentient life or perceiving substance', she says, it is easily understood 'how one body can wound or bring pain or pleasure to another body, because things of one or of a similar nature can easily affect each other'.[73] This similarity extends

[69] *Ibid.*, p. 53. [70] *Ibid.* [71] *Ibid.*, ch. 8, sect. 2, p. 58.
[72] *Ibid.*, sect. 3, p. 59. [73] *Ibid.*

not only to sense and perception, in her view, but also to the common extension, divisibility, and penetrability or impenetrability of created substances.

Thus the 'spiritual' conception of created things advocated by Conway has a notable resemblance to the 'materialist' conception that Cavendish advocates. Henry More held that if an immaterial substance is extended, it does not necessarily follow that it is also divisible. But both Cavendish and Conway believe that divisibility is a natural concomitant of extension. They support More's view that the soul or spirit is always united to some body or other, but they see the soul and body as different degrees or manifestations of one and the same substance. On this interpretation, Conway's spiritual particles are not quite 'spiritual' in the orthodox sense, because they are always extended and (potentially) divisible and impenetrable. Hutton is right in saying that the attributes Conway gives to body are the attributes that any card-carrying Platonist would expect of soul or spirit: life, perception, and self-motion.[74] But in the eyes of More and his contemporaries, Conway's single substance also has some typically *material* attributes. In this sense, Conway has more affinities with Cavendish than first appears to be the case. They have unorthodox conceptions of bodies, as alive, self-moving, perceptive, and penetrable, and they have materialistic views of the soul, as extended, divisible and capable of being impenetrable. These parallels in their monistic theories of created substance are not adequately captured by those labels typically given to their views.

The similarities between Conway and Cavendish also extend to characterisations of matter or body as a female principle. Cavendish employs the symbol of woman-as-nature to celebrate the autonomy of nature and the self-moving power of matter. She does not identify reason with masculine power or control over the natural world. Nature is characterised as the 'chief Mistress' and human knowledge or art is simply the 'Drudgery-maid'.[75] Conway, on the other hand, draws an analogy between the love between males and females, and love between souls and bodies. Her argument relies upon the supposition that men and women love one another because they have the same nature. In other words, she points out the *similarities* rather than the differences between men and women. In this sense, one might say that Conway avoids those metaphorical associations between gender and reason that have led to the exclusion of women from intellectual discourse. Conway does not characterise

---

74 Hutton, 'Anne Conway, Margaret Cavendish'.   75 Cavendish, *Philosophical Letters*, p. 36.

the male–female relationship as one based on inequality in order to illustrate a dominant–subordinate relationship between the soul and body. Furthermore, this egalitarianism is echoed in other passages where spirit and bodies are likened to husband and wife:

In every visible creature there is body and spirit, or a more active and a more passive principle, which are appropriately called male and female because they are analogous to husband and wife. For just as the normal generation of human beings commonly requires the conjunction and cooperation of male and female, so too does every generation and production, whatever it may be, require the union and simultaneous operation of these two principles, namely spirit and body. Moreover, spirit is light or the eye looking at its own proper image, and the body is the darkness which receives this image. And when the spirit beholds it, it is as if someone sees himself in a mirror. But he cannot see himself reflected in the same way in clear air or in any diaphanous body, since the reflection of an image requires a certain opacity, which we call body. Nevertheless, it is not an essential property of anything to be a body, just as it is not a property of anything to be dark. For nothing is so dark that it cannot become bright.... In the same way, light which is created can turn to darkness.[76]

Lois Frankel suggests that this passage reflects the fact that spirit, activity, light, and maleness are valued more highly in Conway's system than matter, passivity, darkness, and femaleness.[77] Frankel attributes this dichotomous thinking to Conway's Platonist and kabbalistic influences. But Conway's philosophy also significantly departs from these sources. The above quotation can also be interpreted as expressing an equal relationship between male–female couples, rather than one between inferiors and superiors: there is a co-dependency between body and spirit, just as there is a relationship of mutual cooperation between wives and husbands.[78] The regeneration of body and spirit, like the reproduction of human beings, requires two principles acting together in harmony. Although creatures may become 'more and more spiritual' as they approach perfection, according to Conway these beings will still be united to some body or other, and they will remain (to some extent) extended, divisible, and impenetrable, because 'the distinction between spirit and body is only modal and incremental, not essential and substantial'.[79] In this

---

[76] Conway, *Principles*, ch. 6, sect. 11, p. 38.

[77] Frankel, 'Anne Finch, Viscountess Conway', p. 46.

[78] There is a similar observation in More's *Antidote*: 'And here I appeal to any man, whether the contrivance of *Male* and *Female* in living Creatures, be not a genuine effect of *Wisdom* and *Counsel*; for it is notoriously obvious that these are made one for the other, and both for the continuation of the *Species*' (More, *Antidote Against Atheism*, p. 122).

[79] Conway, *Principles*, ch. 6, sect. 11, p. 40.

case, as in the argument by analogy, Conway draws on the connections, rather than the disparities, between males and females to make a further point about the parallels between the spiritual and material. She also says that the 'internal productions of the mind' (thoughts) are our inner children, 'and all are masculine and feminine; that is, they have a body and spirit'.[80] The mind is not characterised as exclusively 'masculine' in contrast to the 'feminine' body.

In sum, Conway's philosophy raises the ontological status of bodies by making them alive, sentient, and capable of self-motion, and by giving material attributes to the soul; in her philosophical system, she blurs essential distinctions between body and spirit, making them one and the same substance; and she makes a positive association between the body and femaleness. Furthermore, because Conway does not recognise any essential difference between the body and soul, their relationship is commonly depicted as interdependent. In all these respects, Conway's system has many notable similarities to modern-day feminist responses to dualism.

II

But while there are strong affinities between the views of Conway and Cavendish on created substance, there are crucial respects in which their philosophies *as a whole* fundamentally diverge. The main point of difference lies in their conception of the relationship between God and the created world: for Cavendish, the one created substance completely differs from God, whereas for Conway, the one created substance has essential affinities with the divine.

At first glance, it may appear that Conway's primary concern is to highlight the *differences* between God and the created world. Like Henry More, Conway is especially keen to disassociate her writings from those of the Dutch Jewish philosopher, Baruch (or Benedict) de Spinoza (1632–77). Spinoza's *Tractatus Theologico-Politicus* (1670) and his posthumous *Ethics* (1677), aroused violent hostility in Conway's lifetime. His most controversial thesis was the identification of God with nature. In the *Tractatus*, Spinoza says that 'Nature's power is nothing but the power of God.'[81] He asserts that human beings participate in God's nature, and that God 'communicates his essence to our minds without employing

---

[80] *Ibid.*, p. 39.
[81] Baruch Spinoza, *Tractatus Theologico-Politicus*, translated by Samuel Shirley, with an introduction by Brad S. Gregory, second edition (Leiden: Brill, 1991), p. 71.

corporeal means'.[82] In the *Ethics*, this idea is further justified and developed: God and nature together, according to Spinoza, constitute the one infinite substance in the universe. In the seventeenth century, Spinoza's views were widely regarded as a barely disguised form of atheism. Conway herself says that such ideas are 'to the detriment of true piety, and in contempt of the most glorious name of God'.[83] If God and his creatures were one and the same substance, this leads to the absurdity that 'sin and devils would be nothing but parts of the slightest modification of this divine being'.[84]

In the *Principles*, Conway spells out the differences between her own views and Spinoza's reviled form of pantheistic monism. She asserts that Spinoza 'confounds God and creatures and makes one being of both, all of which is diametrically opposed to our philosophy'.[85] In her philosophy, God is *pure spirit*, utterly without corporeality and divisibility; whereas created substances are both body and spirit – they have spatial dimensions, and they are divisible and impenetrable (to a greater or lesser degree). It follows that God is also *essentially* immutable; he cannot change because he is outside of time and indivisible; whereas daily experience teaches us that creatures, who are both temporal and corporeal (to various degrees), are essentially mutable.[86] Thus God and the creatures are distinct substances.

Like Cavendish, Conway also defines her philosophy against Hobbes's mechanistic materialism. It might be suggested that in Conway's philosophy every creature is either material or corporeal. Conway herself does not deny this point, but rather asserts that 'by material and corporeal, or by matter and body, I mean something very different from Hobbes'.[87] Hobbes makes the same mistake as Descartes – he ignores the most noble, 'spiritual' attributes of body: vitality, perception, and the capacity for greater fruition. In agreement with Cavendish, Conway affirms that Hobbes is wrong to think that there are only mechanical motions in nature.

Nevertheless, implicit in this criticism of Hobbes is a feature of Conway's philosophy that distances her from Cavendish and brings Conway closer to later seventeenth-century women philosophers. Although Conway is no avowed feminist, her metaphysics draws on a principle that underpins the feminist ideas of Astell and Masham: the idea that all of God's creatures have a purpose as part of the divine plan,

---

[82] Spinoza, *Tractatus Theologico-Politicus*, p. 64.   [83] Conway, *Principles*, ch. 9, sect. 1, p. 63.
[84] *Ibid.*, ch. 6, sect. 5, p. 31.   [85] *Ibid.*, ch. 9, sect. 3, p. 64.
[86] *Ibid.*, sect. 5, p. 65.   [87] *Ibid.*, sect. 6, p. 65.

or that all events in nature are arranged by divine wisdom for an end or 'final cause'. In the *Principles*, Conway specifically promotes the view that all creatures are designed to perfect themselves toward a greater spirituality. She says that every created being is capable of becoming 'more perfect and more excellent to infinity', although none can ever reach that infinity.[88]

The ancient view that there is a final or 'intending causality' in nature is not uncommon among seventeenth-century English thinkers. The Cambridge Platonists uphold teleological forms of explanation against Descartes' view that philosophers ought not to inquire into final causes. In his *Principles of Philosophy* (1644), Descartes says that

It is not the final but the efficient causes of created things that we must inquire into. When dealing with natural things we will, then, never derive any explanations from the purposes which God or nature may have had in view when creating them <and we shall entirely banish from our philosophy the search for final causes>. For we should not be so arrogant as to suppose that we can share in God's plans.[89]

Descartes' attitude toward final causality is consistent with his attempt to reduce all the sciences to a purely mechanical physics. For Descartes, the proper scientific study of nature involves seeing the material world as a purely mechanical system and considering nothing but efficient causes.

Descartes' rejection of teleology or 'final cause' explanations was strongly opposed in England. Lamprecht notes that English writers 'were made suspicious at once by the fact that Descartes had entirely rejected the teleological argument which was a bulwark of faith among bishops and ecclesiastics generally'.[90] Ralph Cudworth complains that Descartes disarms the world 'of that grand argument for a Deity, taken from the *Regular Frame* and *Harmony of the Universe*'.[91] He claims that those theorists who allow no '*Final* nor *Mental Causality*' (disposing things in order to Ends) have been strongly suspected for Friends to Atheism'.[92] Instead, he favours Aristotle's system because Descartes

makes God to contribute nothing more to the Fabrick of the World, than the Turning round of a *Vortex* or Whirlpool of Matter; from the fortuitous Motion of which, according to certain General Laws of Nature, must proceed all this Frame of things that now is, the exact Organization, and successive Generation of Animals, without the Guidance of any Mind or Wisdom. Whereas *Aristotle's* Nature is no Fortuitous Principle, but such as doth Nothing in Vain, but all for Ends, and in everything pursues *the Best*.[93]

---

88 *Ibid.*, ch. 6, sect. 6, p. 33.
89 Descartes, *Principles of Philosophy*, in *Philosophical Writings*, vol. 1, pp. 202–3.
90 Lamprecht, 'The Role of Descartes in Seventeenth-Century England', 222.
91 Cudworth, *True Intellectual System*, p. 175.   92 *Ibid.*, p. 154.   93 *Ibid.*, p. 54.

For Cudworth, More, and others, to ignore final causality is akin to suggesting that order in nature comes about through chance, rather than by the design of a providential God.

In the same spirit, teleology is a guiding principle behind Conway's philosophy. Against Descartes' recommendations, she uses final causality as an explanatory tool for her theory of created substances. Like the Platonists, Conway says that 'the divine power, goodness, and wisdom has created good creatures so that they may continually and infinitely move towards the good'.[94] She maintains that all creatures must have the capacity for motion, because otherwise they cannot move toward perfection. This is also her justification for claiming that no creature can be reduced to its smallest part. If something were to be divided into its smallest part, she says, then its motion would cease, 'for it is the nature of all motion that it breaks down and divides something into finer parts'.[95] Instead, every creature, by nature, is either in motion or has the capacity for motion, 'by which means it progresses and grows to its ultimate perfection'.[96] We should not claim that God can reduce a creature to its smallest part, because 'To do this would be contrary to the wisdom and goodness of God. For if every motion or operation would cease in some creature, that creature would be entirely useless in creation and would be no better than if it were pure nothingness and utter non-being.'[97] Conway concedes that it is possible for material things to be broken down into smaller parts. But when 'concrete matter is so divided that it disperses into physical monads, then it is ready to resume its activity and become spirit'.[98] The more spiritual a being becomes, the closer it progresses toward God, the highest spirit.

Furthermore, Conway believes that because all creatures are capable of greater perfection without end, no particular creature can be entirely separated or disconnected from other beings:

For if a creature were entirely limited by its own individuality and totally constrained by and confined within the very narrow boundaries of its own species to the point that there was no mediator through which one creature could change into another, then no creature could attain further perfection and greater participation in divine goodness, nor could creatures act and react upon each other in different ways.[99]

Conway uses the same argument against atomism. If one atom were separate from all fellow creatures, then it could do nothing to perfect itself and

---

[94] Conway, *Principles*, ch. 6, sect. 6, p. 32.   [95] *Ibid.*, ch. 3, sect. 9, p. 20.
[96] *Ibid.*, ch. 2, sect. 6, p. 14.   [97] *Ibid.*, ch. 3, sect. 9, p. 20.   [98] *Ibid.*
[99] *Ibid.*, ch. 6, sect. 5, p. 32.

become greater or better; therefore, it cannot be part of God's creation.[100] To suggest otherwise, she notes again, 'obscures the glory of the divine attributes', namely God's supreme benevolence and wisdom.[101] By a similar logic, there must be a 'middle nature', or mediating substance between God and his creatures, enabling the creatures to attain greater participation in divine goodness; and this mediator is Christ.[102]

Finally, Conway also argues against the concept of dead matter. She says that there cannot be any such thing as matter that completely lacks life, motion, and perception. If matter is incapable of reason, then it is difficult to see how it can 'acquire greater goodness to infinity'.[103] On this view, matter would be a useless part of creation, a notion that would cast doubt on God's wisdom. Instead, Conway says, if we carefully consider the divine attributes we must see that

since God is infinitely good and communicates his goodness to all his creatures in infinite ways, so that there is no creature which does not receive something of his goodness, and this as fully as possible, and since the goodness of God is a living goodness, which possesses life, knowledge, love, and power, which he communicates to his creatures, how can any dead thing proceed from him or be created by him, such as mere body or matter, according to the hypothesis of those who affirm that matter cannot be changed into any degree of life or perception? It has truly been said that God does not make death. It is equally true that he did not make any dead thing, for how can a dead thing come from him who is infinite life and love? Or, how can any creature receive so vile and diminished an essence from him (who is so infinitely generous and good) that it does not share any life or perception and is not able to aspire to the least degree of these for all eternity? Did not God create all his creatures to this end, namely, that they be blessed in him and enjoy his divine goodness in their various conditions and states? Moreover, how could this be possible without life and perception?[104]

Given that every creature shares in the communicable attributes of God, there can be no such thing as dead matter that is incapable of life, movement, and sense. Dead matter is rather 'completely non-being, a vain fiction and Chimera, and an impossible thing'.[105]

The Platonic and kabbalistic view that all creatures have an innate capacity to perfect themselves, and *become more like God*, thus occupies a central position in Conway's metaphysics. This is one of the main points of difference between Conway and Cavendish. Conway's conception of God's affinities with his creation accounts for several key features of her

---

[100] *Ibid.*, ch. 7, sect. 4, p. 54.   [101] *Ibid.*, ch. 6, sect. 5, p. 32.   [102] *Ibid.*, ch. 8, sect. 3, p. 60.
[103] *Ibid.*, ch. 7, sect. 2, p. 46.   [104] *Ibid.*, pp. 44–5.   [105] *Ibid.*, pp. 45–6.

theory: why all creatures have the capacity for motion, why creatures can never be reduced to their smallest parts, or into separate, individual atoms, and why no particle of matter is dead, inactive, or without perception. Like the Cambridge Platonists, Conway takes pains to emphasise the *spiritual purpose* behind creation in the explication of her theory. Cavendish's one created substance, by contrast, does not have the capacity to become more spiritual, or to perfect itself; it has no significant affinities with God, and is completely unlike him for all eternity.

III

So although there are great similarities in the ontological theories of Cavendish and Conway, there is a vast gulf between their attitudes toward theology and philosophy. Both Hutton and Clucas acknowledge this contrast. Hutton points out that for Conway theology and philosophy are inseparable, whereas for Cavendish they are not.[106] In fact, Cavendish maintains that faith and natural philosophy must be kept apart: 'Faith and Reason are two contrary things, and cannot consist together.'[107] In the *Philosophical Letters*, she complains that some philosophers,

drawing Divinity to prove Sense and Reason, weaken Faith so, as their mixed Divine Philosophy becomes meer Poetical Fictions, and Romancical expressions ... Truly, *Madam*, I wish their Wits had been less, and their Judgments more, as not to jumble Natural and Supernatural things together, but to distinguish either clearly, for such Mixtures are neither Natural nor Divine.[108]

Clucas notes that Cavendish advocates an 'extrinsic theism' in the sense that her system does not appeal to God's attributes in the construction of its principles, whereas Conway holds the view that knowledge of the world can be deduced *a priori* from our understanding of God's attributes.[109]

This divergence between Conway and Cavendish can be traced to differing theological assumptions about God and his relationship to the created world. Conway upholds the 'intellectualist' view that God's primary attribute is his supreme wisdom; Cavendish, on the other hand, asserts the 'voluntarist' belief that God's will and power can override his rationality.

An intellectualist, according to John Henry, maintains that God 'had no choice but to create the world in accordance with the moral demands

---

[106] Hutton, 'Anne Conway, Margaret Cavendish'.   [107] Cavendish, *Philosophical Letters*, p. 210.
[108] *Ibid.*, p. 13.   [109] Clucas, 'The Duchess and Viscountess', p. 134.

placed upon Him by His own goodness and in accordance with the essential relationships inherent in the nature of things'.[110] Ralph Cudworth takes a typical intellectualist position in his *True Intellectual System of the Universe*. One of his principal aims is to show that there are certain essential features in the world, or 'Something in its own *Nature, Immutably* and *Eternally Just*, and *Unjust*',[111] which is not subject to the divine will. In his 'Preface to the Reader', Cudworth says that he challenges those theorists who claim that God's will is 'in no way Regulated or Determined, by any *Essentiall* and *Immutable Goodness*, and *Justice*; or that he hath nothing of *Morality* in his *Nature*, he being onely *Arbitrary Will Omnipotent*'.[112] The dialectic concerning God's omnipotence and his intellect in the seventeenth century can be interpreted as a dispute concerning the role of contingency and necessity in the natural world. In *Divine Will and the Mechanical Philosophy*, Margaret Osler says that 'Theologians who emphasized God's rationality were more inclined to accept elements of necessity in the creation than those who emphasized his absolute freedom and concluded that the world is utterly contingent.'[113]

The intellectualist theological outlook – that there are certain necessary features of creation that not even God can change – is present in Conway's views that God cannot reduce creatures to their smallest parts, that no creature can exist independently of another, and that God cannot create dead matter. She suggests that God is bound to create the world in accordance with his supreme benevolence and wisdom: he would not create something that had no chance of achieving perfection or salvation. Conway also says that there can be no indifference of will in God, because this too would be an imperfection.[114] She claims that everything God does must have a reason, or is dictated by wisdom. One corollary of this view is the belief that one can discover the basic principles of reality through reason: if God created the world by exercising his rationality, and if humans partake in the divine rationality, then we must be able to understand that world through a process of pure reasoning.[115] Conway develops her metaphysics along the same lines by theorising about what the divine attributes necessarily imply for his creation – especially the attributes of matter.

[110] John Henry, 'Henry More Versus Robert Boyle: The Spirit of Nature and the Nature of Providence', in Hutton (ed.), *Henry More (1614–1687)*, p. 62.
[111] Cudworth, *True Intellectual System*, sig. A3[v].   [112] *Ibid.*, sig. A3[r].
[113] Margaret J. Osler, *Divine Will and the Mechanical Philosophy: Gassendi and Descartes on contingency and necessity in the created world* (Cambridge: Cambridge University Press, 1994), p. 10.
[114] Conway, *Principles*, ch. 3, sect. 2, p. 16.
[115] See Henry, 'Henry More Versus Robert Boyle', p. 64.

Voluntarists, on the other hand, believe that God's omnipotence can override his rationality. For voluntarists, according to Margaret Osler, there is no guarantee that the course of nature will be predictable or capable of being understood by human reason. This is because God is not constrained to act in accordance with the laws he himself created. Everything other than God, according to this viewpoint, is utterly contingent. Margaret Cavendish advocates this conception of the deity when she maintains that 'nothing is impossible with God'.[116] Those who place a limit on God's power measure omnipotence merely by human rules of logic, 'as if God were not able to work beyond Nature, and Natural Reason or Understanding'.[117] She says: 'I wonder how man can say, God is Omnipotent, and can do beyond our Understanding, and yet deny all that he is not able to comprehend with his reason.'[118] She even claims that 'God's Power may make a Vacuum, yet Nature cannot.'[119]

This voluntarist outlook leads Cavendish to assert, against the Cambridge Platonists, that God is capable of endowing matter with the capacity for perception and self-motion. 'Matter stands in no need to have some Immaterial or Incorporeal substance to move, rule, guide and govern her, but she is able enough to do it all her self, by the free gift of the Omnipotent God.'[120] According to Cavendish, God is able to give nature the power to act independently of his guidance; nature is the designer itself, with no need of God's perpetual direction.

In *The True Intellectual System*, published five years after Cavendish's death, Ralph Cudworth objects to this concept of nature as independent of the deity. Although Cudworth does not refer to Cavendish by name, his reference to her philosophy is unmistakable:

we are not ignorant, that some, who seem to be Well-Wishers to Atheism, have talk'd sometimes of *Sensitive* and *Rational Matter*, as having a mind to suppose, *Three* several sorts of *Matter* in the Universe, Specifically different from one another, that were Originally such, and Self-existent from Eternity; namely, *Senseless, Sensitive* and *Rational*: As if the *Mundane System* might be conceived to arise, from a certain Jumble of these *Three several sorts* of *Matter*, as it were scuffling together in the Dark, without a God, and so producing Brute Animals and Men. But as this is a mere Precarious *Hypothesis*, there being no imaginable accompt to be given, how there should come to be such an Essential Difference betwixt *Matters*, or why this Piece of Matter should be *Sensitive*, and that *Rational*, when

---

[116] Cavendish, *Philosophical Letters*, p. 15.   [117] *Ibid.*, p. 458.   [118] *Ibid.*, p. 199.
[119] *Ibid.*, p. 452.   [120] *Ibid.*, pp. 194–5.

another is altogether *Senseless*; so the Suggestors of it are but mere *Novices in Atheism*, and a kind of Bungling *Well-wishers* to it.[121]

Cudworth claims instead that we ought to attribute order in the material world to an intellectual principle or 'mental causality' that executes the divine plan. Cavendish, however, had already anticipated Cudworth's objection in her *Letters*. She says that 'if man (who is but a single part of nature) hath given him by God the power of free will of moving himself, why should not God give it to Nature?'[122] Cavendish believes it is unhelpful to appeal to fanciful notions such as incorporeal plastic nature, when the idea of self-moving matter can adequately explain natural phenomena. She is opposed to multiplying substances beyond necessity: an all-powerful God ought to be able to order nature in the simplest way. That is to say, she cannot imagine why God 'should make an Immaterial Spirit to be the Proxy or Vice-gerent of his Power, or the *Quarter-Master General of his Divine Providence* . . . when he is able to effect it without any Under-Officers, and in a more easie and compendious way, as to impart immediately such self-moving power to Natural Matter, which man attributes to an Incorporeal Spirit'.[123] Cavendish stresses that Nature is intelligent: 'she knows how to order her parts and actions wisely; for as she hath an Infinite body or substance, so she has an Infinite life and knowledg; and as she hath Infinite life and knowledg, so she hath an infinite wisdom'.[124] Cavendish denies that it is atheistic to say that nature is wise and self-moving. This theory tends to support God's existence because nature's wisdom and free power of moving could proceed only from an omnipotent and infinitely wise being.[125]

Overall, the main point of difference between Cavendish and Conway is not just a matter of Cavendish advocating that 'Where Reason ends, Faith begins,'[126] and Conway maintaining that faith and reason are compatible. The divergence between Cavendish and Conway also lies in their differing conceptions of God's role in his creation. Cavendish holds

---

[121] Cudworth, *True Intellectual System*, p. 137. Cudworth also says that 'The *Numen* which the Hylozoick Corporealist pays all his Devotions to, is a certain blind *Shee-god* or *Goddess*, called *Nature* or the *Life of Matter*' (p. 107). 'Hylozoism' is the view that all material things are invested with life or with an inner vital principle. This doctrine is often contrasted with 'panpsychism', the view that the basic constituent parts of nature have mental properties. For a discussion on hylozoism and panpsychism in the seventeenth century, see Guido Giglioni, 'Panpsychism *versus* Hylozoism: An Interpretation of Some Seventeenth-Century Doctrines of Universal Animation', *Acta Comeniana* 11 (1995), 25–44.
[122] Cavendish, *Philosophical Letters*, p. 95.
[123] *Ibid.*, p. 215. The italicised phrase is quoted from Henry More's *Immortality of the Soul* (III.vi.13).
[124] Cavendish, *Philosophical Letters*, p. 144.   [125] *Ibid.*, p. 164.   [126] *Ibid.*, p. 211.

that the created world is contingent on God's power and will, whereas Conway maintains that created substances are necessarily the way they are due to God's goodness and wisdom.

In so far as they challenge Descartes, More, and Hobbes, in their ontological views Conway and Cavendish are remarkably similar. Conway, like Cavendish before her, challenges the strict division between soul and body. In the contingent, created world, Conway says, the soul and body do not differ essentially, but together they make up one type of substance; body is a kind of solidified spirit, and spirit a kind of volatile body. For Conway, as for Cavendish, questions about how the soul interacts with the body are no longer perplexing once it is granted that the soul is of one nature and substance with the body. Because Conway collapses distinctions between spirit and body, and avoids gender-biased characterisations of the soul–body relationship, she can also be said to anticipate recent feminist critiques of dualism.

But Cavendish and Conway have very different conceptions of God's relationship to his creation. Conway emphasises that no part of the created world is dead or redundant, because if this were so it would be contrary to the wisdom and goodness of God. Instead, all created beings have life, motion, and perception – features that enable them to strive toward perfection. In the following chapters, I show that similar teleological and intellectualist principles provide significant inspiration for the later seventeenth-century writers, Mary Astell, Damaris Masham, and Catharine Trotter Cockburn. Astell, Masham, and Cockburn are not monists, but in their metaphysical writings we see some of the last direct challenges to the Cartesian legacy in England.

4

Mary Astell

Mary Astell was one of the foremost defenders of women in late seventeenth-century England. In a time when women were seen as intellectually deficient, she embraced Descartes' philosophy in support of arguments for the equal rational capacities of the sexes, and she used those arguments to oppose the inferior education bestowed upon women. For this reason, Astell is typically regarded as a Cartesian. Hilda Smith describes Astell as 'a dedicated Cartesian, but one of a particularly religious bent';[1] Ruth Perry believes that 'Cartesian rationalism was the very cornerstone of her feminism';[2] Margaret Atherton defends Astell's 'Cartesian conception of reason';[3] and others emphasise that Descartes' account of subjectivity enables Astell to see the soul, rather than the body, as her true self.[4] At first glance, then, the consensus opinion would appear to place Astell in opposition to modern feminist critics of Cartesianism who allege that Descartes' rationalist philosophy implicitly excludes women by idealising a conception of reason that is stereotypically masculine. If one accepts this view, then Astell's feminist arguments are somewhat limited: despite valorising female rationality, they depend upon a conceptual framework that precipitates women's exclusion from the intellectual sphere.

In this chapter, I show that Astell's feminism is clearly indebted to Descartes, but I also examine the ways in which her metaphysical views diverge from the 'modern Cartesians' of her time. This divergence is most evident in her letters to the 'English Malebranche', John Norris, who published their correspondence in 1695 as *Letters Concerning the Love of God, Between the Author of the Proposal to the Ladies and Mr. John Norris*. In the

---

[1] Smith, *Reason's Disciples*, p. 119.
[2] Perry, 'Radical Doubt and the Liberation of Women', 491.
[3] Atherton, 'Cartesian Reason and Gendered Reason', pp. 27–32.
[4] Gallagher, 'Embracing the Absolute', 34, 35. See also Joan K. Kinnaird, 'Mary Astell and the Conservative Contribution to English Feminism', *The Journal of British Studies* 19:1 (1979), 62.

final part of this exchange, Astell puts forward a non-Cartesian theory of soul–body interaction, influenced by Descartes' early English critics, the Cambridge Platonists. The philosophical themes arising from this correspondence, and developed in Astell's later works, provide evidence that Cartesianism is not the only significant influence in Astell's thought. For this reason, modern feminist criticism of Astell's writings may not be entirely justified.

I

Although only four years separate the publication of Conway's *Principles* and Astell's first treatise, *A Serious Proposal to the Ladies* (1694), the two philosophers belong to completely different generations. Whereas Conway's early education was influenced by the rise of Cartesianism and the Platonic renaissance in mid-seventeenth-century England, Astell's first foray into philosophy was in the late-seventeenth century, and her most common target is John Locke.[5] Nevertheless, both Astell and Conway have Cambridge Platonism as a common source of inspiration. While Conway gained her philosophical education through a correspondence with More, Astell was educated by her uncle, Ralph Astell, a curate who was a student of Emmanuel College in the heyday of Cambridge Platonism.[6] Born in Newcastle-upon-Tyne on 12 November 1666, Mary Astell was the first child of Mary Errington and Peter Astell, a gentleman and member of the Company of Hostmen. From an early age she faced an uncertain and possibly dismal future. Her father's death in 1678 left the family in financial straits, and without a reasonable dowry Astell could not expect to marry someone of her own social standing. She apparently decided on a writing career as an alternative to marriage (she remained single all her life), and after her mother's death in 1684, she moved to London, probably with the intention of pursuing this ambition.[7]

---

5 For Astell's criticisms of Locke, see Richard Acworth, *The Philosophy of John Norris of Bemerton* (1657–1712) (New York: Georg Olms Verlag, 1979), p. 238; Ruth Perry, 'Mary Astell and the Feminist Critique of Possessive Individualism', *Eighteenth Century Studies* 23 (1990), 444–57; Patricia Springborg, 'Mary Astell (1666–1731), Critic of Locke', *American Political Science Review* 89 (1995), 621–33; Patricia Springborg, 'Astell, Masham, and Locke: Religion and Politics', in Smith (ed.), *Women Writers*, pp. 105–25; Kathleen M. Squadrito, 'Mary Astell's Critique of Locke's View of Thinking Matter', *Journal of History of Philosophy* 25 (1987), 433–9; and Kathleen M. Squadrito, 'Mary Astell', in Waithe (ed.), *A History of Women Philosophers*, vol. III, pp. 87–99.
6 On Ralph Astell and the Cambridge school, see Ruth Perry, *The Celebrated Mary Astell: An Early English Feminist* (Chicago: Chicago University Press, 1986), pp. 49–51.
7 This account of Mary Astell's life is taken from my article 'Mary Astell (1666–1731)', *British Philosophers, 1500–1799*, edited by Philip B. Dematteis and Peter S. Fosl, *Dictionary of Literary Biography* 252 (2002), 3–10.

Astell was saved from hardship by the financial support and friend-ship of a group of gentlewomen, including Lady Ann Coventry, Lady Elizabeth Hastings, and Lady Catherine Jones. From the 1690s onward, Astell lived near her friends in Chelsea, where she spent her time, like a true Cartesian, teaching herself the basic principles of philosophy and religion. Unable to read French,[8] Astell's understanding of Descartes was derived from English translations, popularisations, and commentaries on his work. She almost certainly read Henry More's *The Immortality of the Soul* and *An Account of Virtue* (1690). She probably also read More's corre-spondence with John Norris in *The Theory and Regulation of Love* (1688).[9] In all of Astell's writings,[10] there are impressions left by these English works: she is critical of those philosophers who denigrate the spiritual or rational aspects of human beings; like Cudworth and More, she opposes any form of 'atheistic' materialism in which the material world is en-tirely disconnected from the spiritual; and she upholds a providentialist interpretation of the natural world.

Astell's earliest venture into serious philosophical writing is with 'the last of the Cambridge Platonists', John Norris. Their epistolary exchange, initiated by Astell on 21 September 1693 and concluded one year later, was privately published at Norris's suggestion. The principal focus of the *Letters* is on the Malebranchean view that one must desire and love God above everything else. Astell's part of the correspondence was highly praised by her contemporaries. Leibniz and Thomas Burnet of Kemnay both expressed their admiration,[11] the bluestocking Sarah Chapone re-garded the work as Astell's most 'sublime',[12] and Mary Evelyn recom-mended 'Mr Norrises letters to the Seraphick Lady' to Ralph Bohun[13]

---

[8] In a letter to Norris, dated 15 February 1693, Astell says that 'I am exceedingly pleas'd with *M. Malbranch's* Account of the Reasons why we have no Ideas of our Souls, and wish I cou'd read that ingenious Author in his own Language, or that he spake mine' (Astell and Norris, *Letters*, p. 149).

[9] John Norris encourages Astell to read this work (see Norris to Astell, 13 November 1693; in *ibid.*, p. 73).

[10] Astell's works are (in order of publication): *A Serious Proposal To the Ladies* (1694); *Letters Concerning the Love of God* (1695); *A Serious Proposal To The Ladies, Part II* (1697); *Some Reflections Upon Marriage* (1700); *Moderation truly Stated* (1704); *A Fair Way With The Dissenters And Their Patrons* (1704); *An Impartial Enquiry Into The Causes Of Rebellion and Civil War In This Kingdom* (1704); *The Christian Religion, As Profess'd by a Daughter Of The Church of England* (1705); and *Bart'lemy Fair: Or, An Enquiry after Wit* (1709).

[11] Gerhardt (ed.), *Die Philosophischen Schriften*, vol. 11, pp. 569–70, and vol. 111, p. 199.

[12] See Perry, *The Celebrated Mary Astell*, p. 82.

[13] Mary Evelyn to Ralph Bohun, 7 April 1695; in the British Library, London, the 'Evelyn Papers' (uncatalogued). She says that 'I suppose Mr Norrises letters to the Seraphick Lady with her answers and the same Ladyes proposalls to the Ladyes in a litle treatise are not unknowne to you.' I am grateful to Dr Frances Harris in the MSS Department for referring me to Evelyn's letters.

and her son. 'Not that I recomend them from my owne judgment or liking,' Evelyn says, 'but the witts and those of the clergy think them worth reading, I confesse the Notions in the letters are so refined I dare not give my oppinion the woman has a good Character for virtue and is very litle above twenty which adds to her praise, to be so early good and knowing.'[14]

These epistles incorporate many of Astell's central philosophical beliefs. In one letter to Norris, dated 31 October 1693, Astell gives an indication of her later feminist concerns. 'Fain wou'd I rescue my Sex,' she says,

> or at least as many of them as come within my little Sphere, from that Meanness of Spirit into which the Generality of 'em are sunk, perswade them to pretend some higher Excellency than a well-chosen Pettycoat, or a fashionable Commode; and not wholly lay out their Time and Care in the Adornation of their Bodies, but bestow a Part of it at least in the Embellishment of their Minds, since inward Beauty will last when outward is decayed.[15]

Prior to the publication of the *Letters*, Astell realised this ambition with the anonymous *A Serious Proposal to the Ladies*. Written by 'a Lover of her Sex', the proposal is a carefully reasoned argument for the establishment of a female academic institute. According to her biographers, Astell's college did not materialise due to the suspicion that it was a call for the restoration of Catholic nunneries.[16] A wealthy woman, who might have been Princess Anne of Denmark (later Queen Anne), was willing to contribute £10,000 to Astell's plan, but was dissuaded by Gilbert Burnet, the Bishop of Salisbury, who warned her that it looked like preparing a way for popery. *A Serious Proposal to the Ladies Part II* (1697) is dedicated to the princess and emphasises that the institute would be more academic than monastic. Disappointed that no one was roused to build her college, Astell wrote this work to provide a philosophical method for women to practise at home.

In both the first and second parts of the *Proposal*, Astell's arguments are based on ideas borrowed from Descartes' *Discourse on the Method*, *Principles of Philosophy*, and *Passions of the Soul*. Her sources of inspiration include Descartes' view that reason is by nature equal in all human beings, his challenge to ancient authorities, his mistrust of custom and

[14] Mary Evelyn to John Evelyn, 2 November 1695; in the British Library, London, the 'Evelyn Papers' (uncatalogued).
[15] Astell to Norris, 31 October 1693; in Astell and Norris, *Letters*, p. 49.
[16] Ballard, *Memoirs of Several Ladies*, p. 383.

unexamined prejudices, his emphasis on the self-sufficiency of the mind, and his rigorous method of thought.

Astell was not the first writer to apply Descartes' philosophical approach to the issue of women's education. In 1673, a Frenchman named François Poulain de la Barre published a work titled *De l'Égalité des Deux Sexes* (translated into English as *The Woman as Good as the Man* in 1677).[17] In this work, Poulain de la Barre argues that common opinions about the intellectual inferiority of women are based on ill-grounded prejudices and the authority of the ancients. Following Cartesian method, he submits these unexamined opinions to the 'Rule of Verity', the notion that whatever we can clearly and distinctly perceive is true. He points out that the soul is of one and the same nature in all human beings; the spirit itself has no sex, so the difference between the sexes cannot be on these grounds. Furthermore, men and women are *also* equal in terms of the disposition of their sensory organs: the 'impressions of sense', he says, are almost identical in both sexes.[18] Hence women (like men) must also have minds capable of knowing truth, and 'ought to put themselves in condition of avoyding the Reproach, of having stifled a Talent, which they might put to use'.[19]

There is no evidence that Mary Astell read Poulain de la Barre's work,[20] but it is likely she was familiar with his ideas – there are striking similarities both in the language and content of their arguments. Astell draws on Descartes' egalitarian concept of reason in her first letter to Norris, dated 21 September 1693. Justifying her own incursions into philosophy, she says: 'For though I can't pretend to a Multitude of Books, Variety of Languages, the Advantages of Academical Education, or any Helps but what my own Curiosity afford; yet, *Thinking* is a Stock that no Rational Creature can want, if they but know how to use it.'[21] In

---

[17] On Poulain de la Barre, see Madeleine Alcover, *Poulain de la Barre: une aventure philosophique* (Paris-Seattle-Tubingen: Papers on French Seventeenth-Century Literature, 1981); Michael A. Seidel, 'Poulain de la Barre's *The Woman as Good as the Man*', *Journal of the History of Ideas* 35:3 (1974), 499–508; Marie Louise Stock, *Poulain de la Barre: A Seventeenth-Century Feminist* (PhD diss.: Columbia University, 1961); Siep Stuurman, 'Social Cartesianism: François Poulain de la Barre and the Origins of the Enlightenment', *Journal of the History of Ideas* 58 (1997), 617–40; and Siep Stuurman, 'From Feminism to Biblical Criticism: The Theological Trajectory of François Poulain de la Barre', *Eighteenth-Century Studies* 33:3 (2000), 367–82. Other related works by Poulain de la Barre are *De l'education des dames* (1674) and *De l'excellence des hommes* (1675).
[18] Poulain de la Barre, *The Woman as Good as the Man*, p. 103.   [19] *Ibid.*, p. 125.
[20] See Kinnaird, 'Mary Astell and the Conservative Contribution', 60, n. 27; Perry, *The Celebrated Mary Astell*, pp. 71–2, n. 36; and Florence M. Smith, *Mary Astell* (New York: Columbia University Press, 1916), p. 177.
[21] Astell to Norris, 21 September 1693; in Astell and Norris, *Letters*, p. 2.

the *Proposal*, she repeats this notion to urge other women to take up intellectual studies. She says that 'All have not leisure to Learn Languages and pore on Books, nor Opportunity to converse with the Learned; but all may Think, may use their own Faculties rightly, and consult the Master who is within them'.[22] If women can reason about a dress or an estate, then they can also reason about more serious matters.

In her arguments against stereotypical views of women, Astell finds support in Descartes' mistrust of custom. Like Poulain de la Barre, she points out that common beliefs about women's innate irrationality are ill founded. If women are intellectually slow, she says, it is only because custom has prevented them from sharpening their natural intelligence. Ignorance and a poor education lay the foundation of women's vices, and imitation and custom perpetuate them. She observes that

Women are from their very Infancy debar'd those Advantages, with the want of which, they are afterwards reproached, and nursed up in those Vices which will hereafter be upbraided to them. So partial are Men as to expect Brick where they afford no Straw; and so abundantly civil as to take care we shou'd make good that obliging Epithet of *Ignorant*, which out of an excess of good Manners, they are pleas'd to bestow on us![23]

Astell argues that women have to look only within themselves to see that they possess a rational faculty. If they were educated to improve their reason, then they would not appear to be so intellectually deficient. Women's 'Incapacity, if there be any, is acquired not natural; and none of their Follies are so necessary, but that they might avoid them if they pleas'd themselves.'[24] A transformation, Astell maintains, can easily be effected through study and discipline.

Also in the spirit of Cartesianism, Astell encourages women to value their intellectual natures, rather than their bodies. There are no arguments in Astell's *Proposal* for the view that women's souls are wholly distinct from their bodies.[25] But she upholds what Alison Jaggar calls a 'normative dualism': an extreme reverence for human rationality.[26]

---

[22] Mary Astell, *A Serious Proposal to the Ladies, Parts I and II*, edited by Patricia Springborg (London: Pickering and Chatto, 1997), p. 119.
[23] Astell, *Proposal I*, p. 10.   [24] *Ibid.*
[25] Astell does present a version of the real distinction argument in her 1705 work, *The Christian Religion*. Her formulation is impressive for the fact that it anticipates Margaret Wilson's 'epistemological' interpretation of Descartes' argument. On this topic, see O'Neill, 'Astell, Mary (1666–1731)', in Craig (ed.), *Routledge Encyclopedia of Philosophy*, vol. 1, p. 528; Astell, *The Christian Religion*, p. 250; and Wilson, *Descartes*, p. 189.
[26] Alison Jaggar, 'Liberal Feminism and Human Nature', in *Feminist Politics and Human Nature* (Totowa, New Jersey: Rowman and Littlefield, 1983), p. 40.

Astell urges women to consider the welfare of their 'true selves', their *souls*, and she rails against the 'unthinking mechanical way of living, when like Machins we are condemn'd every day to repeat the impertinencies of the day before'.[27] She encourages her female readers to break with tradition and history, and to rely on their own introspective capacities to acquire knowledge. 'Let us learn to pride ourselves in something more excellent than the invention of a Fashion,' she says, 'And not entertain such a degrading thought of our own *worth*, as to imagine that our Souls were given us only for the service of our Bodies, and that the best improvement we can make of these, is to attract the eyes of men.'[28] In a later work, *The Christian Religion*, Astell upholds the same theme, saying that

it can never be suppos'd that GOD Created us, that is our Minds, after His own Image, for no better purpose than to wait upon the Body, whilst it Eats, Drinks, and Sleeps, and saunters away a *Useless Life*;...GOD, whose Works are all in Number, Weight, and Measure, cou'd never form a Rational Being for so trivial a purpose; since a little more Mechanism than what He has bestow'd upon some Brutes, wou'd qualifie us sufficiently for those Employments.[29]

In the second part of the *Proposal*, Astell expounds Cartesian rules of thought for the improvement of women's minds.[30] Her method is borrowed from Descartes' contemporaries, Antoine Arnauld (1612–94) and Pierre Nicole (1625–95), the co-authors of the highly influential *Logic or the Art of Thinking* (1662).[31] This treatise, also known as the *Port-Royal Logic*, is designed for those who have never studied formal logic. Arnauld and Nicole stress the importance of cultivating good judgement in practical, everyday life, and the need to exercise reason (as well as faith) in religious matters. Their emphasis is not on teaching the rules of valid inference, so much as how to avoid reasoning from false premises. Toward this end,

[27] Astell, *Proposal I*, p. 32.   [28] *Ibid.*, p. 8.
[29] Astell, *The Christian Religion*, p. 114. *The Christian Religion* is a 418-page treatise in the form of a letter to Catherine Jones. Regarded as the definitive statement of Astell's religious and philosophical views, this work is designed to acquaint women with the rational principles behind their religious convictions. Astell also aims to meet common threats to religious orthodoxy. Her main targets are Locke's *Essay Concerning Human Understanding* (1690), *Reasonableness of Christianity* (1695), his 'letters' to Edward Stillingfleet, the Bishop of Worcester, as well as Masham's *Discourse*, and the anonymous *The Ladies Religion* (1697). There is no modern edition of *The Christian Religion*.
[30] Irish philosopher George Berkeley plagiarises whole passages from this part of the *Proposal* in his 1714 work *The Ladies Library*.
[31] Astell seems to have read the 1693 English translation of this work (see Springborg's comments in Astell, *Proposal II*, p. 183, n. 17). For a modern edition, see Antoine Arnauld and Pierre Nicole, *Logic or the Art of Thinking*, translated and edited by Jill Vance Buroker (Cambridge: Cambridge University Press, 1996).

they provide a method for attaining truth, taken almost verbatim from Descartes' *Discourse on the Method*.[32]

Whereas Astell is concerned in part I of the *Proposal* that women be educated in a formal institution, in part II she is more concerned that women be able to educate themselves. She says: 'Can you be in Love with servitude and folly? Can you dote on a mean, ignorant and ignoble Life? An Ingenious Woman is no Prodigy to be star'd on, for you have it in your power to inform the World, that you can every one of you be so, if you please your selves.'[33] Like Arnauld and Nicole, Astell believes that self-education is necessary for the sake of one's *spiritual* welfare. Women must gain an understanding of the principles behind their religious beliefs for themselves, and this requires some knowledge of the 'art of thinking'. In a later work, she points out that 'A Blind Obedience is what a Rational Creature shou'd never pay, nor wou'd such an one receive it did he rightly understand its Nature. For Human Actions are no otherwise valuable than as they are conformable to Reason, but a blind Obedience is an Obeying *without Reason*, for ought we know *against it*.'[34]

Astell's rules of logic are paraphrased from the fourth part of the *Art of Thinking*. Her methodology does not require any specialised training, only the exercising of one's natural reason. She teaches women that they must begin by defining the terms of the question under consideration and by putting aside all irrelevant matters. They must reason only about things of which they have clear and distinct ideas, making sure that they have cut themselves off from 'all our former Prejudices, from our Opinion of Names, Authorities, Customs and the like'.[35] She stresses that 'Knowledge in a proper and restricted Sense and as appropriated to Science, signifies that clear Perception which is follow'd by a firm assent to Conclusions rightly drawn from Premises of which we have clear and distinct Ideas.'[36] Drawing directly on the *Art of Thinking*, she maintains that a good philosopher always conducts her thoughts in an orderly manner, from the most simple to the most complex, judging no further than she perceives, and taking nothing for truth that is not evidently known to be so.[37]

---

[32] For Astell's explicit references to Descartes, *see Proposal I*, p. 24; and *Proposal II*, pp. 123, 165.

[33] *Ibid.*, p. 72.

[34] Astell, *Reflections upon Marriage*, p. 75. Shortly after the second part of the *Proposal*, Astell published her second most popular feminist work, *Some Reflections Upon Marriage* (1700), written in response to the unhappy situation of her Chelsea neighbor, Hortense Mancini, the Duchess of Mazarin. In this work, Astell offers a general assessment of marriage, and laments that the institution has been defiled by the 'ill Choice' and 'foolish Conduct' of men and women.

[35] Astell, *Proposal II*, p. 89.   [36] *Ibid.*, p. 102.   [37] *Ibid.*, pp. 126–8.

In sum, these are the views that have led scholars to regard Astell as first and foremost a Cartesian. Like Descartes and his followers, Arnauld and Nicole, Astell formulates a method whereby certainty can be achieved only by detaching oneself from the senses, the imagination, and the passions. Truth, according to Astell, consists in clear and distinct perceptions grasped by the pure intellect alone.

By contrast, late twentieth-century feminists are extremely critical of these aspects of Cartesian thought. Cartesianism has been attacked for its emphasis on the self-sufficiency of the mind, the radical separation between the mind and body, and the denigration of the senses, body, matter, and nature. In the context of pre-existing associations between women and matter, Descartes' philosophy is seen as having further negative consequences for stereotypes of femininity. Genevieve Lloyd believes that, with the advent of Cartesianism,

> The way was thus opened for women to be associated with not just a lesser presence of Reason, but a different kind of intellectual character, construed as complementary to 'male' Reason. This crucial development springs from the accentuation of women's exclusion from Reason, now conceived – in its highest form – as an attainment.[38]

If one accepts Lloyd's view, then Astell's feminist arguments appear to be defective: despite championing female reason, she relies on concepts that lead to women's exclusion from intellectual discourse. Far from overthrowing prejudices about women, Astell's writings (it would appear) are complicit in maintaining the status quo. She valorises the self-sufficiency and autonomy of the mind, she criticises and shuns a life devoted solely to the body, and she distinguishes between the inferior, untrained reason of most women, and the superior reason achieved by disassociating the mind from the senses.

II

Nevertheless, Astell's letters to John Norris show that, despite her reverence for reason, she is extremely critical of his theory of soul–body relations. Although Norris has been called a Cambridge Platonist, this label is something of a misnomer given that he was an Oxford-trained advocate of Nicolas Malebranche's philosophy. Malebranche was one of the leading French disciples of Cartesian philosophy in the seventeenth

---

[38] Lloyd, *The Man of Reason*, p. 50.

century. His theory of causation, known as *occasionalism*, is a rather unorthodox blend of Cartesianism and Augustinian theology, according to
which there is no genuine interaction between the soul and body. The
Cambridge Platonists, on the other hand, claim that there is a 'vital congruity' or a 'plastic nature' between the soul and body that enables the
two substances to interact. Although Norris was initially supportive of
the Platonist theories, from 1688 he was an avowed occasionalist.

Like Anne Conway and Margaret Cavendish, Norris develops his
metaphysical views in response to the Cartesian conception of matter.
All three writers, like Elisabeth of Bohemia, acknowledge that if matter
consists only in extension, then it is inconceivable how it could cause any
effect in a thinking substance. But they come up with different solutions
to this difficulty. Cavendish and Conway see the problem as grounds
for rejecting dualism and for accepting the view that matter is alive and
intelligent. Norris, like his mentor Malebranche, accepts dualism and
maintains that there is no real causal interaction between soul and body.
Material things, Norris says, are completely without power or force, and
all bodies are utterly disconnected from souls. Instead he believes that
there is a perfectly harmonious *correlation* between the soul and body,
orchestrated by God.[39]

Norris gives his reasons for this view in an essay titled 'A Discourse
Concerning the Measure of Divine Love, with the Natural and Moral
Grounds upon which it stands', in the third volume of his *Practical
Discourses* (1693).[40] It is a common belief, he says, that bodies have some
inherent qualities that are analogous to our sensations. But there is no
more reason to suppose that 'there is such a Quality as Heat, resem-
bling what you feel in Fire, then you have to conclude *Pain* to be in a
Needle'.[41] There is nothing conceivable in bodies but magnitude, figure,
and motion, so they cannot possibly have any other essential qualities.
This is a view held by many seventeenth-century thinkers, including
Galileo, Descartes, Boyle, and Locke. But these men are mistaken, Norris
says, in supposing that material objects still have the power to cause our
sensations in some way, because 'the very same Reasons which prove that

[39] On Norris's philosophy, see Acworth, *The Philosophy of John Norris*; Charles McCracken,
Malebranche and British Philosophy (Oxford: Clarendon Press, 1983), pp. 156–79; and Flora
Isabel MacKinnon, *The Philosophy of John Norris* in Philosophical Monographs (Baltimore:
Psychological Review Publications, 1910).
[40] John Norris, *Practical Discourses Upon several Divine Subjects* (London: S. Manship, 1693), vol. III,
pp. 1–83.
[41] *Ibid.*, p. 25.

Bodies have not any Qualities in them like our Sensations, do also prove that they do neither produce Sensations in us'.[42] If bodies are mere magnitude, figure, and motion, then they cannot produce 'sentiments of the mind'. This is because there is no proportion or affinity between the cause and the effect: a material thing cannot 'produce an Effect more Noble and Excellent and of an Order so very much higher than it self'.[43] Furthermore, he says, bodies affect each other through impact and resistance.[44] But the body cannot move the soul in the same way, since the soul is penetrable: 'And therefore since Spirits make no resistance against Bodies, it is not possible that Bodies should have any Action, or make any Impression upon Spirits.'[45]

Norris believes instead that we must look to forces outside of bodies to explain apparent causal relations between the body and soul. Only a being of infinite wisdom and power could produce all things by the immediate efficacy of will. Hence Norris believes that God must be the only causal agent, and the only efficient cause of all sensations is divine intervention. Material things, on the other hand, are merely the *occasions* for that intervention. When the sun shines in my eyes, it is God who gives me the sensations of heat and light. ''Tis not the most delicate Fruit, or the richest Perfume, that delights either our Tast or our Smell,' he says, 'but 'tis God alone that raises Pleasure in us by the Occasion of these Bodies.'[46] Similarly, when I will my leg to kick, my volition is merely the occasion for God to intervene and make my leg move.

Norris promotes this theory in his letters to Astell. While material objects may be the conditions or occasions of our sensations, he says, they are not necessary conditions. In a letter of 13 November 1693, he writes that

> though according to the Law of this State Pain be always occasioned by some Motion or Change in the Parts of the Body, yet since 'tis the Soul that truly feels it, and GOD that truly raises it, I can easily conceive, that GOD can, if he pleases, raise the Sensation of Pain in her though no Change be made in the Body, nay though she had no body at all. That GOD for instance can raise

---

[42] *Ibid.*, p. 32.   [43] *Ibid.*, p. 28.
[44] Norris markedly differs from Malebranche on this point. Malebranche's occasionalism is just as much a theory about body–body relations as soul–body interaction (see Steven Nadler, *Malebranche and Ideas* (Oxford: Oxford University Press, 1992), p. 4). For Norris, however, occasionalism applies *only* to soul–body relations, and not to body–body relations; one body can be the efficient cause of motion in another body through impact. On Norris's position, see John Norris, *An Essay Towards the Theory of the Ideal or Intelligible World . . . Part II* (London: S. Manship, 1704), pp. 223–4, 231–3; Norris, *Practical Discourses*, vol. III, pp. 34–5; and McCracken, *Malebranche and British Philosophy*, p. 172, n. 52.
[45] Norris, *Practical Discourses*, vol. III, p. 34.   [46] *Ibid.*, p. 55.

the Sensation of Burning in the Soul without any Impression of Fire upon her Body.[47]

Even if the material world did not exist, we could still have the sensations and ideas we currently have. In fact, Norris believes that we can never really know that there are actual bodies outside our souls causing or 'occasioning' our sensations.

Norris uses this philosophical basis to argue that God must be the sole object of our love. He maintains that we love only that which brings us pleasure, and because God is the only truly causally efficacious being, only he can be the cause of our pleasure. Consequently, God alone is deserving of our love.[48] After all, no causally inefficacious being could be 'a fit or reasonable object of love' if it never really causes our pleasure. The following passage from Norris's later work, *An Essay Towards the Theory of the Ideal or Intelligible World* (1704), aptly illustrates these moral and metaphysical views:

Reflect then first of all, what a dead unactive thing Matter is, and withal, how poor and empty the Material is in comparison of the intellectual World. And accordingly, whether such an unactive empty Being, that is so without Power or Force, and without Form and Void, can be a fit or reasonable Object of thy Love? ... 'tis plain that Bodies cannot act upon our Souls, nor cause in them the least Pleasure or the least Pain, the lowest Taste, or the faintest Smell, or any other Sensation ... Those Odours, those Savours, nay, even that *Light* and those *Colours* which are imagin'd to be in Bodies, are really not in them, but in our selves. And yet we Court them and Commend them, and say that one shines, and another has a fine Perfume, *&c.* But they, poor Creatures, have none of those Finenesses, Excellencies, or Beauties (*Figure* only excepted) which we think we see in them, and for which we admire them, but are, as it were, mere *Caput Mortuum*, or *Terra Damnata* in the Language of the Sons of Hermes, utterly void and destitute of all those agreeable Prettinesses, those charming Graces which the Poetical imagination of Philosophers, like the Passion of Lovers, has confer'd upon them, and the *Blushes* of the Morning are as much a Fiction as *Aurora* it self. Indeed 'tis all Fiction, Complement, Fallacy, Dream, Imposture and Man walks in a *vain shew*, among Cheats and Delusions, empty Representations, and false Appearances, and the World is to him as some *inchanted* Place, where he is abused by resemblances of things that are not, and is imposed upon by all his Senses. For in short, the Perfections of material Beings are the mere Creatures of his Fansie; those Beauties which he thinks he perceives without, are really in himself, and he carries about him the World that he admires.[49]

[47] Norris to Astell, 13 November 1693; in Astell and Norris, *Letters*, p. 62.
[48] More accurately, Norris says that God alone deserves a love of *desire*, whereas creatures deserve only a love of *benevolence*.
[49] Norris, *Essay Towards the Theory II*, pp. 252–5.

Here it is significant that Norris expresses not only a contempt for the material world, but a symbolic alignment of femaleness with matter. In Lloyd's view, this passage would not be an isolated instance of sexist metaphor, but part of a tradition in which philosophers advocate a transcendence of natural or material things, and in which the feminine is associated with what must be transcended or excluded. Those men who with 'the passion of lovers' court sensual delights with praises of 'fine perfumes', are warned that they will soon be disappointed. In reality, Norris says, they are destitute of all those 'agreeable prettinesses' and 'charming graces'. The philosopher must regard his 'beloved' with disdain. The object of his admiration is likened to the mythical goddess 'Aurora', a type of *belle dame sans merci* who bewitches and enchants unwary men. In short, the same values that enable Norris to hold the material world in contempt, are implicitly directed toward women when he characterises that material world as female. Women do not really belong to the intellectual world, and without 'form' can never hope to aspire to such. The truly rational man, Norris suggests, must overcome the body, matter, and *femaleness*.

It is fitting, therefore, that Astell challenges these particular aspects of Norris's philosophy: the view that God is the only efficient cause of our sensations, the idea that matter is worthless and causally impotent, and the claim that there is no real interaction between the soul and body.

Although Astell's early objections are not directed at Norris's occasionalism, one can detect seeds of dissent throughout their exchange. In her first letter, Astell expresses a difficulty she found when reading volume three of Norris's *Practical Discourses*.[50] She points out that if God is the only true cause of all our sensations, then he is also the only true cause of our pain. Yet we do not love that which causes us pain, and thus 'if the Author of our Pleasure be upon that account the only Object of our Love, then by the same reason the Author of our Pain can't be the Object of our Love'.[51] For, Astell says,

if we must Love nothing but what is Lovely, and nothing is Lovely but what is our Good, and nothing is our Good but what does us Good, and nothing does us Good but what causes Pleasure in us; may we not by the same way of arguing say, That that which Causes Pain in us does not do us Good, (for nothing you say does us Good but what Causes Pleasure) and therefore can't be our Good,

---

[50] Although Astell does not name 'A Discourse Concerning the Measure of Divine Love', her comments indicate that she is referring to this essay in particular.
[51] Astell to Norris, 21 September 1693; in Astell and Norris, *Letters*, p. 5.

and if not our Good then not Lovely, and consequently not the proper, much less the only Object of our Love?[52]

According to Astell, Norris's argument leads to the paradox that the cause of our sensations is both the object of our love and of our aversion. To avoid the inconsistency, she suggests that 'that which Causes Pain does us Good as well as that which Causes Pleasure',[53] and that we ought to love God because he alone does us good, not merely because he is the author of our pleasure. Pain is not inflicted needlessly or callously, but for the sake of what is best.

In his reply of 13 October 1693, Norris concedes that we must love God in spite of, not because he causes our pain, and that pain comes from God 'only indirectly and by Accident'.[54] But in her next letter, of 31 October 1693, Astell plays down the 'accidental' part, saying that 'though Pain considered abstractedly is not a Good, yet it *may* be so circumstantiated, and always *is* when God inflicts it as to be a Good'. Thus we ought to love God because, in his infinite wisdom, he 'designed Pain as well as Pleasure in order to our Happiness'.[55] According to her moral theory, it is not enough to love God simply because he is the cause of our pleasure. We must love him even though he inflicts pain, because he intends for these sensations, like pleasurable ones, to contribute to our overall good.

The basis of Astell's criticisms of Norris is her conception of God. Like Conway and the Cambridge Platonists, Astell holds a type of intellectualist theology. While Norris emphasises God's causal power, Astell maintains that God's omnipotence is constrained by his wisdom and goodness: a supremely rational and perfectly benevolent being could cause pain only to bring about good. In the *Proposal*, Astell spells out the same idea: 'GOD being Infinitely Wise, all his Judgments must be Infallible, and being Infinitely Good he can will nothing but what is best, nor prescribe any thing that is not for our Advantage.'[56] And in *The Christian Religion*, she says that 'when we say that GOD cannot do a thing, we do not at all question Almighty Power, or set any sort of *limits to Infinite Wisdom*; we only question the fitness of the thing to be done, and mean no more than that such a thing is not suitable to the Perfection of the Divine Nature'.[57] Astell believes that God always does what is 'best and most becoming His Perfections, and cannot act but according to the essential

[52] *Ibid.*, pp. 4–5.   [53] *Ibid.*, p. 6.   [54] Norris to Astell, 13 October 1693; *ibid.*, p. 17.
[55] Astell to Norris, 31 October 1693; *ibid.*, pp. 33, 34.   [56] Astell, *Proposal II*, p. 153.
[57] Astell, *Christian Religion*, p. 416.

Nature and Reason of things'.[58] There are no arbitrary features, such as pain, in God's universe: he uses his supreme wisdom to create the 'best of all possible worlds'.

Astell's notion of infinite wisdom is responsible for her eventual rejection of Norris's occasionalism. Six weeks after the correspondence had officially ended, Astell launched an attack on the central premise of Norris's philosophy: the view that God is the only efficient cause of our sensations. Astell's letter and Norris's reply appear as an appendix to the published volume of the correspondence. In her letter, dated 14 August 1694, Astell objects 'First, That this Theory renders a great Part of GOD's Workmanship Vain and Useless' and 'Secondly, That it does not well comport with his Majesty'.[59] For the first, Astell argues that if external objects are not able to produce our sensations, then these objects cannot serve any relevant purpose. Yet, if this is so, then Norris's theory is contrary to the idea that an infinitely wise being creates nothing in vain: it would be unnecessary for God to give us the inclination to believe that material things cause our sensations when he himself causes them:

That this Theory renders a great Part of *GOD's* Workmanship vain and useless, it may be thus argued. Allowing that Sensation is only in the Soul, that there is nothing in Body but Magnitude, Figure and Motion, and that being without Thought itself it is not able to produce it in us, and therefore those Sensations, whether Pleasure or Pain, which we feel at the Presence of Bodies, must be produced by some higher Cause than they; yet if the Objects of our Senses have no natural Efficiency towards the producing of those Sensations which we feel at their Presence, if they Serve no further than as positive and arbitrary Conditions to determine the Action of the true and proper Cause, if they have nothing in their own Nature to qualifie them to be instrumental to the Production of such and such Sensations, but that if *GOD* should so please (the Nature of the things notwithstanding) we might as well feel Cold at the presence of fire as of water, and heat at the Application of Water or any other Creature, and since *GOD* may as well excite Sensations in our Souls without these positive Conditions as with them, to what end do they serve? And then what becomes of that acknowledged Truth that *GOD* does nothing in vain, when such Variety of Objects as our Senses are exercised about are wholly unnecessary?[60]

---

[58] *Ibid.*, p. 95.   [59] Astell to Norris, 14 August 1694; Astell and Norris, *Letters*, p. 278.
[60] *Ibid.*, pp. 278–80. This objection anticipates John Locke in his 'Remarks Upon some of Mr. Norris's Books, Wherein he asserts F. Malebranche's Opinion of Our Seeing all things in God', in *A Collection of Several Pieces of Mr. John Locke*, second edition (London: R. Francklin, 1739). Locke's essay was written in 1693 and first published in 1720. He observes that 'if the perception of colours and sounds depended on nothing but the presence of the object affording an *occasional cause* to God Almighty to exhibit to the mind, the Ideas of figures, colours and sounds; all that nice and curious structure of those organs is wholly in vain' (p. 48).

An infinitely wise being, Astell suggests, would not permit such super-fluous features in his design. Norris's idea of a God who could make us feel cold at the presence of fire offends Astell's belief in a supremely rational deity. In *The Christian Religion*, this same principle is the basis for her claim that 'not the least Particle of Body doth totally Perish'. She believes that it does not 'consist with the Wisdom and Majesty of the Great Creator to Annihilate His Works. For He does nothing in vain, and can't be Suppos'd to Make a Creature with a design to Destroy or Unmake it'.[61]

Astell's second objection is that Norris's theory does not comport well with God's majesty. She implies that it would be beneath a perfect being to be constantly intervening in earthly events, when he could simply create an instrument to enact his will. Instead Astell asks

Why therefore may there not be a *sensible Congruity* between those Powers of the Soul that are employed in Sensation, and those Objects which occasion it? Analogous to that vital Congruity which your Friend Dr. *More* (*Immortality of the Soul, B. II. Chap. 14. S. 8.*) will have to be between some certain Modifications of Matter, and the plastick Part of the Soul, which Notion he illustrates by that Pleasure which the preceptive Part of the Soul (as he calls it) is affected with by good Musick or delicious Viands, as I do this of *sensible* by his of *vital Congruity*, and methinks they are so symbolical that if the one be admitted the other may. For as the Soul forsakes her Body when this vital Congruity fails, so when this sensible Congruity is wanting, as in the Case of Blindness, Deafness, or the Palsie, & c. the Soul has no Sensation of Colours, Sounds, Heat and the like, so that although Bodies make the same Impression that they used to do on her Body, yet whilst it is under this Indisposition, she has not that Sentiment of Pleasure or Pain which used to accompany that Impression, and therefore though there be no such thing as Sensation in Bodies, yet why may there not be a *Congruity* in them by their Presence to draw forth such Sensations in the Soul? Especially since in the next place, it seems more agreeable to the Majesty of GOD, and that Order he has established in the World, to say that he produces our Sensations *mediately* by his Servant Nature, than to affirm that he does it *immediately* by his own Almighty Power.[62]

Astell implies that there is a natural efficacy in bodies to produce sensa-tions in the soul. She accepts Norris's claim that sensations do not reside in the material objects themselves. But against Norris, she suggests that there is something in the body, a 'sensible congruity', that promotes its in-teraction with the soul, and enables the body to cause sensations. Insofar as material bodies are connected to, or have a correspondence with,

[61] Astell, *Christian Religion*, pp. 247–8.
[62] Astell to Norris, 14 August 1694; in Astell and Norris, *Letters*, pp. 280–2.

certain plastical powers in the soul, they do 'really better our condition', they do 'contribute to our happiness or Misery', and they do 'in some sense produce our Pleasure or Pain'.[63] God's 'Servant nature', according to Astell, acts as a causal agent in the natural world, making material things 'necessary Instruments', rather than mere 'occasions'.[64]

Astell's theory of a sensible congruity between 'certain Modifications of Matter, and the plastick Part of the Soul' owes its origins to More's doctrine of the spirit of nature and Cudworth's theory of plastic nature. Like Astell, Cudworth believes that 'it seems not so agreeable to Reason... that Nature as a Distinct thing from the Deity should be quite Superceded or made to Signifie Nothing, God himself doing all things Immediately'.[65] Instead, Cudworth tries to strike a balance between mechanistic and occasionalist-style philosophies, claiming that

since neither all things are produced Fortuitously, or by the Unguided Mechanism of Matter, nor God himself may reasonably be thought to do all things Immediately and Miraculously; it may well be concluded, that there is a *Plastic Nature* under him, which as an Inferior and Subordinate Instrument, doth Drudgingly Execute that Part of his Providence, which consists in the Regular and Orderly Motion of Matter.[66]

This plastic nature is a spiritual intermediary between spirit and matter that gives material things life and activity, when they would otherwise be dead and passive. Henry More likewise claims that the union between spirit and matter cannot be explained in mechanical terms, but only in terms of a 'vital congruity' between the plastic part of the soul and the body.[67] Astell refers to a passage in *The Immortality of the Soul* (book 2, chapter 14, section 8) where More claims that this congruity is 'chiefly in the *Soul* it self', but that it can also be in matter. More says that

it is termed *Vital* because it makes the *Matter* a *congruous* Subject for the Soul to reside in, and exercise the functions of life. For that which has no *life* it self, may tie to it that which has. As some men are said to be tied by the teeth, or tied by the ear, when they are detained by the pleasure they are struck with from

[63] *Ibid.*, p. 284.
[64] Norris objects by saying that 'even Instruments belong to the Order of efficient Causes, though they are less principal ones, and 'tis most certain that God has no need of any, since his Will is efficacious itself' (Norris to Astell, 21 September 1694; *ibid.*, pp. 306–7). This counter-objection is not very strong, because one might still ask: if God has no need of material objects, and 'his Will is efficacious itself', then why do such objects even exist?
[65] Cudworth, *True Intellectual System*, p. 150.   [66] *Ibid.*
[67] On the topic of vital congruity, see Hutton, 'Anne Conway Critique d'Henry More'.

good Musick or delicious Viands . . . Now as we see that the *Perceptive* part of the Soul is thus vitally affected with that which has no life in it, so it is reasonable that the *Plastick* part thereof may be so too; That there may be an Harmony betwixt Matter thus and thus modified, and that Power that we call *Plastick*, that is utterly devoid of all Perception. And in this alone consists that which we call *Vital Congruity* in the prepared Matter, either to be organized, or already shaped into the perfect form of an Animal.[68]

In the same chapter, More calls the spirit of nature the '*Inferiour Soul of the World*',[69] and says that matter enjoys a vital congruity with this part of the soul. Likewise, in an earlier letter to Norris (31 October 1693), Astell explains her theory of sensation with reference to the 'inferior' and 'superior' parts of the soul.[70] The inferior part, she says, corresponds to sensible objects, it feels sensations of pain, colour, and so on; whereas the superior or intellectual part, comprised of the understanding and will, is capable of knowing abstract truths.[71]

There are also similarities between Astell's views and those of Anne Conway. Conway emphasises that every created thing has a spiritual dimension, and that there can be no such thing as dead matter. 'For suppose that this dead matter, or body, has assumed all forms and has changed into all kinds of shapes, both the most regular and precise. What use is this body or matter since it lacks life and perception?'[72] Conway believes instead that every particle of matter has the ability to perfect itself. Though Astell does not espouse a thoroughgoing perfectionism or monistic vitalism, she too highlights the spiritual *telos* of material things. Astell's main criticisms of Norris rely on pointing out the final, as well as the efficient, causes of material things: their *purpose* in God's grand design. In her objections to Norris, she emphasises that God created material things for a reason; if his philosophy fails to account for the purposefulness of matter, it is therefore inadequate.

Overall, there are significant differences between Astell's metaphysical views and those of Norris. Astell advocates a theory of causation in which she reinstates the causality of the body and re-affirms its connection with the soul. She believes that the body is capable of a sympathetic interaction with the soul and that material things are necessary, not

---

[68] More, *Immortality of the Soul*, pp. 263–4. [69] *Ibid.*, p. 266.

[70] Although Astell borrows this notion from Norris's *Christian Blessedness*, she takes the distinction more literally than he intended. In a letter dated 13 November 1693, Norris claims that he cannot form a 'clear Idea of any such Parts', and he only meant for the distinction to be a figure of speech (*Letters*, p. 60).

[71] Astell to Norris, 31 October 1693; *ibid.*, p. 37. [72] Conway, *Principles*, ch. 7, sect. 2, p. 46.

arbitrary features of the created world. Norris, on the other hand, advocates a transcendence of material bodies, while at the same time associating matter with femaleness. This matter is rendered unnecessary, causally impotent, and incapable of affecting the soul. In Astell's metaphysics, however, material things *do* serve a purpose, and they *can* act as true causal agents. It is not the case, as Norris says, that they are mere 'empty representations' – they have the capacity to produce those 'finenesses' and 'those excellencies' that he denies them. In these respects, Astell's views resemble the orthodox Cartesian position on soul–body interaction, according to which the soul and body *are* capable of influencing one another. But with her theory of a 'sensible congruity', Astell goes beyond the typical Cartesian stance: her theory not only empowers and enlivens matter (when it would otherwise be dead and inert), but also avoids an extreme form of dualism. The doctrine of plastic nature to which she appeals introduces a 'middle way', an intermediary sphere that bridges the gulf between spiritual and material substances. As John Passmore says, 'once such an intimate communion between reason and matter is admitted to be possible, the sharp edge of dualism is blunted'.[73] In Astell's metaphysical outlook, the polarities that make the female–male symbolism appropriate for Norris to express the relations between the soul and material bodies, are thus undermined.

Of course, Astell's final objections to Norris's theory of causation are only tentative. She does not go on to formulate a detailed theory of the 'sensible congruity' between the soul's sensations and the material objects that cause them. There is no mention of any 'plastick part of the soul', for example, when she details the relationship between the soul and the body in the second part of the *Proposal*. Here she simply writes:

not to enter too far into the Philosophy of the Passions, suffice it briefly to observe: That by the Oeconomy of Nature such and such Motions in the Body are annext in such a manner to certain Thoughts in the Soul, that unless some outward force restrain, she can produce them when she pleases barely by willing them, and reciprocally several Impressions on the Body are communicated to, and affect the Soul, all this being perform'd by the means of the Animal Spirits. The Active Powers of the Soul, her Will and Inclinations are at her own dispose, her Passive are not, she can't avoid feeling Pain or other sensible Impressions so long as she's united to a Body, and that Body is dispos'd to convey these Impressions.[74]

John Passmore, *Ralph Cudworth: An Interpretation* (Cambridge: Cambridge University Press, 1951), p. 28.
Astell, *Proposal II*, p. 161. Here Astell's interpretation of soul–body interaction may have been influenced by More's *Account of Virtue* (see *Proposal II*, p. 165).

Nonetheless, in this passage Astell deliberately avoids an occasionalist interpretation (there is no mention of God's causal agency), and she does say that the body is 'dispos'd to convey' sensible impressions to the soul. In her later works, Astell apparently decides to suspend her judgement on the matter, for example, when she says in the second part of the *Proposal* that 'We know and feel the Union between our Soul and Body, but who amongst us sees so clearly, as to find out with Certitude and Exactness, the secret ties which unite two such different Substances, or how they are able to act upon each other?'[75] Likewise, in *The Christian Religion*, she says 'neither do I comprehend the Vital Union between my Soul and Body...though I am sure that it is so'.[76] For Astell, like Descartes in the correspondence with Elisabeth, the issue of soul–body relations is a subject that the human intellect cannot penetrate. But this eventual agnosticism on the topic does not mean that we should discount Astell's criticisms of Norris – especially when they are consistent with her central philosophical and theological beliefs.

III

There are, moreover, significant continuities between Astell's feminist and metaphysical views. It is important to remember that when Astell values rationality over the body, she is reacting against stereotypical views of women as *mere* material objects or 'machines' devoid of reason. 'For if we do not live like Machines', she says, 'but like Reasonable Creatures, that is if we Observe, Examine and Apply whatever comes under our Cognizance, every Turn in our own and our Neighbours Life will be Useful to us.'[77] In both the *Letters* and the *Proposal*, Astell's objectives are the same: to re-affirm the worth of a part of God's creation that has been rendered purposeless by re-affirming its connection with the spiritual–intellectual realm.

In fact, the same principle that leads Astell to reject an utter separation between the soul and body – the dictum that *God creates nothing in vain* – also leads her to reject the view that women are not fully rational. In the second part of the *Proposal*, Astell says that 'GOD does nothing in vain, he gives no Power or Faculty which he has not allotted to some proportionate use, if therefore he has given to Mankind a Rational Mind, every individual Understanding ought to be employ'd in somewhat worthy of it.'[78] In *The Christian Religion*, she says that the author of our being would

[75] *Ibid.*, p. 101.   [76] Astell, *Christian Religion*, p. 51.   [77] Astell, *Proposal II*, p. 163.
[78] *Ibid.*, pp. 118–19.

not allow any superfluities in his supremely intelligent design; thus, 'If GOD had not intended that Women shou'd use their Reason, He wou'd not have given them any, for He does nothing in vain.'[79] Astell warns that when a woman is taught that her duty is to serve men, or to live a life devoted solely to the body, she is taught to disregard her obligations to God. Astell stresses instead that women must be educated so that their rationality is exercised toward higher virtues, and not neglected as vain and useless. 'For unless we have very strange Notions of the Divine Wisdom,' she says, we must admit that 'Our Powers and Faculties were not given us for nothing.'[80]

This theological aspect to Astell's feminist arguments clearly distinguishes her writings from those of Poulain de la Barre. In *The Woman as Good as the Man*, Poulain de la Barre does not expand on the religious significance of women's education. Yet even when propounding the Cartesian method in the second *Proposal*, Astell's examples of self-evident principles reflect her strong religious and moral beliefs. 'If it be farther demanded what these Principles are?' she says, 'no body I suppose will deny us one, which is, *That we ought as much as we can to endeavour the Perfecting of our Beings, and that we be as happy as possibly we may.*'[81] She emphasises that women must use their rational faculties to move closer toward perfection and God, 'the Supream and Universal Reason':[82]

For since GOD has given Women as well as Men intelligent Souls, why should they be forbidden to improve them? Since he has not denied us the faculty of Thinking, why shou'd we not (at least in gratitude to him) employ our Thoughts on himself their noblest Object, and not unworthily bestow them on Trifles and Gaities and secular Affairs? Being the Soul was created for the contemplation of Truth as well as for the fruition of Good, is it not as cruel and unjust to preclude Women from the knowledge of one, as well as from the enjoyment of the other?[83]

'A desire to advance and perfect its Being,' she says, 'is planted by GOD in all Rational Natures, to excite them hereby to every worthy and becoming Action.'[84] A supremely rational God would not have given women this desire unless he required them to act on it. Therefore, she says, women must be educated to use their reason to raise themselves toward perfection.

---

[79] Astell, *Christian Religion*, p. 6.   [80] Astell, *Proposal II*, p. 149.   [81] *Ibid.*, pp. 82–3.
[82] Astell, *Christian Religion*, p. 13.   [83] Astell, *Proposal I*, p. 22.   [84] *Ibid.*, p. 12.

This 'theological' outlook brings Astell closer to her scholastic predecessor, Anna Maria van Schurman.[85] In her *Dissertatio*, Schurman presents a series of syllogisms in favour of women's aptitude for study.[86] Like Astell, she urges women to pursue knowledge, not for the sake of intellectual endeavour alone, but to move closer to God and the salvation of the soul. In her second syllogism, Schurman argues that 'Whoever has a desire for sciences and arts is suited to study sciences and arts. But women by nature have a desire for arts and sciences. Therefore [all arts and sciences are fitting to women].'[87] In defence of the first premise, Schurman appeals to the notion that 'nature makes nothing in vain'; if human beings have this desire by nature, it is there for a reason.[88] In defence of the second, she draws on Aristotle's view that every human being has a natural desire for knowledge, and that 'what belongs to the whole species also belongs to single individuals'.[89] In other arguments, Schurman relies on a conception of human beings as created by God for a specific purpose, and the idea that 'their own highest perfection is proper to all creatures and that toward that end it is necessary to struggle with all their strength'.[90] These same scholastic and theological principles are reflected in Astell's arguments.

In sum, Astell's criticisms of Norris stem from her convictions about God's supreme wisdom. She argues that if the material world serves no purpose (is unable to affect our souls), then God will have created something in vain; but a supremely wise being does nothing in vain; therefore the material world must serve some purpose (it *is* able to affect our souls). Astell applies the same teleology in her arguments for women's education that she uses in her criticisms of Norris. She points out that if women are endowed with a rational faculty that serves no purpose, then God will have created something in vain; but God does nothing in vain;

---

[85] Astell also anticipates the theological arguments of eighteenth-century feminist Mary Wollstonecraft (1759–97). In *A Vindication of the Rights of Woman* (1792), Wollstonecraft holds the view that God's omnipotence is limited and regulated by his wisdom. Women, she says, partake in this divine wisdom, in so far as they are rational and immortal beings. Therefore, according to Wollstonecraft, women's morals must be 'fixed on the same immutable principles as those of man' (Mary Wollstonecraft, *A Vindication of the Rights of Woman*, edited with an introduction by Miriam Brody (Harmondsworth: Penguin, 1992), p. 88). Against Rousseau, she says that 'if . . . there were to be rational creatures produced, allowed to rise in excellence by the exercise of powers implanted for that purpose; if benignity itself thought fit to call into existence a creature above the brutes, who could think and improve himself, why should that inestimable gift . . . be called, in direct terms, a curse?' (*ibid.*, p. 94). For other similarities between Astell and Wollstonecraft, see John McCrystal, 'Revolting Women: The Use of Revolutionary Discourse in Mary Astell and Mary Wollstonecraft Compared', *History of Political Thought* 14 (1993), 189–203.
[86] On the significance of Schurman's choice of form, see van Eck, 'The First Dutch Feminist Tract?'
[87] Schurman, *Whether a Christian Woman*, p. 28.   [88] *Ibid.*   [89] *Ibid.*   [90] *Ibid.*, p. 30.

therefore women are endowed with a rational faculty that must serve
some purpose. In both cases Astell regards created things as purposeful
and there for the sake of some greater goal. These features of the created
world contribute toward, and are evidence of, God's supreme design.
Astell's teleological beliefs further lead to a re-establishing of connections
between the material and spiritual: to be purposeful, material things must
have a sympathetic interaction with spiritual beings; similarly, women
must be more than mere bodies to fulfil their divine purpose.

Finally, these beliefs also inform Astell's conception of reason. In her
article on 'Cartesian Reason and Gendered Reason', Margaret Atherton
notes that while Astell gives a high evaluation to reason, she does not
believe that the rational mind can completely transcend or exclude the
body. Astell, she says, does not regard a life based on reason as a *rival* to
a life based on the body; human beings, in her view, can be neither pure
cogitation nor pure mechanism. Like Elisabeth of Bohemia, Astell sees
bodies as making a contribution to human life that cannot be ignored. In
the second part of the *Proposal*, Astell says it is a mistake 'of our Duty as our
Happiness to consider either part of us singly, so as to neglect what is due
to the other. For if we disregard the Body wholly, we pretend to live like
Angels whilst we are but Mortals; and if we prefer or equal it to the Mind
we degenerate into Brutes.'[91] Despite the fact that Astell believes the soul
should govern the body, she says that it is actually impossible for humans
to lead a life that is identified solely with the soul. We cannot live like
those 'few Scrupulous Persons' who neglect the body for ascetic reasons;
to do so is 'inconsistent with a Human Frame'.[92] In this sense, Astell
does not wholeheartedly support a conception of reason that opens the
way for femininity to be associated with a lesser type of thought. Neither
does she advocate that the soul can be completely autonomous, or that
we can completely ignore the body.

It is clear that Cartesianism is not the only significant feature of Astell's
thought. On the one hand, Astell undoubtedly finds support in Cartesian
ideas for her plan to establish a female academy. On this philosophical
basis, she dismisses customary perceptions about female intellectual de-
ficiency, and exhorts women to exercise their natural reason. When her
proposal is ignored, Astell advocates Cartesian method as a course of
study that women can pursue at home. Anybody can attain knowledge,
she argues, so long as they begin with self-evident ideas in the mind, and
proceed from simple to complex ideas in an orderly, rigorous manner.

---

[91] Astell, *Proposal II*, p. 158.   [92] *Ibid.*

In this way, all women can examine the rational principles behind their moral beliefs for themselves. These arguments are indebted to various Cartesian philosophers, including Descartes himself, Antoine Arnauld, Pierre Nicole, and probably also Poulain de la Barre. Yet although Astell is a strong advocate for Cartesian reason, there are other equally relevant principles at work in her writings. Like Anne Conway, Astell demonstrates that she has thought consistently about what God's attributes imply for his creation. If one were to sum up her guiding philosophical principle, it would most likely be that 'there is not a greater boldness and *presumption* than in *affirming* that God does any thing in vain'.[93] In short, Astell argues that God has designed a harmonious order in which each part is suited to its end, and there is no waste or lost labour. She opposes any view of women in which their reason is denied, neglected, or made redundant: a supremely wise being, she says, would not have endowed women with a rational faculty if he had not wished them to use it. Thus, she says, they must not be encouraged to act as though they were mere mechanical bodies. Similarly she believes that matter is not without purpose or connection to the spiritual world. Astell rejects Norris's conception of matter as without power or force and supports a theory of causation in which matter is revitalised and its connection with the spiritual world re-established. On this interpretation, Astell supports a metaphysical framework that allows her to avoid some of the gender-biases modern feminists identify in Cartesianism. Her philosophy raises the ontological status of those stereotypically 'feminine' categories of matter, nature, and the body.

[93] Astell, *Christian Religion*, p. 405.

5

Damaris Masham

In 1696 there appeared a scathing reply to the Astell–Norris letters in an anonymous work titled *A Discourse Concerning the Love of God*. This short tract was written by Damaris Masham, the daughter of Ralph Cudworth and a close friend of the empiricist philosopher John Locke. Ignoring Astell's criticisms of Norris, Masham attacks both writers for espousing an impractical or 'unserviceable' moral theory, rather than one based on common sense. She accuses Astell and Norris of opposing the 'daily Sense and Experience of all Mankind'.[1] It is obvious, she says, that creatures are designed for a sociable life, and that they can no more love and desire God alone than fishes can fly in the air. In addition to the Astell–Norris letters, Masham targets Norris's 'Discourse Concerning the Measure of Divine Love' and Astell's first *Serious Proposal to the Ladies*.[2]

Masham's remarks sparked defensive responses from both Astell and Norris. In their replies, both writers misattribute the work to Locke – a mistake which is understandable given that Masham's arguments are steeped in the empiricist philosophy of Locke's *Essay Concerning Human*

---

[1] Masham, *Discourse*, p. 92. The *Discourse* was translated into French in 1705 by Pierre Coste, the first translator of Locke's *Essay* into French, and published in Amsterdam as *Discours Sur L'Amour Divin*. Jean Le Clerc reviewed the translation in his *Bibliothèque Choisie* 7.

[2] On this debate, see Acworth, *The Philosophy of John Norris*, pp. 172–80, 237–8; Hutton, 'Damaris Cudworth, Lady Masham', 34–7; Perry, *The Celebrated Mary Astell*, pp. 73–82, 87–97; Springborg, 'Astell, Masham, and Locke', pp. 105–25; and Springborg, 'Introduction' to Astell, *Proposal*, pp. xiv–xix. I find it perplexing that Springborg says she can 'find no direct reference to the Astell–Norris correspondence' in the *Discourse* (pp. 114–15, n. 34). The running title for the first edition of the Astell–Norris *Letters* is 'Letters Philosophical and Divine', and Masham makes explicit reference to the 'Letters Philosophical and Divine' on pp. 15, 20, and 121. She also alludes to Astell on pp. 27, 78, 120, and 126. There is evidence that Masham had a copy of the *Proposal* in her library when writing the *Discourse*. Locke's journal for 22 December 1694 reads:

> 'To Oates,
> Delivered to my Lady Masham
> Mrs Astels Proposal to ye Ladies
> Mr Norris's letters.' (Bodleian Library, University of Oxford,
> Locke MS f. 10, fol. 251)

Understanding (1690). Masham has been variously described as a 'blue-stocking admirer' of Locke,[3] someone who 'adopted Locke's views',[4] a 'Lockean feminist',[5] and 'a clear and ardent exponent' of Locke's ideas.[6] Others have even maintained that Masham 'sat loyally' at Locke's feet as a pupil, or that she wrote 'under the inspection of Mr. Locke'.[7] On the basis of their brief but heated exchange, Masham and Astell are typically regarded as philosophical adversaries: Astell a disciple of Norris, Masham a devout Lockean. Commenting on their differences, Ruth Perry says that 'All of this was predictable: that Masham's position would be as sensible and down-to-earth as Astell's was abstract and idealist, that Masham would focus on life-on-earth while Astell stressed preparation for the hereafter. Like seconds in the duel between Locke's empiricism and Norris's idealism, their exchange is a fascinating reprise of that debate.'[8] Patricia Springborg also observes that in this debate 'Astell proved to be the spiritual daughter of Ralph Cudworth and Masham the Platonist consort of Locke.'[9]

In this chapter, however, I argue that there are many affinities between the philosophical views of Astell and Masham. In a 12 March 1743 letter to George Ballard, Thomas Rawlins observes that 'Lady Masham . . . was supposed to be Author of Mrs Astells Serious Proposal to the Ladies.'[10] This supposition is not as absurd as it may seem because both Masham and Astell are champions of women's education, and believe that women ought to improve their rationality to become useful members of society.[11] In addition, they challenge Norris's occasionalist metaphysics: they do not regard material things as causally impotent, they do not believe that bodies are unable to affect souls, they believe in interaction between the corporeal and incorporeal worlds, and they both ground these views on a teleological conception of the created world. These similarities

---

3 Irvin Ehrenpreis, 'Letters of Advice to Young Spinsters', in *The Lady of Letters in the Eighteenth Century* (Los Angeles: 1969), p. 14.

4 Christabel Osborne, 'Masham, Damaris', in *Dictionary of National Biography*, vol. xii, p. 1298.

5 Bridget Hill (ed.), 'Introduction' to *The First English Feminist: 'Reflections Upon Marriage' and Other Writings by Mary Astell* (Aldershot: Gower Publishing Co., 1986), p. 50.

6 Ada Wallas, *Before the Bluestockings* (London: G. Allen and Unwin, 1929), p. 95.

7 Benjamin Rand (ed.), *The Correspondence of John Locke and Edward Clarke*, reprint of 1927 edition (New York: Plainview, 1975), p. 14; and Ballard, *Memoirs of Several Ladies*, p. 333.

8 Perry, *The Celebrated Mary Astell*, p. 97.   9 Springborg, 'Introduction' to Astell, *Proposal*, p. xv.

10 Thomas Rawlins to George Ballard, 12 March 1743; in the Bodleian Library, University of Oxford, Ballard MS 41, fol. 231.

11 Although Masham's feminist ideas do not appear in print until her second work, *Occasional Thoughts in Reference to a Vertuous or Christian Life* (London: A. and J. Churchil, 1705), in her 1682 poem, 'When deaths cold hand shall close my eyes', she touches on the topic of women's reason. It is possible that her poetry was passed around scribal publication circles and that, in this way,

between their views can, to some extent, be traced back to their common Cambridge–Platonist backgrounds.

I

Damaris Masham was born in Cambridge on 18 January 1659 and educated by her father, the Cambridge Platonist Ralph Cudworth.[12] According to George Ballard, Masham developed a reputation for 'uncommon learning and piety' in her youth.[13] She met the philosopher John Locke around 1681 and became his close companion and correspondent for more than twenty years. Locke lived with Masham and her husband, Sir Francis Masham,[14] in Essex for the last thirteen years of his life. In one letter to Philippe van Limborch, dated 13 March 1691, Locke describes

---

Masham developed a reputation amongst her peers for her defences of women. For example, in the poem she says

> And our weak Sex I hope will then
> disdaine yt Stupid ignorance
> w:^{ch} was at first impos'd by men
> their owne high merits to inhance
> and now pleads custome for pretense
> to banish knowledg witt and sense
> Long have we here condemned been
> to Folly and impertinence
> but then it surely will be seene
> There's in our Souls no difference
> when we no longer Fetterd are
> but like to them o[ur] selves appeare.

This poem is in the Lovelace collection of John Locke's papers in the Bodleian Library, University of Oxford (Locke MS c.32, fol. 17). It recently appeared in *Kissing the Rod: An Anthology of Seventeenth-Century Women's Verse*, edited by Germaine Greer, Susan Hastings, Jeslyn Medoff, and Melinda Sansone (New York: The Noonday Press, 1988), pp. 315–23.

[12] For articles on Masham, see Lois Frankel, 'Damaris Masham: A Seventeenth-Century Feminist Philosopher', *Hypatia* 4:1 (1989), 80–90, and her 'Damaris Cudworth Masham', in Waithe (ed.), *A History of Women Philosophers*, vol. 111, pp. 73–85; Hutton, 'Damaris Cudworth, Lady Masham', and 'Like Father Like Daughter?'; Sheryl O'Donnell, ' "My Idea in Your Mind": John Locke and Damaris Cudworth Masham', in *Mothering the Mind*, edited by Ruth Perry and Martine Brownley (New York: Holmes and Meier, 1984), pp. 26–46; Sheryl O'Donnell, 'Mr Locke and the Ladies: The Indelible Words on the *Tabula Rasa*', *Studies in Eighteenth-Century Culture* 8 (1979), 151–64; Luisa Simonutti, 'Damaris Cudworth Masham: una Lady della Repubblica delle Lettere', in *Scritti in Onore di Eugenio Garin* (Pisa: Scuola Normale Superioire, 1987), pp. 141–65; Springborg, 'Astell, Masham, and Locke', pp. 105–25; and Sue Weinberg, 'Damaris Cudworth Masham: A Learned Lady of the Seventeenth Century', in *Norms and Values: Essays on the Work of Virginia Held*, edited by Joram Graf Haber (Lanham: Rowman and Littlefield, 1998), pp. 233–50.
[13] Ballard, *Memoirs of Several Ladies*, p. 332.
[14] Damaris married Sir Francis Masham (1649–1723) in June 1685. He was the third baronet of Oates in Essex, a member of Parliament, and a widower with nine children. Together they had one son, Francis Cudworth Masham, who was baptised on 8 June 1686.

Masham as 'a remarkably gifted woman'. 'The lady herself,' he says, 'is so much occupied with study and reflection on theological and philosophical matters, that you could find few men with whom you might associate with greater profit and pleasure.'[15] Masham's early letters to Locke reveal a sound understanding of the neoplatonic views of Cudworth, Henry More, John Smith, and Joseph Glanvill.[16] It is also possible that Masham had heard of Anne Conway's writings. John Covel writes of an occasion when Conway stayed with Cudworth in the Master's Lodge at Christ's College, Cambridge;[17] and Masham's mother, Damaris Cradock, was second cousin to Conway.[18] Francis Mercury van Helmont, one of Conway's closest friends, was also one of Masham's guests at her home in Essex, and Leibniz refers to Conway in a letter to Masham, saying that he would not have ventured to discuss intellectual matters with a woman if he had not been familiar with the perspicacity of other English ladies, such as 'Mad. la Comtesse de Connaway'.[19] In one letter to Locke, dated 9 March 1682, Masham says 'That I have no Ill Opinion of the Platonists I confess, nor ought you to wonder at That seeing I have spent the Most of my Life amongst Philosophers of that Sect in whom I have always found the most Vertue and Friendship.'[20] Later she jokes about her poetry that 'the Vehicles of the Platonists (whatever the Vortices of Des Cartes were) were Always much more my Favourites then the Muses'.[21] Despite the strong influence of Locke's empiricism on her mature thought, Masham never fully abandons these Platonist roots.[22]

Besides the *Discourse*, Masham wrote one other philosophical work, *Occasional Thoughts in Reference to a Vertuous or Christian Life*, published anonymously in 1705. Among her extant papers are letters to Locke,

[15] Locke to Philippe van Limborch, 13 March 1691; in *The Correspondence of John Locke*, edited by E. S. de Beer, 8 vols. (Oxford: Clarendon Press, 1976–82), no. 1375, p. 237.

[16] *Ibid.*, nos. 684, 687, 688, 695, 696, 699, and 1040.

[17] Dr Covel, Cudworth's successor, recalls that on one occasion 'My Lord and Lady Conway & their whole attendance were entertain'd by D:ʳ Cudworth many dayes, & were lodged partly at his private, & partly in the publick Lodgings & they all supped (at a Commencement night) in yᵉ Publick Hall'. See 'Christ College in Cambridge 1719. An Account of yᵉ Master's Lodgings in yᵉ College, and of his private Lodge by it self' in *Correspondence of Dr Covell*, vol. II (in the British Library, Add. MS 22,911, fol. 228).

[18] See J. C. Whitebrook, 'Samuel Cradock, Cleric and Pietist (1620–1706) and Matthew Cradock, First Governor of Massachusetts', *Congregational Historical Society Transactions* 5 (1911–12), 183.

[19] Leibniz to Masham, 14/25 December 1703; in Gerhardt (ed.), *Die Philosophischen Schriften*, vol. III, p. 337.

[20] Damaris Cudworth (later Masham) to John Locke, 9 March 1682; in de Beer (ed.), *The Correspondence of John Locke*, no. 690, p. 493.

[21] Masham to Locke, 15 September 1685; *ibid.*, no. 830, p. 735.

[22] On this topic, I am influenced by Hutton, 'Damaris Cudworth, Lady Masham', and 'Like Father Like Daughter?'

Limborch, Leibniz, Anthony Ashley Cooper (the third Earl of Shaftes-
bury), and Jean Le Clerc, including the first biographical sketch of
Locke, and several poems. Masham also had a correspondence with John
Norris prior to the publication of the *Discourse*. In 1688, Norris dedicated
his *Theory and Regulation of Love* to Masham, referring to 'The Esteem,
where with your Ladyship honour'd my former writings'. He praises her
as 'a Person of such nice and refined Sense, and whom *Nature* and your
own *unassisted Curiosity* have Conspired to accomplish beyond what the
Present Age can *parallel*, Or (unless you Ladyship will be perswaded to
bequeath some Monument of your extraordinary Genius to the world)
the *Future* will ever *believe*'.[23] In his *Reflections upon the Conduct of Human Life*
(1690), Norris also compliments Masham for being 'so much a *Mistress*'
of the works of Descartes and Malebranche.[24] It must have been a sad
irony for Norris that the first 'monument' to her intellect was the *Discourse*,
an unequivocal attack on his philosophy. Masham's break with Norris
was personal as well as philosophical: in 1692, Locke accused Norris of
breaking the wax seal on one of his letters to Masham;[25] and Masham
apparently became offended when Norris failed to omit a mistaken reference to her 'blindness' in the first edition of the *Reflections*.[26] At around
the same time, Masham also became sympathetic to the empiricist views
of Locke, a permanent resident in her home from 1691.

  In Masham's arguments against Astell and Norris, she draws on both
the common-sense philosophy of Edward Stillingfleet, the Bishop of
Worcester,[27] and the epistemology of Locke's *Essay*. This combination
may appear odd, because Stillingfleet is now chiefly remembered as
Locke's adversary.[28] But Masham blends their views to challenge what

---

[23] John Norris, *The Theory and Regulation of Love. A Moral Essay. In Two Parts. To which are added
Letters Philosophical and Moral between the Author and Dr Henry More* (Oxford: Henry Clements, 1688),
pp. ii–v.

[24] John Norris, *Reflections upon the Conduct of Human Life: With reference to the Study of Learning and
Knowledge. In a Letter to the Excellent Lady, the Lady Masham* (London: S. Manship, 1690), p. 62.

[25] For more details, see Charlotte Johnston, 'Locke's *Examination of Malebranche* and John Norris',
Journal of the History of Ideas 19 (1958), 551–8.

[26] In a letter to William Molyneux, 22 February 1697, Locke says of Masham that 'She has, 'tis true,
but weak eyes, which Mr. Norris, for reasons he knew best, was resolv'd to make blind ones. And
having fitted his epistle to that supposition, could not be hinder'd from publishing it so; though
my lady, to prevent it, writ him word that she was not blind' (de Beer (ed.), *The Correspondence of
John Locke*, no. 2202, p. 9).

[27] Masham knew Stillingfleet personally and, prior to her marriage, sometimes stayed with his
family in London.

[28] See Richard H. Popkin, 'The Philosophy of Bishop Stillingfleet', *Journal for the History of Philosophy*
9 (1971), 303–20, and Robert Carroll, *The Common-Sense Philosophy of Religion of Bishop Edward
Stillingfleet, 1635–1699* (The Hague: Nijhoff, 1975).

she sees as a tendency toward 'enthusiasm'[29] in the writings of Astell and Norris. Stillingfleet maintains that all theological and philosophical explanations of the world must be answerable to common sense.[30] One might say that he wields a 'common-sense razor' in his writings: his method dictates that one should never go beyond the bounds of sense without necessity. He practises this methodology to defend orthodox Anglicanism, warning that 'If once an unintelligible Way of Practical Religion become the Standard of Devotion, no Men of Sense will ever set themselves about it; but leave it to be understood by mad Men, and practis'd by Fools.'[31]

Following Stillingfleet's lead, Masham sets out to show that a religious or moral theory based on occasionalism is 'out of the reach of common Sense'.[32] She believes that 'if it were generally receiv'd and Preach'd by our Divines, that this Opinion of Seeing all things in God was the Basis upon which Christianity was built, Scepticism would be so far from finding thereby a Cure, that it would spread itself much farther amongst us than it has yet done'.[33] In her *Discourse*, she targets the Astell–Norris view 'that Mankind are obliged strictly, as their Duty, to love with Desire, nothing but God only', as well as the metaphysical argument that Norris offers in support of this belief: 'That God, not the creature, is the immediate, efficient Cause of our Sensations.'[34] In the first instance, Masham differs from Astell, but in the second, she brings up almost the very same objections to Norris's occasionalism. In both cases, Masham is against those theorists who advocate a transcendence or conquering of the material world in favour of a life devoted solely to the rational mind.

The primary difference between Masham and Astell lies in their views concerning the love of creatures. Like Norris, Astell believes that creatures deserve only a love of *benevolence*, a disinterested love motivated by altruism and charity. God, on the other hand, merits a love of *desire*; she believes that we must desire him as our good.[35] This is the case because an absolutely perfect being could want nothing that we could wish for him, therefore he does not need our benevolence; and the creatures, being imperfect, could never satisfy our desires. Astell maintains that even

---

[29] In seventeenth-century texts, an 'enthusiast' is someone who holds extravagant and visionary opinions not grounded in reason.

[30] By 'common sense' Stillingfleet means that any philosophical explanation must conform to a reasonable person's everyday beliefs and intuitions.

[31] Quoted in Masham, *Discourse*, p. 6.   [32] *Ibid.*, p. 29.   [33] *Ibid.*, p. 71.   [34] *Ibid.*, p. 7.

[35] On Norris's treatment of the traditional scholastic distinction between a love of benevolence and a love of desire, see Acworth, *The Philosophy of John Norris*, pp. 156–60.

if bodies were able to affect minds (as she had argued), God would still be the only deserved object of our love of desire:

allowing that Bodies did really better our Condition, that they did contribute to our Happiness or Misery, and did in some Sense produce our Pleasure or Pain, yet since they do not *will* it, do not act voluntarily but mechanically, and all the Power they have of affecting us proceeds intirely from the Will and good Pleasure of a superior Nature, whose Instruments they are, and without whose Blessing and Concurrence they could not act, therefore they are not proper Objects of our Love or Fear, which ought wholly and intirely to be referred to him, who freely acts upon our Souls, and does us good by these involuntary and necessary Instruments.[36]

We must love God alone with a love of desire because he is still the author of our good, even when using instruments to perform his will. Arguing by analogy, Astell points out that 'If a bountiful Person gives me Money to provide my self Necessaries, my Gratitude surely is not due to the Money but to the kind Hand that bestowed it.'[37]

By contrast, Masham believes that creatures can be loved with both a love of desire and a love of benevolence. While Astell and Norris define love as a movement in the soul towards good, Masham defines it as 'that Disposition, or Act of the Mind, we find in our selves towards any thing we are pleas'd with'.[38] Here Masham echoes Locke's remark in the *Essay* that 'our Ideas of Love and Hatred, are but the Dispositions of the Mind, in respect of Pleasure and Pain in general, however caused in us'.[39] Locke claims that 'the Being and Welfare of a Man's Children or Friends, producing constant Delight in him, he is said constantly to *love* them'.[40] Masham likewise says, almost verbatim, that we love our child or friend because their being is a pleasure to us.[41] But she takes this definition further than Locke by applying it to the distinction between a love of benevolence and a love of desire. The disposition of love, Masham says, 'cannot be distinguish'd into different Acts of wishing well, and desiring; which are other different Acts of the Mind, consequential to Love, according to the difference of the Object'.[42] Benevolence and desire, in other words, are simply acts that follow from love, depending on the loved object. We may love our children with a love of desire when they are away from us, and yet at the same time we may also wish good

[36] Astell to Norris, 14 August 1694; in Astell and Norris, *Letters*, pp. 284–5.
[37] *Ibid.*, p. 282.   [38] Masham, *Discourse*, p. 18.
[39] John Locke, *An Essay Concerning Human Understanding*, edited by Peter H. Nidditch (Oxford: Clarendon Press, 1979), II.xx.5, p. 230.
[40] *Ibid.*, II.xx.5, p. 230.   [41] Masham, *Discourse*, p. 18.   [42] *Ibid.*, pp. 18–19.

for them.[43] In short, Masham believes that the creatures are capable both of being a good *to* us and of receiving good *from* us. The only difference between our love of creatures and the love of God is that we ought to love God above all things.[44] So Masham diverges from Astell in that she believes that we may still desire material things as our good, whether or not they are the efficient causes of our pleasure. If occasional causes are always necessarily accompanied by a particular effect, according to Masham, then they may still be goods to us the same as if they were efficient causes:

> Or must we think a beautiful Flower has not the same Appearance, whether it be believ'd that God has lodg'd a power in the Flower to excite the Idea of its Colour in us, or that he himself exhibits the Idea of its Colour at the presence of that Object? If the Flower is either way equally pleasing (as certainly it is) then it is also equally desireable.[45]

There is no reason why the love of creatures should exclude the love of God, any more than 'the Love of Cherries should exclude the love of our Friend that gives them us'.[46]

Furthermore, in Masham's view, we can love God only *after* we have loved other people: 'if we lov'd not the Creatures, it is not conceiveable how we should love God'.[47] Following Locke, Masham denies that we have any innate moral principles; all our ideas are derived from sensation or reflection on the mind's activities.[48] No human being is born with the notion that 'we ought to love and desire God alone'; it is not a self-evident truth. Human beings must 'know many other Truths before we come to know this; which is a Proposition containing many complex ideas in it'; and we are not capable of framing such propositions 'till we have been long acquainted with pleasing Sensations'.[49] In other words, we can love God only if we have an *idea* of love; and to attain the idea of love, we

---

[43] *Ibid.*, p. 24.
[44] Masham says that because God is the most perfect being, we ought to 'pay the highest Tribute of Affection, and Adoration, to him that our Natures are capable of' (*ibid.*, p. 45).
[45] *Ibid.*, pp. 31–2.   [46] *Ibid.*, p. 88.   [47] *Ibid.*, p. 62.
[48] In the later work, *Occasional Thoughts*, Masham is more explicit:

> To see what light we receive from Nature to direct our Actions, and how far we are Naturally able to obey that Light, Men must be consider'd purely as in the state of Nature, *viz.* as having no extrinsick Law to direct them, but indu'd only with a faculty of comparing their distant Ideas by intermediate Ones, and Thence of deducing, or infering one thing from another; whereby our Knowledge immediately received from *Sense*, or *Reflection*, is inlarg'd to a view of Truths remote, or future. (*Occasional Thoughts*, pp. 60–1)

[49] Masham, *Discourse*, p. 66.

must first experience sensations of pleasure in our interactions with other creatures. It is therefore unreasonable to propose that humans can love God alone, in the same way that it is unreasonable 'for the Fishes (if they were capable of it) to propose, or pray to God, that they might fly in the Air like Birds; or Ride Post-Horses as Men do'.[50] It is obvious, according to Masham, that human beings are designed by God to love other creatures. 'To say that Religion unfits us for it, is to reproach the Wisdom of God as highly as it is possible.'[51]

Finally, Masham also explicitly attacks Astell for her *Letters* and the *Proposal*. In 'The Preface' to the *Letters*, Astell modestly describes her own writings as 'crude Rapsodies'. Masham replies that 'Pompous Rhapsodies of the Soul's debasing her self, when she descends to set the least part of her Affections upon any thing but her Creator . . . are plainly but a complementing God with the contempt of his Works, by which we are most effectually led to Know, Love and Adore him.'[52] Masham also claims that Astell's letters are 'not the Productions of Philosophical Disquisition'[53] and describes her as 'a young Writer, whose Judgment may, perhaps, be thought Byassed by the Affectation of Novelty'.[54] She warns that Norris's opinions are in danger of 'introducing, especially amongst those whose Imaginations are stronger than their Reason, a Devout way of talking'.[55] She even makes pointed references to the *Proposal*, stating that Norris's type of unbridled enthusiasm 'can End in nothing but Monasteries, and Hermitages; with all those Sottish and Wicked Superstitions which have accompanied them where-ever they have been in use'.[56] The basis of Masham's criticisms is the view that it is more reasonable to assume that God has created human beings to enjoy a sociable life. Masham concludes the *Discourse* by saying that

As for Monasteries, and Religious Houses, (as they are call'd) all who are acquainted with them, know that they are nothing less than what is pretended; And serve only to draw in Discontented, Devout People, with an imaginary Happiness. For there is constantly as much Pride, Malice, and Faction, within those Walls, as without them; And . . . very often as much licentiousness.[57]

Masham sees the *Proposal* for an academy for women as a natural extension of Astell's view that we must love God alone with a love of desire, and thus rejects Astell's feminist plans as impractical and utopian. She interprets Astell as encouraging women to withdraw from the world, rather than offering a reasonable proposal for social reform.

[50] *Ibid.*, pp. 82–3.   [51] *Ibid.*, p. 123.   [52] *Ibid.*, p. 27.   [53] *Ibid.*
[54] *Ibid.*, p. 78.   [55] *Ibid.*, p. 120.   [56] *Ibid.*   [57] *Ibid.*, p. 125.

In sum, Masham's Lockean views on morality set her apart from Astell. Like Locke, Masham believes that our idea of love originates with our sensations. On these grounds, Masham rejects Astell and Norris's distinction between love of benevolence and love of desire, and claims that we must love the creatures before we can love God, else we can have no idea of love. Consequently Masham rejects a life devoted solely to the life of the mind.

In these respects, Masham also disrupts what Lloyd sees as the basis of women's exclusion from intellectual discourse in that period: a stark polarisation between the superior 'masculine' trait of reason, and those inferior categories metaphorically associated with femininity, such as the body and the senses. When Masham argues against the Astell–Norris conception of love, Masham emphasises that the love of other creatures is necessary if we are to love the deity: we would not be able to love him unless we loved these things first, because the idea of love can be acquired only through *sensory experience* of other creatures. For this reason also, Masham's moral thought is interpreted as stereotypically 'feminine' in that she emphasises the social ties between human beings. Lois Frankel points out that theorists such as Nancy Chodorow believe that child-rearing practices encourage males to define their masculinity in terms of detachment and separation.[58] Females, on the other hand, are raised to see their identity in terms of relation and connection. Frankel claims that Masham's moral theory is representative of the 'female experience' in that it emphasises a social life rather than a solitary, contemplative existence. Although it is difficult to accept that there is a homogeneous 'female experience', it cannot be denied that Masham raises the moral status of those metaphysical categories that have been traditionally associated with the feminine in philosophical texts of the early modern period, such as the senses, the body, and matter.

Masham's book provoked responses from both Norris and Astell. Norris wrote 'An Admonition Concerning two late Books call'd *Discourses of the Love of God*', appended to the fourth volume of his *Practical Discourses* (1698). His essay is also a response to Daniel Whitby's *Discourse of the Love of God* (1697), another attack on Norris's theory of love. In his 'Admonition', Norris mistakenly attributes Masham's *Discourse* to Locke. Norris criticises 'him' (Masham) for the 'unkindness and disrespect he expresses towards me';[59] and complains that there is a 'spiteful Ayr'

---

[58] See Lois Frankel's two articles: 'Damaris Masham', 86–9, and 'Damaris Cudworth Masham', pp. 80–3.

[59] John Norris, *Practical Discourses Upon several Divine Subjects* (London: S. Manship, 1698), vol. iv, pp. 381–2.

running throughout the book.[60] But he does not engage with Masham on a philosophical level. Toward the end of the essay Norris says: 'I was inclining once to have made some Remarks upon the particular Arguments, together with other incidental Passages that run through the Bulk of their Discourses, but a Kind and Ingenious Hand has saved me that Pains in relation to Mr. L.–'.[61] Mary Astell is the 'kind pen' to whom Norris refers, and her response is *The Christian Religion*.[62]

Although *The Christian Religion* was published nine years after the *Discourse* appeared, Astell takes particular offence against Masham's remarks about 'pompous rhapsodies' and 'driving Folks into *Monasteries*'.[63] Astell says that

This is not a place to take notice, how those who are so severe upon their Neighbours for being wanting (even in Private Letters writ without the design of being Publish'd) in that exactness of *Expression* which ought to be found in *Philosophical Disquisitions*, do themselves confound the notion of Love with the sentiment of Pleasure, by making Love to *consist barely in the act of the Mind toward that which pleases.*[64]

Astell believes that equating love with pleasure poses a problem for moral agency: since we cannot help being pleased with that which pleases, then this type of love is beyond our voluntary control; if we love something bad or evil, we are not free to do otherwise. For this reason, it is far better to define love as an intellectual endeavour of the soul toward good. Astell also takes up Masham's assertion that every man's experience confutes the view that no creature is a good to us,[65] saying she would allow this 'just so much and no more than they will allow me, That *the daily sense and experience of Mankind* disproves what a great Philosopher asserts when he tells us, That *Flame* is not *Hot and Light*, nor *Snow White and Cold*, nor *Manna White and Sweet*'.[66] Astell suggests that if all philosophical explanations must be answerable to common sense (as Masham suggests), then, by the same light, Locke's theory of secondary qualities is highly questionable. Overall, Astell apparently finds nothing in the *Discourse* to make her revise her opinions about the love of God and his creatures.

---

[60] *Ibid.*, p. 382.   [61] *Ibid.*, pp. 423–4.   [62] Acworth, *The Philosophy of John Norris*, p. 177.
[63] Astell, *Christian Religion*, pp. 138, 140–2. Astell says that 'none that I know of plead for Monasteries, strictly so call'd, in *England*, or for any thing else but a reasonable provision for the Education of one half of Mankind, and for a safe retreat so long and no longer than our Circumstances make requisite' (p. 142).
[64] Astell, *Christian Religion*, pp. 131–2.   [65] Masham, *Discourse*, p. 25.
[66] Astell, *Christian Religion*, p. 131.

II

Nevertheless, Masham and Astell do agree on one key issue: unlike Norris, they oppose any theory in which real interaction between souls and bodies is denied. In the *Discourse*, Masham seems to arrive independently at Astell's objection that Norris's theory 'renders a great Part of God's Workmanship Vain and Useless'.[67] Masham argues that if material beings are causally inefficacious, and if it is God himself who represents the idea of material things to our souls, then our sensory organs must be completely superfluous. But if this is so, she says, then it is contrary to the idea that God is supremely wise, because a perfect being would have eliminated any arbitrary features from his design. Hence Masham accuses Norris of detracting 'from the Wisdom of God, in framing his Creatures like the Idols of the Heathen, that have Eyes, and see not; Ears, and hear not, *& c*'.[68] She says that if we believe that creatures are the occasional, rather than the efficient causes of our sensations, then

> the Wisdom of God cannot herein be equally admired, because it is not equally conspicuous. For if God immediately exhibits to me all my Idea's, and that I do not truly see with my Eyes, and hear with my Ears; then all that Wonderful Exactness and curious Workmanship, in framing the Organs of Sense, seems superfluous and vain; Which is no small reflection upon infinite Wisdom.[69]

In addition, Masham repeats Astell's assertion that Norris's theory does not comport well with God's majesty. Astell implies that it would be beneath a perfect being to be constantly intervening in earthly events, as Norris believes he does. Similarly, Masham says that it is 'unworthy of, and mis-becoming the Majesty of the great God, *who is of Purer Eyes than to behold iniquity*, to be as it were at the beck of his sinful Creatures, to excite in them Sentiments of Delight and Pleasure, whenever they are dispos'd to transgress against his Laws'.[70] Masham takes the same argument further than Astell to claim that Norris's theory forces God to be 'a partner in our wickedness'.[71] An unacceptable consequence

---

[67] Astell to Norris, 14 August 1694; in Astell and Norris, *Letters*, p. 278.
[68] Masham, *Discourse*, pp. 29–31.   [69] *Ibid.*, pp. 31–2.
[70] *Ibid.*, p. 102. Here Masham's comments resemble those in Locke's 'Remarks', written at Oates in 1693. Locke writes 'And so, whatever a man thinks, God produces the thought; let it be infidelity, murmuring, or blasphemy. The Mind doth nothing; his mind is only the mirror that receives the Ideas that God exhibits to it, and just as God exhibits them, the man is altogether passive in the whole business of thinking' ('Remarks', p. 52). If this is so, according to Locke, then Norris resolves all, 'even the thoughts and will of men, into an irresistible fatal necessity' ('Remarks', p. 52).
[71] Masham, *Discourse*, p. 102.

of Norris's theory is that it implies that God *intended* human beings to have sinful desires. On Norris's view, every act that carries our desires towards the creature is sinful, or 'a kind of Spiritual Adultery'.[72] He believes that we love creatures only because we mistakenly believe that *they* are the cause of our pleasure. This last notion takes an interesting turn in the writings of Nicolas Malebranche, Norris's mentor. In his *Christian Conversations*, Malebranche claims that *women* are principally to blame for our early inclinations toward sensible objects.[73] He says that

there is no Woman that has not some traces in her Brain, and motion of her Spirits, which carry her to something sensible. Now when the Child is in the Womb of its Mother, it has the same traces, and the same motion of the Spirits: Therefore in this estate it knows and loves Bodies, and consequently is born a Sinner.[74]

Masham is also opposed to this view. If God is the only true cause of our pleasure, then he is responsible for creating our desires. In other words, 'we are necessitated by God himself'[75] to that which Norris and Malebranche call idolatry, therefore women cannot be blamed.

In short, in her *Discourse*, Masham repeats Astell's final objections to Norris's occasionalist metaphysics: she too believes that his theory is contrary to the wisdom and majesty of God. Not only would it be beneath God's majesty to be constantly exciting pleasure and pain in his creatures, it would also vilify his wisdom and benevolence.

In addition, Masham raises similar objections against Leibniz's system of pre-established harmony. Masham began a correspondence with the German philosopher Gottfried Wilhelm Leibniz in early 1704. Leibniz took an interest in almost every notable woman thinker of the seventeenth century. He shared an intellectual correspondence with his friend and patron, Electress Sophie of Hanover, as well as her sister Elisabeth of Bohemia, Sophie's daughter, Queen Sophie-Charlotte of Prussia, and Caroline of Ansbach, later Queen of England (1683–1737). During his time as family historian for the House of Hanover, Leibniz kept Sophie well informed of the latest philosophical trends. Sophie's skills as

---

[72] *Ibid.*, p. 115.
[73] Elisabeth of Bohemia also took an interest in the *Christian Conversations*, and sent a copy to Leibniz in 1678. For details, see Leibniz, *Philosophical Papers and Letters*, a selection translated and edited, with an introduction, by Leroy E. Loemker, second edition (Dordrecht: D. Reidel, 1969), pp. 209–12. Malebranche makes similar statements about women in his *Elucidations of The Search After Truth* (in Malebranche, *The Search After Truth*, p. 600).
[74] Quoted in Masham, *Discourse*, p. 75.   [75] *Ibid.*, p. 66.

a philosopher were not as refined as those of Elisabeth;[76] but she was extremely curious about intellectual matters, and encouraged the philosophical interests of her daughter, Sophie-Charlotte.[77] At around the same time that Leibniz was urging Sophie and her family to campaign for the English succession, he was also expressing an admiration for English women philosophers.[78] Leibniz makes comparisons between his own philosophy and that of Anne Conway; he praises Mary Astell's part in the correspondence with Norris; and he commends Catharine Trotter Cockburn's defence of Locke. In Hanover, he met with the devotional writer, Elizabeth Burnet, the wife of Gilbert Burnet; and he may have also been familiar with Sophie's correspondent, the feminist polemicist Mary Chudleigh. Not surprisingly, in his first letter to Masham, Leibniz says that he has an extremely good opinion of the minds of English women.

In early 1704, Leibniz heard that Masham intended to send him a copy of her father's *True Intellectual System of the Universe*, and wrote to express his admiration for Cudworth. Leibniz told her that he had himself 'discovered a new country in the intelligible world' and had thereby added a little to Cudworth's system.[79] Masham responded to Leibniz by asking him to spell out his theory of substance. She had read his 'Système nouveau' in *Journal des savants* (1695) and the comments on that essay in the first edition of Pierre Bayle's *Historical and Critical Dictionary* (1696),[80] but she required his clarification on certain points.

In the 'Système nouveau' Leibniz expresses his theory of the true relationship between the soul and body. In the first half of the essay, he claims that matter is nothing but a collection or aggregation of parts.

[76] Leibniz complains that Sophie does not make the effort to understand his writings before she raises objections (see Zedler, 'The Three Princesses', p. 48). On Sophie, see also Maria Kroll, *Sophie Electress of Hanover: A Personal Portrait* (London: Victor Gollancz, 1973).
[77] Sophie-Charlotte's questions inspire Leibniz to write his famous *Theodicy* (1710).
[78] Leibniz also comments on the philosophical opinions of Queen Christina of Sweden; see Loemker (ed.), *Philosophical Papers and Letters*, p. 554.
[79] Leibniz to Masham, early 1704; in Gottfried Wilhelm Leibniz, *Leibniz's New System and Associated Contemporary Texts*, translated and edited by R. S. Woolhouse and Richard Francks (Oxford: Clarendon Press, 1997), p. 203.
[80] The full title of Leibniz's essay is 'Système nouveau de la nature et de la communication des substances, aussi bien que de l'union qu'il y a entre l'âme et le corps' ('New System of the Nature of Substances and their Communication, and of the Union which Exists between the Soul and the Body'). The Woolhouse and Francks volume of *Leibniz's New System* includes an English translation of this paper and of the articles and letters that followed its appearance. The same volume has excerpts from the Masham–Leibniz correspondence, but omits Masham's final letter on Cudworth's philosophy. The correspondence is reproduced in full in Gerhardt (ed.), *Die Philosophischen Schriften*, vol. III. But because Gerhardt omits Masham's emphases for quotations, I have referred to the original manuscripts here.

Located within matter are certain principles of action and perception that Leibniz calls 'substantial forms', 'atoms of substance', 'souls', 'first entelechies', and 'primary forces'. The nature of these substantial forms consists in force; they are the incorporeals that, when united to an extended mass, organise it into a unified body.[81] The human soul is like a superior type of substantial form, endowed with the capacity for abstraction and forming universal ideas. On the question of soul–body interaction, Leibniz says that he can find no intelligible way of explaining how the body transmits or communicates anything to the soul, or vice versa. Yet despite agreeing that no created substance has any real influence upon another, Leibniz rejects occasionalism. He says that advocates of this theory have an unacceptable preference for miracles over natural explanations, and that the 'reason and order of the divine wisdom demands we make no needless recourse to miracles'.[82] Instead, he claims, there is a 'perfect agreement' or an 'adaptation of the soul to the body'.[83] God created the soul so that everything must arise in it from its own inner nature, with a perfect conformity to the things outside it.

In his response to Masham, dated May 1704, Leibniz expands on these points:

For we have experience of bodies acting on one another according to mechanical laws, and of souls producing within themselves various internal actions, but we see no way of conceiving action of the soul on matter, or of matter on the soul, or anything which corresponds to it. For we cannot explain, by the example of any machine whatever, how material relationships – that is to say, mechanical laws – could produce a perception, or how perception could produce a change in the velocity or the direction of animal spirits or other bodies, of whatever subtle or gross kinds.[84]

The inconceivability of any other explanation, he says, and the admirable uniformity of nature, has led him to believe that the soul and the body follow their own separate laws, without corporeal laws being affected by the soul and 'without bodies finding windows through which to exert their influence over souls'.

You will then ask how this agreement of the soul with the body comes about. The defenders of occasional causes hold that God continually adjusts the soul

---

[81] For this point, I am grateful to Eileen O'Neill.
[82] Woolhouse and Francks (eds.), *Leibniz's New System*, pp. 211–12.
[83] In Leibniz's first letter to Masham, in early 1704, he calls this a 'little system of pre-established harmony between substances' (Woolhouse and Francks (eds.), *Leibniz's New System*, p. 203).
[84] Leibniz to Masham, May 1704; *ibid.*, p. 206.

to the body, and the body to the soul. But since that would mean that God had to keep disturbing the natural laws of bodies, it could only involve miracles, and so is not very suitable for philosophy, which has to explain the ordinary course of nature. That is what made me think that it is infinitely more worthy of God's economy and of the uniformity and constant order of his works to conclude that from the start he created souls and bodies in such a way that each following its own laws would match up with the other. It cannot be denied that this is possible for one whose wisdom and power are infinite.[85]

In her reply, dated 3 June 1704, Masham criticises this non-interactionist account of soul–body relations. Leibniz says that his new system is 'more than a hypothesis', but Masham demurs:

it appears not yet to me that this is more than an Hypothesis; for as Gods ways are not limited by our Conceptions; the unintelligibleness or inconceivablness by us of any Way but one, dos not (methinks) much induce a Beleefe of that's being the way which God has chosen to make use of. Yet such an inference as this from our Ignorance, I remember P. Malbranche (or some other assertor of his Hypothesis) would make in behalf of Occasional Causes: to which Hypothesis, amongst other exceptions, I think there is one, which I cannot (without your help) see, but that yours is alike Liable to and that is from the Organization of the Body; wherin all that Nice Curiositie that is discoverable seeming useless; becomes Superfluous, and Lost labour.[86]

By 'some other assertor', Masham obviously means John Norris. She could not abide by Leibniz's system of pre-established harmony for the same reason that she could not accept Norris's occasionalism: it makes material bodies superfluous and redundant. According to Leibniz, any causal connection between souls and bodies is merely apparent; in reality, they are entirely unrelated to each other. Rather than see this account as a celebration of God's perfections, Masham views it as an affront to divine wisdom. If the soul is self-sufficient, then bodily organs can serve no purpose in creation. Her objections to Norris and Leibniz arise from the same source as Astell's objections to Norris: her intellectualist conception of God's relationship to the natural world.

Masham's criticisms of occasionalism and pre-established harmony are undoubtedly influenced by her father's theological principles. One of Cudworth's main theses in *The True Intellectual System* is that nothing in nature 'floats' without a head and governor, and that God presides

---

[85] *Ibid.*
[86] Masham to Leibniz, 3 June 1704; in the Niedersächsische Landesbibliothek zu Hanover, MS 612, fols. 8–9; and Woolhouse and Francks (eds.), *Leibniz's New System*, p. 209. She also says 'To this difficultie likewise let me add that I conceive not why *Organisme* should be, or can be thought, (as you say is) *Essential to Matter*' (*ibid.*).

over everything. Cudworth opposes those mechanical theories that render God an 'idle Spectator' in his creation, thus making 'his Wisdom altogether Useless and Insignificant, as being a thing wholly Inclosed and shut up within his own breast, and not at all acting abroad upon any thing without him'.[87] But he also challenges the view that God does everything 'Immediately and Miraculously'.[88] The theory of plastic nature is essential to Cudworth's system, because it strikes a medium: it is 'a living Stamp or Signature of Divine Wisdom' in the created world, and yet it does not require God to exert a 'Sollicitous Care or Distractious Providence'.[89]

In her letters to Leibniz, Masham defends Cudworth's theory of plastic nature. From 1703 to 1706, Jean Le Clerc published selections from *The True Intellectual System* in his new journal, *Bibliothèque Choisie*.[90] Masham wrote to Le Clerc on 18 June 1703 to thank him for the respect he showed her father.

> Your extract of the first Chapter of the *Intellectual System of the Universe*; wherein you have givn so advantageous an Idea of that work, as Joyn'd to the Authoritie your Judgment Carrys, will (I doubt not) Highly recommend it to all the Learned World; to whom I have too often desir'd it should be more knowne, not to be extreamly Pleas'd in your Resolution of makeing it be so.[91]

But Masham had cause to be dismayed when controversy grew up around the publication. As each issue of the periodical appeared, the French scholar Pierre Bayle (1647–1706) published his own highly critical response to Cudworth's philosophy.[92]

Plastic nature or 'plastic powers' are the executors of God's grand design, his causal instruments in the natural world. These incorporeal spirits have the formative power to determine the organisation, growth, vitality, and movement of living things. But while plastical powers within the universe act like minds in that they are purposeful, they

---

[87] Cudworth, *True Intellectual System*, p. 148.   [88] *Ibid.*, p. 150.   [89] *Ibid.*, pp. 150, 155.

[90] For further details see Rosalie Colie, *Light and Enlightenment: A Study of the Cambridge Platonists and the Dutch Arminians* (Cambridge: Cambridge University Press, 1957), pp. 117–44, and Susan Rosa, 'Ralph Cudworth in the *République des Lettres*: The Controversy about Plastick Nature and the Reputation of Pierre Bayle', *Studies in Eighteenth-Century Culture* 23 (1994), 147–60.

[91] Masham to Le Clerc, 18 June 1703; in the Amsterdam University Library (UVA), MS J.58ᵛ. In a later letter to Le Clerc, dated May 1704, Masham writes that 'No one can have more respect for the memorie of a Dead Parent or Freind than I have for my Fathers; and it is no little satisfaction to me to see that a work of his, thought excellent by the best Judges of such a Performance, will be by your means more knowne in the World than it has hitherto been' (MS J.57.b).

[92] These rejoinders were published in Henri Basnage de Beauval's *Histoire des Ouvrages des Savants* and in Bayle's *Continuations des pensées diverses sur la comète*.

are also unconscious and non-deliberative in their activities.[93] Against this view, Bayle claims that Cudworth's theory of an insensible plastic nature implies that matter might conceivably exist and act by itself, independently of God.[94] Bayle suggests that the doctrine is atheistic in tendency, because it makes it unnecessary to suppose that wherever purpose is exhibited, God must be at work; in short, it appears to make God superfluous.

In a letter to Le Clerc, dated 21 June 1705, Masham says 'I could heartilie wish that you were at Libertie to answer the objections of Mr Bayle.' She expresses her fears that no one will be able to present convincing arguments against him:

> Of what I have read, some Things seem'd to me very well; and others I fear'd Mr Bayl would take advantage from. The Systematical Men will hardly I doubt be able to answer him thorowly, but especially the Calvinistical; in whose Orthodoxie he is so intrench'd, that those Divines can scarce have one faire Blow at him. And it is really sad to see that whilst such Teachers of the People do with so cruel heat (as they too often do) fall upon some men onely for dissenting from them in Opinions which are no Doctrines of Christianitie; and represent for dangerous Heretics such (for example) as You are; they at the same time are forc'd patiently to hear Religion ridicul'd without dareing to oppose the man who dos it, from a Feare (but too Just) that they should thereby afford him matter of greater Triumph.[95]

In frustration, it seems, Masham formulates her own counter-objections in a letter to Leibniz, dated 20 October 1705. Masham criticises Bayle for saying that God cannot make an unconscious agent act for wise ends unless God himself is giving perpetual direction to material causes (*i.e.*, unless occasionalism is true). Masham says:

> my Fathers Hypothesis is methinks sufficiently secur'd from *the Retorsion of Atheists*, without being *in the same case* with any one which makes God the immediate Efficient Cause of all the Effects of Nature. Since my Father dos not therein[96] assert (as Mʳ Bayle says he dos) That *God has been able to give to Creatures a Facultie of Produceing Excellent Works (viz such as is the Organization of Plants and Animals) seperate from all Knowledge* &c.: but onely a Facultie of Executeing instrumentally his Ideas or Designs, in the Production of such *Excellent Works*: so that (*according to him*) *there*

---

93 Masham says that plastic natures can be likened to 'habits' in humans, such as 'those of singing and danceing: which shall oftentimes direct the motions of body, or voice without any consideration of what the next note, or motion should be' (Masham to Leibniz, 20 October 1705; in Hanover, MS 612, fol. 23ᵛ). Here she echoes Cudworth, *True Intellectual System*, p. 157.

94 Colie, *Light and Enlightenment*, p. 138.

95 Masham to Le Clerc, 21 June 1705; in the Amsterdam University Library (UVA), MS J.57.c.

96 Masham crosses out '(in effect)' here.

is (differently from what Mr Bayle asserts of his Hypothesis) *an inseparable union betwixt the Power of Produceing Excellent Works, and the Idea of theire Essence, and manner of Produceing them*: and it seems to me that there can be no pretence to the *Retorsion of Atheists* unless it were asserted, That God had been able to give to Creatures a Facultie of Produceing *excellent works*; the Ideas whereof never were in any understanding: But my Father is so far from asserting any such thing as this, that he holds the Operations of the Plastick Nature to be *essentially and necessarilie Dependent* on the ideas in the Divine Intellect.[97]

In short, God gives creatures a faculty of executing his 'ideas' instrumentally. These ideas or essences must have existed prior to the existence of the creatures, and, moreover, they must have existed in a mind. From this we can conclude that plastic nature is essentially and necessarily dependent on the ideas in the divine mind: the plastical powers could never be autonomous.[98] Matter does not have the power to act independently of God; it has 'onely a Pow'r to Execute the Ideas of a Perfect Mind; if there were no *Mind* in the universe; this Pow'r in the Matter must Lye for ever Dormant and unproductive, of any such Excellent Work as is spoken of'.[99]

From these remarks, it is not obvious that Masham holds Cudworth's theory as her own. Nevertheless, her argument does depend upon a presupposition that underlies her earlier objections to Norris and Leibniz. In her defence of Cudworth's doctrine of plastic nature, Masham once again makes the divine mind or *divine wisdom* a fundamental premise in her argument.[100] Like Astell, Masham has an intellectualist conception of the divine attributes. Her aim is to promote the wisdom of God against the imputations of occasionalism, and to affirm the harmony and order he has established in the world.[101] This is why Masham's views bear similarities to those of Astell. In defending her father's theory of plastic nature, Masham emphasises the connections, relations, and interactions between matter and spirit. Material things are not radically separate or detached from spirits and God. Just as Astell draws

---

[97] Masham to Leibniz, 20 October 1705; in Hanover, MS 612, fols. 22–3; and Gerhardt (ed.), *Die Philosophischen Schriften*, vol. III, pp. 370–1.

[98] Cudworth writes that 'if there had been no *Perfect Mind* or *Intellect* in the World, there could no more have been any *Plastick Nature* in it, then there could be *an Image in the Glass* without a *Face*' (*True Intellectual System*, p. 172).

[99] Masham to Leibniz, 20 October 1705; in Hanover, MS 612, fol. 23; and Gerhardt (ed.), *Die Philosophischen Schriften*, vol. III, p. 371.

[100] For this point, I am indebted to Hutton's 'Like Father Like Daughter?'

[101] In *Occasional Thoughts*, Masham's intellectualism is more explicit. She says that the divine will is 'one steady, uniform, unchangeable result of infinite Wisdom and Benevolence, extending to and including All his Works' (p. 69).

upon the idea of a plastic faculty connecting the soul to its material body, so too does Masham emphasise the spiritual aspects of material things.

Masham's wider theories about soul and body are, however, more radical than Astell's. While Masham is passionate about defending her father's views, in other parts of the correspondence with Leibniz, she expounds her own independent theories on substance, drawing together the views of Locke and Henry More. In an early letter to Leibniz (8 August 1704), Masham argues against the system of pre-established harmony by stating that she has no positive idea of the essence of 'atoms of substance'. She says that

> your Negation of theire haveing any Dimensions, makes theire Existence (I confess) inconceivable to me; as not being able to conceive an existence of that which *is No Where*. If the Localitie of these substances were accounted for by theire being as you [say] they are always in Organiz'd Bodies, then they are somewhere: But if these *Atomes de Substance* are somewhere then they must have some extension, which you deny of them.[102]

Instead Masham believes that '*Extension* is...inseparable from the notion of All Substance'.[103] On this point, she goes against her father's teaching. In the preface to *The True Intellectual System*, Cudworth says that distinct from the body there is a substance that is indivisible, penetrable, and self-active. But whether 'this *Substance* be altogether *Unextended*, or *Extended* otherwise then *Body*,' he says, 'we shall leave every man to make his own Judgment'.[104] In his fifth chapter, however, he claims that those who cannot conceive of unextended substances allow their imaginations to impose on their reason. He says that the notion that 'whatsoever is *Unextended*, and hath no *Distant Parts*, one without another, must therefore needs be *Nothing*, is no *Common Notion*, but the *Spurious Suggestion* of *Imagination* only, and a *Vulgar Errour*'.[105]

But Masham's views do have an affinity with Cudworth's Cambridge colleague, Henry More, who had argued that the soul is extended. Masham adds weight to More's arguments by appealing to Locke's claim that knowledge can come only from our perception of the agreement or disagreement of ideas. More specifically, she says that

---

[102] Masham to Leibniz, 8 August 1704; in Hanover, MS 612, fols. 8ᵛ–9; and Woolhouse and Francks (eds.), *Leibniz's New System*, p. 216.
[103] Masham to Leibniz, 8 August 1704; in Hanover, MS 612, fol. 12ᵛ; and Woolhouse and Francks (eds.), *Leibniz's New System*, p. 216.
[104] Cudworth, *True Intellectual System*, 'The Preface to the Reader', n.p.   [105] *Ibid.*, p. 780.

wherever I have no Idea of a thing; or Demonstration of the Truth of any Proposition the Truth of which is inconceivable by me, I cannot, and conclude that I ought not to assent to what is asserted of either: since should I once do this I know not where I should stop; what should be the Boundaries of Assent. Or why I might not Beleeve alike one thing as well as another.[106]

Masham tells Leibniz that she cannot form a positive *idea* of unextended substance, and therefore she has no conception 'from whence I can affirm, or Deny, any thing Concerning it'.[107] On the other hand, she does have some conception of two substances, one of extension without solidity, the other of solid extension.[108]

The same principles that lead Masham to affirm that all substances are extended, lead her also to the Lockean view that it is conceivable for God to annex thought to a system of solid extension. Locke's observation about 'thinking matter' stems from his belief that we have only an obscure and confused idea of substances. Drawing on Locke's argument in the *Essay* IV.iii.6, Masham asks whether God could not conceivably

add (if he so Pleas'd) the *Power of Thinking* to that Substance which has *Soliditie?* *Soliditie* and *Thought* being both of them but attributes of some unknown Substance, and I see not why it may not be one and the same which is the common support of Both these; there appearing to me no Contradiction in a co-existence of *Thought* and *Solidity* in the same Substance.[109]

Masham says that this hypothesis is just as conceivable as Leibniz's hypothesis of God creating an unextended substance and then uniting it to an extended thing. In both cases, the substances underlying the attributes are unknown. Yet, according to Masham, Leibniz's theory is at a disadvantage for two reasons: first, his system makes material things redundant, and, second, it is not possible to conceive of unextended substances. Although we have only an obscure idea of substance in general, it is reasonable to affirm 'that God should give *Thought* to a Substance which I know not, but whereof I know some of its attributes [*e.g.* extension], than to another suppos'd Substance of whose Being I have no Conception at all [*i.e.* unextended substance]'.[110]

[106] Masham to Leibniz, 3 June 1704; in Hanover, MS 612, fol. 9; and Gerhardt (ed.), *Die Philosophischen Schriften*, vol. III, p. 351.
[107] Masham to Leibniz, 8 August 1704; in Hanover, MS 612, fol. 12ᵛ; Woolhouse and Francks (eds.), *Leibniz's New System*, p. 217.
[108] For my understanding of this topic, I am indebted to Robert Sleigh, 'The Masham–Leibniz Correspondence: What does it tell us about Masham?', presented at the 'Seventeenth-Century Women Philosophers' conference in Amherst, Massachusetts, November 1997.
[109] Masham to Leibniz, 8 August 1704; in Hanover, MS 612, fol. 13; and Woolhouse and Francks (eds.), *Leibniz's New System*, p. 217.
[110] *Ibid.*

Masham was not the only early modern woman to perceive difficulties in Leibniz's metaphysics. Sophie, Electress of Hanover, also raises objections to Leibniz's view that the rational soul is immaterial. In a letter to Leibniz, dated 2 June 1700, Sophie reports a dispute between her son and Gerhard Wolter Molanus, the Abbot of Loccum.[111] Her son, the Elector George Louis, claims that thought must be material in so far as it is composed of things that come to us through the sensory organs: 'one cannot think of anything without making for oneself an idea of things that one has seen, heard, or tasted'.[112] Molanus responds along Cartesian lines that the soul is a thinking and really distinct from the body. Sophie rejects his position, taking the side of her son; and she asks Leibniz to act as a mediator in their dispute. In his reply (12 June 1700), Leibniz agrees with Molanus, but rejects the Cartesian viewpoint. Instead Leibniz claims: (i) that we obviously have thoughts that are not acquired through the senses (such as the ideas of force, unity, and so on); and (ii) that we only acquire the *representations* or *ideas* of material things through the senses, not the things themselves. He elaborates with reference to his theory of 'unities' or monads, as well as the system of pre-established harmony. But his arguments fail to convince Sophie: in a later letter (27 November 1702), she confesses that for her the term 'immaterial' is in fact unintelligible.

Sophie's last point echoes Damaris Masham's claim that she cannot have an idea of unextended substance. On the question of genuine soul–body interaction, Leibniz says he can find no intelligible way of explaining how the soul has a causal influence on the body, or vice-versa. But Masham cannot accept his non-interactionist theory of causation for the same reason that she cannot accept occasionalism: it makes matter redundant and superfluous. Instead Masham appears to favour an alternative, almost *anti-dualist*, viewpoint that blends both Cambridge–Platonist and Lockean presuppositions concerning substances: the view that every substance has extension, and the idea of thinking matter.

It is not difficult to see how Masham's views may have feminist significance. In the theories of Norris, Malebranche, and Leibniz, matter occupies an inferior place and has no real connection with the spiritual-intellectual world. Lloyd sees this radical separation between mind and matter as a typical feature of western philosophy; she believes that such theories opened the way for women, who are traditionally associated

---

[111] For details of this dispute, I am indebted to Zedler, 'The Three Princesses', pp. 48–9; and Aiton, *Leibniz*, pp. 257–62.

[112] Sophie to Leibniz, 2 June 1700; quoted in Zedler, 'The Three Princesses', p. 49.

with matter and the body, to become associated with a lesser intellectual character. In Malebranche's theory, the metaphorical association is made literal. Women, he says, are primarily to blame for our love of bodies; a child is born a sinner by virtue of its physical contiguity with its mother. But in Masham's writings there is no such denigration of matter, nature, and the body; instead material things are a necessary feature of reality, capable of interacting with spirits. As Lois Frankel says

Male philosophers have traditionally associated women with nature, the earth, the body, and everyday or 'worldly' things in general, while associating men with God, the spirit, and 'otherworldly' things. One form of feminist response might be to reject such dualistic stereotypes; another, which Masham embraces to a certain extent, is to rehabilitate the female side of the dichotomy.[113]

This 'rehabilitation' is certainly evident in Masham's rejection of occasionalism and her belief in the causal efficacy of matter. Masham also disarms the Cartesian dualist theory of substance by maintaining that all substances are extended, and by supporting Locke's suggestion that it is possible for matter to think.

III

I now show that Masham premises her feminist arguments on the same presuppositions as Astell. Typically, the origins of Masham's feminist arguments are traced to the new egalitarian concept of reason prevalent in the seventeenth century.[114] But there is scant evidence that Cartesian reason or method, in particular, is the inspiration behind Masham's feminism. Like Astell, Masham believes that the ignorance of men is to blame for the inferiority of women: men deprive women of the valuable education needed to cultivate their reason. And, like Astell again, Masham's feminist anger originates in certain teleological principles.

Masham's only feminist work, *Occasional Thoughts*, was written around 1703, and was revised and corrected for publication in 1705 after Locke's death in 1704. Like the *Discourse*, this work has been attributed to Locke and was even published as *Thoughts on Christian Life by John Locke esq* in 1747. Richard Gwinnett writes to Elizabeth Thomas about *Occasional Thoughts*, in June 1705, saying that

[113] Frankel, 'Damaris Cudworth Masham', p. 82.
[114] See, for example, Atherton's 'Cartesian Reason and Gendered Reason', p. 20.

This little *Posthumous* Treatise of Mr Locke, I take to be nothing inferiour to the more elaborate Works of that ingenious Author, except in the Stile, which is sometimes perplexed, and in many Places forced and stiff; not unlike the Writings of Mr Boyle, which may be reasonably attributed to the hasty and negligent Manner wherein these Thoughts were penned... However, the Excellency of the Matter, and the Usefulness of the Observations, contained in this small sketch, makes sufficient Compensation for all the Faults that can be found in the Expression.[115]

The work was popular in women's intellectual circles: Locke's friend Elizabeth Burnet offered to lend Masham's book to Catharine Trotter Cockburn;[116] and Elizabeth Thomas appears to have read it on Gwinnett's recommendation.[117]

Ruth Perry believes that Masham partly re-wrote the work in response to some of Astell's points in *The Christian Religion*.[118] But Perry's reasons for saying this are unclear. There is actually more evidence that Masham was *positively* inspired by the second part of Astell's *Proposal* (1697). In this work, Astell claims that women will find knowledge useful, not just for their souls, but for the management of their families and relations with their neighbours. The education of children, she wryly observes, should 'be laid by the Mother, for Fathers find other business, they will not be confin'd to such a laborious work, they have not such opportunities of observing a Childs Temper, nor are the greatest part of 'em like to do much good, since Precepts contradicted by Example seldom prove Effectual'.[119] The idea that the improvement of women's reason will benefit the education of children, is taken up by Masham in the latter half of *Occasional Thoughts*.

The foundation of Masham's feminism, like Astell's, is the belief that a supremely wise and benevolent God would not have endowed women with reason, if he did not intend for them to exercise their rational faculties toward perfection. Masham points out that

no one is Born into the World to live idly; enjoying the Fruit and Benefit of other Peoples Labours, without contributing reciprocally some way or other, to the good of the Community answerably to that Station wherein God... has

---

[115] Elizabeth Thomas and Richard Gwinnett, *Pylades and Corinna: or, Memoirs of the Lives, Amours, and Writings of Richard Gwinnett and Mrs Elizabeth Thomas* (London: Edmund Curll, 1731), p. 90.

[116] Trotter (Cockburn) to Burnet, 12 November 1705; in Cockburn, *The Works*, vol. ii, p. 190.

[117] See Thomas and Gwinnett, *Pylades and Corinna*, p. 93. Gwinnett also comments on *Occasional Thoughts* that 'what in my opinion deserves the highest Praise, is the principal design of the Book, which is to recommend the Improvement of the Fair Sex, by a more ingenious and learned Education that is now customary, or even commendable among them' (p. 92).

[118] Perry, *The Celebrated Mary Astell*, p. 96.　　[119] Astell, *Proposal II*, pp. 149–50.

plac'd them; who has evidently intended Humane kind of Society and mutual Communion, as Members of the same Body, useful every one each to other in their respective places.[120]

Women, Masham says, must be educated for the sake of order and harmony in society. Mothers, after all, are the early educators of men, and if mothers are not educated, then the education of men will suffer too. She observes that if women are lacking in knowledge, then they are 'much more to be pitty'd than blam'd',[121] because

the information and improvement of the Understanding by useful Knowledge, (a thing highly necessary to the right regulation of the Manners) is commonly very little thought of in reference to one whole Sex, even by those who in regard of the other, take due care hereof. But to this omission in respect of one Sex, it is manifestly very much to be attributed, that that pains which is often bestow'd upon the other, does so frequently, as it does, prove ineffectual Since the actual assistance of Mothers, will (generally speaking) be found necessary to the right forming of the Minds of their Children of both Sexes; and the Impressions receiv'd in that tender Age, which is unavoidably much of it passed among Women, are of exceeding consequence to Men throughout their Lives, as having a strong and oftentimes unalterable influence upon their future Inclinations and Passions.[122]

Masham refers to the 'impression' that women make on their children, just as Malebranche refers to the influence of mothers on foetuses. In both cases, the influence is negative: women are made responsible for those prejudices and passions that prevent men from attaining knowledge. But Masham's point is obviously very different. Malebranche simply aligns women with those material influences that must be ignored or transcended in the search for truth. Masham, on the other hand, says that because women make an impression on the minds of children, we ought to improve *women's* understanding. Like Astell, she emphasises that women are intellectual beings, rather than mere material objects.

Masham further believes that it is essential for women to be educated for the sake of their *own* spiritual welfare. She emphasises that 'Women have Souls to be sav'd as well as Men.'[123] They are endowed by God with rational abilities that enable them to understand the principles behind their religious beliefs. She believes that all things in nature are fitly disposed 'to the All-wise ends of their Maker'.[124] But, she says,

[120] Masham, *Occasional Thoughts*, pp. 179–80.   [121] *Ibid.*, p. 161.
[122] *Ibid.*, pp. 7–8.   [123] *Ibid.*, p. 166.   [124] *Ibid.*, p. 231.

be Nature ever so kind to them in this respect, yet through want of cultivating the Tallents she bestows upon those of the Female Sex, her Bounty is usually lost upon them; and Girls, betwixt silly Fathers and ignorant Mothers, are generally so brought up, that traditionary Opinions are to them, all their lives long, instead of Reason. They are, perhaps, sometimes told in regard of what Religion exacts, That they must *Believe* and *Do* such and such things, because the Word of God requires it; but they are not put upon searching the Scriptures themselves, to see whether, or no, these things are so.[125]

Instead women must be taught that 'their Duty is not grounded upon the uncertain and variable Opinion of Men, but the unchangeable nature of things'.[126] As part of the educational process, women must come to value and cherish their *minds* as well as their bodies. Chastity, according to Masham, is an over-rated virtue because stress on chastity gives the impression that a woman's moral duty consists in regulating her *body* alone.[127] Masham observes that although chastity is a duty for both sexes, 'a Transgression herein, even with the aggravation of wronging another Man, and possibly a whole Family thereby, is ordinarily talk'd as lightly of, as if it was but a Peccadillo in a Young Man, altho' a far less Criminal Offence against this Duty in a Maid shall in the Opinion of the same Persons brand her with perpetual Infamy'.[128]

There is evidence, in turn, that the second part of Astell's *Proposal* is influenced by the *Discourse*. Masham's arguments may have encouraged Astell to see individual persons not as self-sufficient entities, but as parts dependent on a larger whole. There are early indications in the *Letters* that Astell finds it difficult to accept Norris's extremism. On 31 October 1693, she wrote that

Sensible Beauty does too often press upon my Heart, whilst *intelligible* is disregarded. For having by Nature a strong Propensity to friendly Love, which I have all along encouraged as a good Disposition to Vertue, and do still think it so if it may be kept within the due Bounds of Benevolence. But having likewise thought till you taught me better, that I need not cut off all Desire from the Creature, provided it were in Subordination to, and for the sake of the Creator: I have contracted such a Weakness, I will not say by Nature (for I believe Nature is often very unjustly blam'd for what is owing to *Will* and *Custom*) but by voluntary Habit, that it is a very difficult thing for me to love at all, without something of Desire.[129]

Masham's criticisms of the *Letters* may have prompted Astell to strengthen these views about love of other people. In the second part of the *Proposal*, Astell writes that

---

[125] *Ibid.*, pp. 162–3. [126] *Ibid.*, p. 17. [127] *Ibid.*, pp. 21–2. [128] *Ibid.*, pp. 154–5.
[129] Astell to Norris, 31 October 1693; in Astell and Norris, *Letters*, pp. 47–9.

It was not fit that Creatures capable of and made for Society, shou'd be wholly Independent, or Indifferent to each others Esteem and Commendation; nor was it convenient considering how seldom these are justly distributed, that they shou'd too much regard and depend on them. It was requisite therefore that a desire of our Neighbours Good Opinion shou'd be implanted in our Natures to the end we might be excited to do such things as deserve it.[130]

Astell, like Masham, emphasises that all human beings are 'Parts of one Great whole, and are by Nature so connected to each other, that whenever one part suffers the rest must suffer with it'.[131]

At the end of the seventeenth century, Mary Astell and Damaris Masham were engaged in a dispute about the love of God. In this exchange, Masham attacks Astell's theory that God ought to be the sole object of our love, and, on Lockean grounds, Masham dismisses Astell's moral views as an affront to everyday experience. Years later, Astell responds to Masham in equally hostile terms, and criticises Masham's definition of love as consisting in nothing but the bare sentiment of pleasure. As a consequence of this exchange, commentators regard these women as opponents or 'seconds in the duel' between Locke and Norris. To some extent, this is a fair evaluation of the moral positions of Masham and Astell. There are, to be sure, important and fundamental differences between their philosophies due to their respective allegiances to Locke and Norris. But despite their exchange of insults, Masham and Astell also have a surprising amount in common. If Masham had paid closer attention to Astell's writings, she would have detected a common theological outlook, inspired by Cambridge Platonism. In Norris's occasionalist philosophy, matter is rendered causally impotent and incapable of affecting the mind. Both Masham and Astell, however, object to any view of matter that suggests that a supremely rational God has rendered it causally ineffective or purposeless. Their objections to Norris depend on the teleological presupposition that God has designed a harmonious order, where each part is suited to its end, and where there is no waste or 'lost labour'. In his infinite wisdom, according to Astell and Masham, God would not have created material things if they did not serve some purpose. Likewise, a supremely wise being would not have endowed women with a rational faculty if he had not wished them to use it.

[130] Astell, *Proposal II*, p. 95.   [131] *Ibid.*, p. 159.

6

Catharine Trotter Cockburn

Catharine Trotter Cockburn (1679–1749) enjoyed two successful careers in her lifetime. In her youth, she was tremendously popular as one of England's first woman writers for the stage; and in her later years, she was celebrated for her philosophical defences of John Locke and Samuel Clarke (1675–1729).[1] Although all of Cockburn's philosophical texts were written and published in the eighteenth century,[2] in style and content she might be considered the last of the seventeenth-century women philosophers in England. Cockburn's works bear all the distinctive marks of early modern women's writing: her feminist views appeal to the equal rational capacities of the sexes, and her philosophical ideas are built upon the foundations of natural reason. From her early *Defence of Locke* (1702) to her final vindication of Clarke, *Remarks upon the Principles and Reasonings of Dr. Rutherford* (1747), Cockburn develops an impressively consistent moral position based upon the human capacity for reason and sociability.[3] In

---

[1] The philosophical articles on Cockburn are: Martha Brandt Bolton, 'Some Aspects of the Philosophy of Catharine Trotter', *Journal of the History of Philosophy* 31:4 (1993), 565–88; Sarah Hutton, 'Cockburn, Catharine (1679–1749)', in Craig (ed.), *Routledge Encyclopedia of Philosophy*, vol. 11, pp. 386–7; Victor Nuovo, 'Cockburn, Catharine (1679?–1749)', in *The Dictionary of Seventeenth-Century British Philosophers*, edited by Andrew Pyle (Bristol: Thoemmes Press, 2000), pp. 191–4; and Mary Ellen Waithe, 'Catharine Trotter Cockburn', in Waithe (ed.), *A History of Women Philosophers*, vol. 111, pp. 101–25.

[2] Cockburn's intellectual works are *A Defence of Mr Ls: Essay of Humane Understanding in answer to the Remarks* (1702); *A Discourse Concerning a Guide in Controversies in Two Letters* (1707); *A Letter to Dr Holdsworth: occasioned by his sermon preached before the University of Oxford* (1726); *A Vindication of Mr Locke's Christian Principles from the Injurious Imputations of Mr Holdsworth* (1726); *Remarks upon Some Writers in the Controversy Concerning the Foundations of Moral Duty* (1743); and *Remarks upon the Principles and Reasonings of Dr. Rutherforth's Essay on the Nature and Obligations of Virtue, in Vindication of the Contrary Principles and Reasonings Inforced in the Writings of the Late Dr Samuel Clarke* (1747). These works, a selection of Cockburn's letters and poems, and the *Fatal Friendship*, were edited by Thomas Birch and published in two volumes as *The Works of Mrs. Catharine Cockburn, Theological, Moral, Dramatic, and Poetical* in 1751. Cockburn participated in the editing of the two volumes, but died before their completion, following several years of ill health, on 11 May 1749.

[3] For a full and detailed discussion on Cockburn's moral views, see Brandt Bolton, 'Some Aspects of the Philosophy of Catharine Trotter', 565–88.

this chapter, I examine the connection between Cockburn's feminist and moral views, as well as the metaphysical themes and principles in her writings. Cockburn did not develop a full-bodied or systematic metaphysical thesis, but there are distinct lines of development in her views on the soul and body, and the concept of substance in general. Furthermore, her writings reveal that she is another English woman who derives inspiration, both directly and indirectly, from the philosophy of the Cambridge Platonists, More and Cudworth. Cambridge Platonism had a profound impact on English women's attitudes toward Cartesian dualism and its successors, occasionalism and the doctrine of pre-established harmony. Like her seventeenth-century forebears, Cockburn is undoubtedly one of 'reason's disciples', but she also develops a metaphysical outlook that opposes Cartesian dualism and the Cartesian theory of substance. In this sense, she might be regarded as another early modern precursor to recent feminist critics of dualism.

I

Catharine Trotter (later Cockburn) was born in London on 16 August 1679, the daughter of Sarah Ballenden and David Trotter, a Scottish naval commander.[4] Following David Trotter's death in 1684, the family lived on a widow's pension from Charles II; but when the king died, they relied solely on the assistance of family and friends. In these impoverished circumstances, Catharine received some form of tuition in Latin and logic.[5] The rest of Cockburn's intellectual education appears to have been self-taught. She is reported to have formulated her own abstract on logic at a very young age; and she learnt French 'by her own application and diligence, without any instruction'.[6] At the age of fourteen,[7] Cockburn's first work, the short epistolary novel *Olinda's Adventures: Or the Amours of a Young Lady*, was published anonymously in Samuel Briscoe's collection *Letters of Love and Gallantry and Several Other Subjects* (1693). This partly autobiographical tale received a modest amount

4 For further biographical details, see Thomas Birch, 'The Life of Mrs. Cockburn', in Cockburn, *The Works*, vol. 1, pp. i–xlviii; Edmund Gosse, 'Catharine Trotter, the Precursor of the Bluestockings', *Transactions of the Royal Society of Literature* 34 (1916), 87–118; Leslie Stephen, 'Cockburn, Catharine (1679–1749)', in *Dictionary of National Biography*, vol. IV, pp. 639–40; and Alison Fleming, 'Catherine Trotter – "the Scots Sappho" ', *Scots Magazine* 33 (1940), 305–14.
5 Birch, 'The Life of Mrs. Cockburn', in Cockburn, *The Works*, vol. 1, p. v.   6 *Ibid.*, p. iv.
7 Victor Nuovo speculates that Cockburn may have been older; see Nuovo, 'Cockburn, Catharine (1679?–1749)', p. 191; and Margarette R. Connor, 'Catharine Trotter: An Unknown Child', *American Notes and Queries* 8:4 (1995), 11–14.

of popularity, and was reissued approximately six times between 1693 and 1724.[8] But today Cockburn is best known as a pioneering woman dramatist. She published five plays, to varied acclaim, from 1695 until shortly before her marriage to the clergyman Patrick Cockburn in 1708, including *Agnes de Castro* (1695), *The Fatal Friendship* (1698), *Love at a Loss* (1700), *The Unhappy Penitent* (1701), and *The Revolution of Sweden* (1706).[9] There are thematic similarities between these dramatic works and Cockburn's later philosophical writings. The plays focus on the regulation of the human passions, and they earned Cockburn a reputation as a 'moral reformer of the stage'.[10] Her dramatic writings teach that it is natural for human beings to be drawn to sensual pleasure, but that such inclinations must be kept in subjection to 'the superior faculty' of reason. In the dedication to Charles Halifax in *The Unhappy Penitent*, Cockburn writes that 'Passion is to be the Noblest frailty of the Mind, but 'tis a Frailty, and becomes a Vice, when cherish'd as an exalted Vertue.'[11] The same idea is developed in Cockburn's later philosophical works, which are largely preoccupied with the topic of moral obligation and virtue.[12]

In 1701, Cockburn took up residence in Salisbury with her sister's family, and remained there till 1706. From that time, Cockburn wrote almost exclusively on theological and philosophical topics. Among Cockburn's circle in Salisbury were several notable intellectuals. Gilbert Burnet, the Bishop of Salisbury, helped Cockburn's mother to renew her pension through Queen Anne, and Cockburn herself developed a friendship with the bishop's new wife, the devotional writer Elizabeth Berkeley Burnet (1661–1709).[13] The Burnets were instrumental in Cockburn's conversion from Catholicism to the Church of England. Elizabeth

[8] See Robert Adams Day's 'Introduction' to Catharine Trotter Cockburn, *Olinda's Adventures: Or the Amours of a Young Lady* (Los Angeles: Augustan Reprint Society no. 138, 1969), p. ii.

[9] These works can be found in *The Plays of Mary Pix and Catharine Trotter*, edited by Edna L. Steeves (New York and London: Garland Publishing, 1982), vol. II. Cockburn also contributed to the *Nine Muses* (1700), a tribute to John Dryden compiled by Delarivière Manley.

[10] Jeslyn Medoff, 'The Daughters of Behn and the Problem of Reputation', in *Women, Writing, History 1640–1740*, edited by Isobel Grundy and Susan Wiseman (London: B. T. Batsford, 1992), p. 44.

[11] Cockburn, *The Unhappy Penitent*, in Steeves (ed.), *The Plays of Mary Pix and Catharine Trotter*, vol. II, sig. A3.

[12] In *Remarks upon the Principles and Reasonings of Dr. Rutherforth's Essay*, Cockburn says that 'It is our fault if we suffer our passions or affections to be our masters: that indeed is not natural, tho' the affections themselves are so; for it is the province of reason to keep them in subjection, to regulate them, and to point out the proper application of them' (Cockburn, *The Works*, vol. II, p. 31).

[13] On Elizabeth Burnet as a writer, see C. Kirchberger, 'Elizabeth Burnet, 1661–1709', *Church Quarterly Review* 148 (1949), 17–51; Ballard, *Memoirs of Several Ladies*, pp. 345–52, 433–4.

Burnet even wrote to her friend John Locke for his assistance, saying of Cockburn that 'I can't but admier that one of such clear thoughts can be of a relegion that puts such schac[k]les on the exercies of thought and reason...I wish you could be an instrument to free her from those erors'.[14] In addition, on Cockburn's behalf, Elizabeth Burnet consulted with philosopher-theologian Samuel Clarke about the topic of the infallibility of the Church.[15]

Gilbert Burnet's cousin, Thomas Burnet of Kemnay (1656–1729), a close friend of Cockburn's, also played a role in her conversion. Thomas Burnet was part of the Hanoverian circle in the time of Electress Sophie, and a correspondent of Sophie-Charlotte, Leibniz, Locke, and Masham.[16] In a letter to Cockburn, dated 18 February 1702, Thomas Burnet writes that 'I am exceedingly glad you have made so good use of your retirement for contemplative study, and should be yet gladder, to hear you had found opportunity for quitting fictitious and poetical study.'[17] In one letter, he writes in praise of Caroline of Ansbach, later Queen of England, and a key intermediary and participant in the Leibniz–Clarke debate.[18] In 1704, there were plans to marry Caroline to the young King Charles of Spain; but she offered such fierce resistance to a Catholic conversion, that the marriage never resulted. 'It pleased God,' Thomas Burnet writes to Cockburn, 'to inspire her with the holy courage and resolution one day, when it was least expected, to declare plainly she would not abandon her religion for any crown.'[19] Burnet commends Caroline's great 'conquest over her own passions', and hopes Caroline's story will be a 'good example' to Cockburn. A few years later, Cockburn renounced her Catholicism, and gave an account of her conversion to the Church of England in *A Discourse Concerning a Guide in Controversies* (1707), a work that includes an anonymous preface by Gilbert Burnet.

The orthodox Anglican circle in Salisbury had a significant impact on the style and content of Cockburn's writing career. After 1701, she

---

[14] Elizabeth Burnet to Locke, 20 June 1702; in de Beer (ed.), *The Correspondence of John Locke*, no. 3153, p. 638. Burnet's spelling is very poor, even for the standards of the time.

[15] See Elizabeth Burnet to Catharine Trotter, [*c.* 1702?]; in the British Library, London, Add. MS 4264, fols. 337–8.

[16] Thomas Burnet of Kemnay apparently initiated a correspondence between Leibniz and Cockburn; see Constance Clark, *Three Augustan Women Playwrights* (New York: Peter Lang, 1986), p. 50.

[17] Thomas Burnet to Catharine Trotter, 18 February 1702; in Cockburn, *The Works*, vol. II, p. 160.

[18] On the significance of Caroline's role in the Leibniz–Clarke exchange, see D. Bertoloni Meli, 'Caroline, Leibniz, and Clarke', *Journal of the History of Ideas* 60:3 (1999), 469–86.

[19] Thomas Burnet to Catharine Trotter, 8 December 1704; in Cockburn, *The Works*, vol. II, pp. 183–4.

not only turns away from drama in favour of philosophy, but advocates a religious and moral outlook that is founded on reason, rather than an unquestioning faith. Her philosophical views are also steadfastly anti-authoritarian and anti-dogmatic. In addition, Cockburn's early acquaintance with Clarke had a lasting impact on her thought: two of her later works defend Clarke's moral theory, and one essay takes up issues in the Leibniz–Clarke correspondence. Other writings suggest that Cockburn regards Caroline as a significant intellectual role model. Furthermore, it is likely that Elizabeth and Gilbert Burnet introduced Cockburn to the writings of Locke and Damaris Masham.[20]

Like Masham, Cockburn was directly inspired by Locke's conception of reason, and indirectly influenced by the view of reason and rational method that gained popularity in England following the rise of Cartesianism. Cockburn shares Locke's cautiousness about the limits of natural reason, and the 'weakness and scantiness of our knowledge'.[21] Like him, she maintains that the only path to knowledge is through ideas derived from sensation and reflection on the mind's activities.[22] She challenges those philosophers who make 'a vain pretence to knowledge of things out of the reach of human understanding'.[23] Like nearly all seventeenth-century women, she believes that school learning largely 'disuse[s] the mind to plain and solid truth';[24] true philosophy can be practised without books or a scholastic background. Cockburn attacks dogmatic authors 'who having with much pains imbibed the opinions of reverenced authors, are unwilling to unlearn all their former knowledge',[25] and therefore subject themselves to 'a willing slavery'.[26] She says that Locke is regarded as 'a troublesome and dangerous innovator', because it is difficult 'for men, who have been used to receive truth in a particular dress, to know her, when stript of those false colours and borrowed ornaments, with which she is too often disguised'.[27]

Cockburn's remarks are echoed by another Locke admirer, the feminist author Mary Chudleigh. In her address 'To the Reader', in *Essays upon Several Subjects* (1710),[28] Chudleigh writes that 'Truth is valuable though she appears in a plain Dress; and I hope they will not slight her because she wants the Ornaments of Language'.[29] She also notes

---

[20] In turn, Thomas Burnet gave Masham a copy of Cockburn's *A Defence of Mr. Locke's Essay of Human Understanding* (1702); see Cockburn, *The Works*, p. 195.
[21] Cockburn, *Defence of Locke*, in *The Works*, vol. 1, p. 87.
[22] *Ibid.*, p. 53.   [23] *Ibid.*, p. 45.   [24] *Ibid.*, p. 45.   [25] *Ibid.*, p. 51.   [26] *Ibid.*, p. 51.
[27] *Ibid.*, p. 48.   [28] This work is dedicated to Sophie, Electress of Hanover.
[29] Chudleigh, *Essays upon Several Subjects*, p. 247.

that 'The greatest part of Mankind are chain'd to what they call their Interest…Reason has no Superiority over them; her Voice is too soft, her Whispers too low to be heard amidst so much Hurry and Noise.'[30] In the same vein, Mary Astell writes that 'Truth tho she is bright and ready to reveal her self to all sincere Inquirers, is not often found by the generality of those who pretend to seek after her, Interest, Applause, or some other little sordid Passion, being really the Mistress they court.'[31] It is not unusual to find truth and reason personified as a woman in seventeenth-century texts, but the remarks of Cockburn, Chudleigh, and Astell have added significance. Locke's ideas were controversial for the fact that they challenged ancient authority and received opinions. In the minds of early modern feminists, the 'truth' of women's intellectual equality is also overlooked because it does not meet particular interests or fit with social customs. In both cases, liberation can occur only when we have freed our minds from the shackles of prejudice. This theme is taken up in Cockburn's dedications and commendatory letters, most of which are addressed to women.

In the dedication to *The Revolution in Sweden* (1706), addressed to Harriett Godolphin (the daughter of the Duke of Marlborough), Cockburn writes:

There are so great Difficulties, and such general Discouragements, to those of our Sex, who wou'd improve their Minds, and employ their Time in any Science or useful Art, that there cannot be a more distinguishing Mark of a Free, and Beneficent Spirit, than openly to condemn that ill-grounded Custom, by giving Countenance and Protection to those, who have attempted against it.[32]

Cockburn hopes that 'an Encouraging Indulgence to the Endeavours of our Sex' will inspire 'some greater Geniuses' to rival the neighbouring nations in their illustrious women, instead of their foppery. Several European women have mastered the difficult sciences, received honours from their academies, and become members of distinguished societies. 'This without doubt is not from any Superiority of their Genius to ours,' Cockburn says, appealing to national pride, 'But from the much greater Encouragement they receive, by the Publick Esteem, and the Honours that are done them.'[33] Like Astell, who embraces the egalitarian implications of Cartesian reason, Cockburn emphasises that

---

[30] *Ibid.*, p. 305.   [31] Astell, *Proposal II*, p. 90.
[32] Cockburn, *The Revolution of Sweden*, in Steeves (ed.), *The Plays of Mary Pix and Catharine Trotter*, vol. II, sig. A2[r–v].
[33] *Ibid.*

'ill-grounded custom' rather than nature is to blame for women's intellectual deficiencies.[34] Where Locke emphasises that ignorance and error are the result of laziness and pride (or *moral* failings, as John Richetti notes),[35] Cockburn ascribes women's ignorance to their disadvantages in a society where they are publicly discouraged from rational pursuits. If European women can make progress in the sciences when granted an 'encouraging indulgence', then with like encouragement, English women might also improve their analytical skills. This patriotic theme is taken up in a panegyric dedicated to Caroline, the 'Verses Occasioned by the Busts in the Queen's Hermitage' (1732). In this piece, Cockburn says that England should vie with 'Gallia' and boast of her own 'Daciers'.[36] She laments that

> those restraints, which have our sex confin'd
> By partial custom, check the soaring mind:
> Learning deny'd us, we at random tread
> Unbeaten paths, that late to knowledge lead.[37]

There is a similar sentiment in Cockburn's defence of Masham against the suggestion that she is merely a mouthpiece for Locke. In a letter to

---

[34] There is evidence that Cockburn's feminist views are directly inspired by Mary Astell's writings. In her prefatory letter to the *Letters Concerning the Love of God*, Astell expresses a desire to excite a 'generous Emulation' in her sex, and inspire them to 'leave their insignificant Pursuits for Employments worthy of them' (Astell and Norris, *Letters*, sig. b5r). Similarly, in her 'Verses', Cockburn writes:

> O! might I thus the blest occasion prove,
> Fair emulation in the sex to move!
> Beholding one, who could but well design,
> Protected thus by royal *Caroline*.
> Important is the boon! nor I alone,
> The female world its influence would own,
> T'approve themselves to thee, reform their taste,
> No more their time in trifling pleasures waste;
> In search of truths Sublime, undaunted soar,
> And the wide realms of science deep explore.

(Cockburn, 'Verses Occasioned by the Busts in the Queen's Hermitage', in *The Works*, vol. II, p. 574.)

[35] John J. Richetti, *Philosophical Writing: Locke, Berkeley, Hume* (Cambridge, Mass.: Harvard University Press, 1983), p. 53.

[36] Anne Dacier (1654–1720), a French scholar, was famous in England for her French translations of Homer. In a letter to Cockburn, dated 18 February 1702, Thomas Burnet praises Dacier, saying 'she never had, nor has her match for a woman in true or useful learning, and that to the highest degree, and is a good reasoner to the boot' (Cockburn, *The Works*, vol. II, p. 163).

[37] Cockburn, 'Verses Occasioned by the Busts in the Queen's Hermitage', *ibid.*, p. 573. These lines echo Mary Astell's observation that 'The field of Truth is large, and after all the Discoveries that have been made by those who have gone before, there will still be untroden Paths, which they who have the Courage and Skill may beat out and beautify' (*Proposal II*, p. 109).

Thomas Burnet of Kemnay, Cockburn says that 'It is not to be doubted, that women are as capable of penetrating into the grounds of things, and reasoning justly, as men are, who certainly have no advantage of us, but in their opportunities of knowledge'.[38] She points out that Masham is known for her superior natural capacities, has made efforts to improve them, and 'no doubt profited much by a long intimate society with so extraordinary a man as Mr. *Locke*'.[39] There is no reason to assume that a woman of her character would pretend to write something not entirely her own.

I pray be more equitable to her sex, than the generality of yours are; who, when any thing is written by a woman, that they cannot deny their approbation to, are sure to rob us of the glory of it, by concluding 'tis not her own; or at least, that she had some assistance, which has been said in many instances to my knowledge unjustly.[40]

Cockburn's defences of women's intellectual nature are firmly grounded in her moral views. In Cockburn's moral philosophy, those individuals who are led by self-interest and passion rather than reason, transgress the 'eternal and immutable' rules of justice and equity. When men deny women 'an equal right… to be treated with justice and honour',[41] they act against the nature and reason of things. This is because

A rational being ought to act suitably to the reason and nature of things: a social being ought to promote the good of others: an approbation of these ends is unavoidable, a regard to them implied in the very nature of such beings, which must therefore bring on them the strongest *moral obligations*.[42]

A society in which women are treated as inferior beings is *morally* impermissible, given its foundations in vanity, pride, and selfishness, rather than reason. These claims are based on a conception of human beings as naturally 'rational and sociable creatures'. In this sense, Cockburn shares the *teleological* perspective on human nature advocated by Astell and Masham.[43] She believes that

Mankind is a system of creatures, that continually need one another's assistance, without which they could not long subsist. It is therefore necessary, that every one, according to his capacity and station, should contribute his part towards the good and preservation of the whole, and avoid whatever may be detrimental to

---

[38] Catharine Trotter to Thomas Burnet, 19 February 1705; in Cockburn, *The Works*, vol. 11, p. 190.
[39] *Ibid.*   [40] *Ibid.*   [41] Cockburn, 'Letter of Advice to her Son', in *The Works*, vol. 11, p. 119.
[42] Cockburn, *Remarks Upon Some Writers* in *The Works*, vol. 1, p. 420.
[43] For details on this teleological aspect to Cockburn's views, see Brandt Bolton, 'Some Aspects of the Philosophy of Catharine Trotter', 572.

it. For this end they are made capable of acquiring social or benevolent affections (probably have the seeds of them implanted in their nature) with a moral sense or conscience, that approves of virtuous actions, and disapproves of the contrary. This plainly shews them, that virtue is the law of their nature, and that it must be their duty to observe it, from whence arises *moral obligation*, tho' the sanctions of that law are unknown.[44]

Cockburn argues that if God had *not* required us to act according to our nature, as rational and sociable beings, then it would be 'inconsistent with that divine wisdom, which we see has fitted all other things to their proper and certain end, to have formed us after such a manner'.[45] An infinitely wise being *cannot* act so contrary to his essential nature;[46] therefore we must conclude that 'the Author of our being does require those things of us, to which he has suited our nature, and visibly annexed our happiness, which he has made the necessary motive of all our actions'.[47]

These views bear a particularly strong resemblance to those of Damaris Masham, who also appeals to the fact that God has intended human beings to act as 'Members of the same Body, useful every one each to other in their respective places.'[48] Women and mothers, Masham says, must be educated for the sake of society, and to fulfil the duties required of them according to the 'unchangeable nature of things'.[49] In the same vein, Cockburn appeals to 'the duties of the mother, friend, and wife' in her 'Verses', claiming that a higher education would assist women to meet their filial obligations, and 'To nobler gain improve their vacant hours'. Furthermore, in *Occasional Thoughts*, a book that Elizabeth Burnet offers to lend to Cockburn,[50] Masham observes that although the Bible teaches that chastity is a duty to both sexes, in practice the moral injunction seems to apply only to women. For a man, transgressions that ruin whole families are often regarded as mere 'peccadillos'; but for a woman, even lesser offences can brand her with 'perpetual Infamy'.[51] Cockburn echoes these same sentiments on the sexual double standard. In her 'Letter of Advice to her Son', Cockburn warns him not to imagine

---

[44] Cockburn, *Remarks Upon Some Writers*, in *The Works*, vol. 1, p. 413.
[45] Cockburn, *Defence of Locke*, in *The Works*, vol. 1, p. 59.
[46] In *Remarks upon the Principles and Reasonings of Dr. Rutherforth's Essay*, Cockburn sums up this idea by saying, like Astell and Masham, that God 'does nothing in vain' (*The Works*, vol. 11, p. 88).
[47] Cockburn, *Defence of Locke*, in *The Works*, vol. 1, p. 59.
[48] Masham, *Occasional Thoughts*, pp. 179–80. [49] *Ibid.*, p. 17.
[50] Cockburn to Thomas Burnet, 12 November 1705; in Cockburn, *The Works*, vol. 11, p. 190. Cockburn was personally acquainted with Masham; see Cockburn to Thomas Burnet, 10 September 1708, in Cockburn, *The Works*, vol. 11, p. 207.
[51] Masham, *Occasional Thoughts*, pp. 154–5.

that women are to be considered only as objects of your pleasure, as the fine gentlemen of the world seem, by their conduct, to do. There is nothing more unjust, more base, and barbarous, than is often practised towards them, under the specious names of love and gallantry; as if they had not an equal right, with those of the other sex, to be treated with justice and honour. What would be thought of a man, who should take advantage of the weakness, credulity, complaisance, or affection of his friend, to ruin at once his innocence, his reputation, his fortune, and peace of mind for ever? Would not everyone readily allow, that this was a great piece of villainy? And yet this very practice towards women passes for a trifle, the amusement of a man of gallantry; and is often made the subject of boast and triumph.[52]

Cockburn urges her son to inquire into the 'ends' for which his passions and appetites were given him: 'the preservation and perfection of our own being, and the benefit of society'.[53] He should avoid letting his natural passions run 'loose and unbridled', and act always in accordance with the rational faculties bestowed upon him by God. For these reasons, he must be respectful in his conduct with women, and equip himself 'with maxims entirely contrary to the notions and common practice of the men of the world'.[54]

In sum, Cockburn's feminist views develop out of a broader conception of human beings as essentially rational and constrained to act in accordance with their rationality. She believes that men ought to behave as 'their being rational animals obliges them to',[55] to treat women with the equity and respect that all rational creatures deserve, and to permit women to improve and perfect their natural faculties. In this sense, Cockburn might be regarded as another early modern woman who bases her feminist arguments on the rational natures of women and the egalitarian implications of Cartesian and Lockean philosophy.

II

Nevertheless, Cockburn's reverence for rationality is not grounded in a rigorously dualist metaphysics. There are few purely metaphysical pieces in Cockburn's works, but there are recurring themes and ideas in her writings that together constitute a distinctive metaphysical position.[56]

---

[52] Cockburn, 'Letter of Advice to her Son', in *The Works*, vol. II, p. 119.

[53] *Ibid.*, p. 118.   [54] *Ibid.*   [55] *Ibid.*

[56] Her principal metaphysical works are *A Letter to Dr Holdsworth: occasioned by his sermon preached before the University of Oxford* (1726); and the 'Cursory Thoughts' prefixed to *Remarks Upon Some Writers in the Controversy concerning the Foundation of Moral Virtue and Moral Obligation; Particularly the translator of Archbishop King's Origin of Evil, and the Author of the Divine Legation of Moses. To which are prefixed,*

The main themes are a Lockean approach to substances, and the blurring of sharp distinctions between the soul and body, spirit and matter.

Cockburn's first defence of Locke was completed in December 1701 at the age of twenty-two, and published anonymously in May the next year. *A Defence of Mr. Locke's Essay of Human Understanding* (1702) vindicates Locke against charges of irreligion. Her opponent is Thomas Burnet (1635?–1715),[57] who attacks Locke's *Essay* for undermining belief in the immortality of the soul. In 1651, Burnet was admitted to Clare Hall, Cambridge, as a student of John Tillotson (1630–94), but followed Ralph Cudworth to Christ's College, and there became a fellow in 1657.[58] Burnet was also a friend of Henry More.[59] In his *Remarks upon an Essay Concerning Humane Understanding* (1697), Burnet identifies two suppositions that he thinks weaken proofs for the immortality of the soul.[60] The first is Locke's claim that the soul does not always think; and the second, that '*God may give, or have given, for any thing we know, to some systems of matter, a power to perceive, and think.*'[61] On these subjects, Burnet echoes More's principal concerns in the *Antidote Against Atheism* and the *Immortality of the Soul*. Burnet is disturbed that if thought can be attributed to matter, then there can be no proof that the soul is distinct from the body; and therefore there will be no guarantee that the soul is immaterial and immortal.

Locke expected a 'storm' of protest to follow the publication of his *Essay*. In his only published reply to Burnet, the short and dismissive 'Answer to "Remarks upon an Essay Concerning Human Understanding &c." ' (1697), Locke writes that 'Before anything came out against my *Essay*... I was told that I must prepare myself for a storm that was coming against it; it being resolved by some men that it was necessary that book of mine should, as 'tis phrased, be run down.'[62] The point of most enduring controversy is a passing statement in IV.iii.6 of the *Essay*,

---

Some Cursory Thoughts on the Controversies concerning necessary Existence, The Reality and Infinity of Space, The Extension and Place of Spirits, and on Dr. Watts's Notion of Substance (1743). The main treatise is hereafter referred to as *Remarks Upon Some Writers*.

57 This Thomas Burnet is not to be confused with Cockburn's close friend and correspondent, Thomas Burnet of Kemnay.

58 Leslie Stephen, 'Burnet, Thomas (1635?–1715)', in *Dictionary of National Biography*, vol. III, pp. 408–10.

59 George Watson, 'Introduction' to Thomas Burnet, *Remarks on John Locke*, edited by George Watson (Doncaster: Brynmill, 1989), p. 15.

60 Burnet's three anonymous works are the *Remarks upon an Essay Concerning Humane Understanding*, the *Second Remarks* (both published in 1697), and the *Third Remarks* (1699).

61 Cockburn, *Defence of Locke*, in *The Works*, vol. I, p. 87. The other concerns of the *Defence*, not examined here, are Locke's foundation of morality, and the idea of 'natural conscience'.

62 Watson (ed.), *Remarks on Locke*, p. 33. Locke's answer is appended to his *Reply to the Right Reverend the Lord Bishop of Worcester's Answer to his Second Letter* (1697).

where Locke says that we cannot know, 'by the contemplation of our own Ideas' of 'matter' and 'thought', whether an omnipotent God 'has not given to some Systems of Matter fitly disposed, a power to perceive and think'.[63] It is just as conceivable that God could superadd a faculty of thinking to matter, as to any other substance, 'since we know not wherein Thinking consists'.[64] This remark is borne of Locke's claim that we have only an obscure and confused idea of substances. Hence one cannot be assured that 'the thing in us which thinks' is immaterial; but nor is it possible to affirm that it is material; in either case, we are equally ignorant.[65]

History reveals that Locke was right to expect criticism.[66] His suggestion was mistakenly interpreted as support for the idea of 'thinking matter', or outright materialism, and hence Locke was vilified as a danger to orthodox religion. Mary Astell's response in *The Christian Religion* is typical of those writers, such as Norris and Stillingfleet, who write against Locke's suggestion that (for all we know) it is possible that God could endow some systems of matter with the power of thought. Her strategy of refutation is to point out inconsistencies in Locke's own writings. In some passages of the *Essay* and in his replies to Stillingfleet, she says, Locke admits that although human understanding is limited, we can have knowledge of the 'Repugnancy of Ideas'.[67] We can know, for example, that it is contradictory to say that a substance is solid and not solid at the same time, or that it is impossible for God to change the essential property of a thing. Astell believes that the ideas of extension and thought are 'repugnant' or incompatible in this way. Thought is the essence of mind, and extension the essence of body; according to Astell, each substance and its essential attribute is necessarily inseparable; therefore we can know that 'an Extended Being does not, cannot Think, any more than a Circle can have the Properties of a Triangle'.[68] Mimicking Masham's criticisms in the *Discourse*, Astell supposes that Locke can hardly despise her arguments as 'the *Rhapsodies* and *Strong Imaginations* of a silly Woman'[69] when they thus proceed by his own principles. But although Astell's argument is perceptive, her critique of thinking matter overlooks a significant difference between Locke's views

---

[63] Locke, *Essay*, IV.iii.6, p. 540.   [64] *Ibid.*, p. 541.
[65] See Michael Ayers, *Locke: Epistemology and Ontology*, 2 vols. (London and New York: Routledge, 1993), vol. II, chapter 4.
[66] For details on the reception of Locke's so-called 'thinking matter' statement, see John Yolton, *Thinking Matter: Materialism in Eighteenth Century Britain* (Minneapolis: University of Minnesota Press, 1983).
[67] Astell, *The Christian Religion*, p. 258.   [68] *Ibid.*, p. 250.   [69] *Ibid.*, p. 256.

and the Cartesian conception of substance.[70] For Locke, it was *not* the case that extension is the essence of body; and, moreover, we can never have a clear idea of the essence or nature of any given substance. In these respects, Locke markedly diverges from Descartes.

Burnet takes a similar misguided approach against Locke's idea of 'cogitant matter'. He begins by noting that what is conceivable by us is also logically possible. Yet, according to our faculties, it is not conceivable that matter should be capable of thought. This is because 'the different operations of the mind or understanding – simple apprehension, judgement, ratiocination – must all lie under the prospect, intuition and correction of some one common principle; and that must be a principle of such perfect unity and simplicity as the body – any part of the body – or any particle of matter is not capable of'.[71]

In her *Defence*, Cockburn does not address this argument; she aims only to defend Locke's remarks against the charge that they have 'dangerous consequences' for religion. In her view, we do not have to establish the soul's immateriality in order to believe that it is immortal. The 'Eastern Pagans', she points out, conceive of the soul as 'matter subtile enough to escape being seen or handled', yet they still maintain that the soul is immortal.[72] In addition, even if the heathens were convinced of the soul's immateriality, they might still think that it returns to 'the universal soul, of which it may be an effluence', or 'inform[s] the next parcel of matter it finds fitted for it'.[73] So, according to Cockburn, belief in the soul's immortality must be established on a firmer basis: that is, by 'consideration of ourselves as rational and free creatures...and of an omnipotent Being, from whom we are, and on whom we depend'.[74] The providence of a wise and just God, she says, makes it extremely likely that if we act in accordance with natural laws, 'the dispensation of rewards and punishments is reserved for a future life'.[75] Furthermore, 'We will suppose the heathen convinced by these arguments, or others to the same purpose; that he owns it is highly reasonable to conclude there must be a future state of rewards and punishments; but he does not so well digest the soul's being immaterial; he has no notion of a substance without any extension.'[76] In this part of her *Defence*, Cockburn does not openly support Locke's suggestion about thinking matter, but

---

[70] Squadrito, 'Mary Astell's Critique of Locke', 438; and Acworth, *The Philosophy of John Norris*, p. 238.
[71] Watson (ed.), *Remarks on Locke*, p. 79.
[72] Cockburn, *Defence of Locke*, in *The Works*, vol. 1, pp. 88–9.
[73] *Ibid.*, p. 90.   [74] *Ibid.*, p. 89.   [75] *Ibid.*, p. 90.   [76] *Ibid.*, pp. 90–1.

she does regard his conception of substances as compatible with her own moral and religious views. The claim that the heathen can still believe in the soul's immortality, *even if he maintains that it is extended*, is especially significant – in later works, Cockburn herself maintains that the soul *is* extended.

Thomas Burnet believes that Locke's claim that the soul does not always think also has 'dangerous consequences' for religion. In the *Essay*, Locke claims that the idea of the soul, a 'spiritual substance', is derived from the blending of simple ideas, such as thinking, desiring, and so on, with our obscure idea of substance in general. But we cannot say that thought is the *real essence* of the soul. Locke points out that whenever we think, we must be sensible of it (this is part of the definition of thought). Yet we are not sensible of thinking when we are in a dreamless sleep. He says that

> I confess my self, to have one of those dull Souls, that doth not perceive it self always to contemplate *Ideas*, nor can conceive it any more necessary for the *Soul always to think*, than for the body to move; the perception of *Ideas* being (as I conceive) to the soul what motion is to the body, not its Essence, but one of its Operations.[77]

In his 'First Remarks', Burnet says 'I wonder how you can observe that your soul sometimes does not think; for when you do observe it, you think.'[78] Cockburn replies that 'Mr. *Locke* says, *men do not think in a sound sleep*; and his reason is, because they are not *conscious* of it, and it is a contradiction to say a man thinks, but is not *conscious* of it; thinking consisting in that very thing of our being conscious of it.'[79] Cockburn points out that Burnet is mistaken because he 'takes the soul, man, and person, to signify the same thing', when Locke had made a careful distinction between these terms.[80] She says that Locke understands 'person' to mean 'self-conscious being', and human being to be 'the soul and body united'. This means that personal identity consists in the same *consciousness*, and not in the same *substance*: 'for whatever substance there is, without consciousness there is no person'.[81] Hence when Burnet says 'I wonder how you can observe that your soul sometimes does not think', he confuses the person ('you') with the soul, when they are not identical.[82]

---

[77] Locke, *Essay*, II.i.10, p. 108.   [78] Watson (ed.), *Remarks on Locke*, p. 27.

[79] Cockburn, *Defence of Locke*, in *The Works*, vol. 1, p. 71. This response is similar to Locke's marginalia on the same topic. He says of Burnet: 'I wonder how you can observe that you sometimes sleep, for when you observe it you are awake' (Watson (ed.), *Remarks on Locke*, p. 27).

[80] Cockburn, *Defence of Locke*, in *The Works*, vol. 1, p. 72.   [81] *Ibid.*, p. 73.

[82] Cockburn develops these themes (Locke's distinction between persons, human beings, and substances) in her later defences of Locke. See *A Letter to Dr Holdsworth: occasioned by his sermon preached*

Cockburn's other main point is that proofs of the soul's immortality do not, and should not, depend upon the contrary supposition, that the soul *always* thinks.[83] This assumption has dangerous consequences for religion because human beings are 'so much in the dark as to those principles, upon which it is established'.[84] Like Locke, Cockburn emphasises that claims to certainty can pose a threat to religious belief. If it were discovered that the soul's immortality is founded upon the obscure notion of immaterial substances, she says, then this could lead to disillusionment. In her concluding remarks on the topic, Cockburn notes that

it is true that we have no idea of the soul but by her operations; but that is no more a reason to conclude, that she is nothing when she does not operate, than when she does, since we are equally ignorant what the soul is, when we do think, as when we do not. I ask what is the soul when she does think? Is she a real permanent substance? What then are her peculiar properties, whereby she is distinguished from other substances? If it be said the power of thinking; I ask, whether she has any other properties from nothing, and from matter? If not, then nothing, or matter, may have the power of thinking. This is plain, if the soul has no essential properties distinct from matter to distinguish her, whereby she alone is capable of the power of thinking, there can be no reason, why matter may not have that power.[85]

Cockburn's justification for this view is the Lockean claim that we have no clearer idea of bodily substance, than we have of spiritual substance; we simply cannot know the essence of either.[86]

Modern commentators point out that Cockburn does not agree with Locke's moral views in every respect in her *Defence*.[87] But Cockburn *is* sympathetic toward Locke's non-dogmatic views about material and spiritual substances. In Cockburn's Locke-inspired metaphysics, we see the culmination of the seventeenth-century's move away from Cartesian philosophy.[88] The earlier female critics of Cartesian dualism – Elisabeth, Cavendish, and Conway – are sceptical about soul–body interaction within the Cartesian framework, but (like Descartes himself) they do not challenge the scholastic notion of substance. Following Locke, Cockburn is circumspect about the limits of human understanding; she accepts his cautious and sceptical attitude toward the idea of substance in general, and adopts a most un-Cartesian attitude toward the soul and

---

before the University of Oxford (1726), and *A Vindication of Mr Locke's Christian Principles* (1727) in *The Works*.

[83] Cockburn, *Defence of Locke*, in *The Works*, vol. 1, p. 70.   [84] *Ibid.*, p. 83.   [85] *Ibid.*, p. 80.
[86] *Ibid.*   [87] Hutton, 'Cockburn, Catharine (1679–1749)', p. 386.
[88] On the topic of Descartes' last direct influence in England, see Lamprecht, 'The Role of Descartes in Seventeenth-Century England', 228–40.

body distinction. In this respect, Cockburn's works signal the end of the Cartesian influence on women philosophers in England.

III

After her marriage to Patrick Cockburn in 1708, Cockburn was diverted from her writings by the duties and cares of family life. But before this hiatus, Cockburn received a substantial amount of high praise for her *Defence*. John Locke himself wrote to Cockburn, saying 'that as the rest of the world take notice of the strength and clearness of your reasoning, so I cannot but be extremely sensible, that it was employed in my defence'.[89] The work also won the approval of one of Locke's supporters, John Toland, the author of the notorious and controversial *Christianity Not Mysterious* (1696).[90] In his book, Toland uses Locke's ideas to undermine the doctrine of the Trinity, the belief that three persons and one divine substance can be reconciled. Toland argues that the doctrine of the Trinity is unintelligible because its key ideas (of substance, nature, and so on) come from neither sensation nor reflection on the mind's activities. His remarks drew Edward Stillingfleet into print against Locke's way of ideas, and thereby sparked the famous Locke–Stillingfleet debate.

Cockburn's response to Thomas Burnet is favourably compared to this exchange. Locke learnt of Cockburn's identity through Elizabeth Burnet, who wrote to him in praise of Cockburn's arguments and her 'modest and unafected stile'.[91] Elizabeth Burnet did not have the same praise for Locke's own polemical writings. In a letter to Locke, dated 22 September 1697, she offers her candid opinion on the Locke–Stillingfleet debate.[92] She observes that Locke is too ready to take personal offence, he is unfair and uncharitable to Stillingfleet, and his comments are often irrelevant or 'a litle too Criticall in observeing small faults'.[93] She also warns Locke that he has 'put the tryall of my Frindship on a pretty hard service',[94] because Stillingfleet is a good friend of hers. In short, she

---

[89] John Locke to Catharine Trottter, 30 December 1702; in de Beer (ed.), *The Correspondence of John Locke*, no. 3234, p. 731.

[90] See Catharine Trotter to Thomas Burnet, 8 August 1704; in Cockburn, *The Works*, vol. 11, p. 175. John Toland was also an admirer of Sophie-Charlotte, the daughter of Leibniz's patron, Sophie. Toland addresses his *Letters to Serena* (1704) to Sophie-Charlotte in response to her questions about the origins of prejudice and idolatry, and the immortality of the soul.

[91] Elizabeth Burnet to Locke, 15 July 1702; in de Beer (ed.), *The Correspondence of John Locke*, no. 3164, p. 650.

[92] Elizabeth Berkeley (later Burnet) to Locke, 22 September 1697; *ibid.*, no. 2315, pp. 197–204.

[93] *Ibid.*, p. 199.   [94] *Ibid.*

thinks it is best for both parties to remain silent in future. By contrast, in a letter to Cockburn, Elizabeth Burnet praises Cockburn's defence of Locke because

the whole is writ short & clear, without affectation of witt or eloquence, needless reflections on your adversary or making him more in the rong then he is, rather bringing him nearer, then driveing him farther from truth, takeing his words in as good a sense as they would baer in which I hartely wish the searchers after truth would imetate you, if they did I am perswaded there would be both more light as well as more charity in the world, then at present while such distructive methods to both are taken can be expected.[95]

Burnet regards Cockburn as a greater devotee to Locke's 'unbiased search for truth' than Locke himself. In the same letter, Burnet says that Gilbert Burnet and John Norris were 'extremly pleased' with Cockburn's *Defence*, and that "tis not without deficulty some can beleeve that any one not breed up to sience & Logick in perticuler could be capable of so close & clear reasoning'.[96]

Thomas Burnet of Kemnay writes to Sophie-Charlotte in Berlin in praise of Cockburn. Sophie-Charlotte replies that she is 'charmed with the agreeable picture which he had drawn of the new Scots Sappho'.[97] Burnet also made Cockburn known to Leibniz and gave him a copy of Cockburn's *Defence*. Leibniz comments on this work in a letter to Electress Sophie, in which he takes issue with Locke, but approves of Cockburn's claim that moral distinctions, such as justice and injustice, are not arbitrary, but founded in the nature of a supremely rational God.[98] It is to Leibniz's credit that he notices telling differences between the moral views of Cockburn and Locke.

Cockburn's friend Elizabeth Burnet also made the acquaintance of Leibniz during her travels abroad. In her travelogue, Burnet writes that on a visit to 'HH' (Herrenhausen, the home of Electress Sophie),

---

[95] Elizabeth Burnet to Catharine Trotter, 19 June 1702; in British Library, London, Add. MS 4264, fol. 155. There are echoes of this critique in Burnet's only published work, the posthumous *A Method of Devotion: Or, Rules for Holy and Devout Living, with Prayers on Several Occasions, and Advice and Devotions for the Holy Sacrament*, second edition (London: Joseph Downing, C. Smith and A. Barker, 1709). She says that 'to dwell long on some Speculations, such as the Disputes of Predestination, of the Trinity, the Union of the Divine and Humane Nature, and the like; such obscure Inquiries beyond the plain Doctrine as delivered in the Scriptures, are not proper Subjects of Meditation'. It is 'safer Believing with Humility, than Disputing with Niceness; which is often the Effect of Pride, the Cause of Divisions, and is an Enemy to Charity' (Burnet, *Method*, p. 86).
[96] Elizabeth Burnet to Catharine Trotter, 19 June 1702; in the British Library, Add. MS 4264, fol. 155.
[97] Birch, 'The Life of Mrs. Cockburn', in Cockburn, *The Works*, vol. 1, p. xxv.
[98] See Gosse, 'Catharine Trotter, the Precursor of the Bluestockings', p. 105.

I saw Mr Libniz he seemed to be a man above 50: Black not of a very agreable aspect, he talks much & fast, but has some empediment in sp:[eech?] . . . he talked allso of Mr Dodwells books & Tolands & of the liberty there was in Eng:[land] to reason on such things; I find strangers are much in the openion that Eng: abounds in Atheistical & infidle princeples.[99]

This last point is especially interesting in light of Leibniz's first letter to Caroline in the dispute with Clarke. In his opening sentence, Leibniz states that 'Natural religion itself, seems to decay (in England) very much. Many will have human souls to be material: others make God himself a corporeal being.'[100] Burnet's remarks provide further evidence that Leibniz was keen to discredit English theology for political as well as philosophical reasons.[101] By drawing Electress Sophie's attention to English 'atheism', Leibniz might have been implying that his personal religious guidance would be required in England upon the Hanoverian succession.

Not surprisingly, given Catharine Cockburn's associations with Locke, Leibniz, and Clarke, and her admiration for Caroline, she takes note of the issues in the Leibniz–Clarke correspondence.

IV

In Cockburn's later work, the 'Cursory Thoughts' prefixed to *Remarks Upon Some Writers* (written *c.* 1739, and published in 1743),[102] the earlier Lockean themes of the *Defence* are revisited and developed in light of eighteenth-century controversies. In *Remarks upon Some Writers*, Cockburn's particular concern is to defend Samuel Clarke's views about the foundation of moral obligation. But in the 'Cursory Thoughts', she focuses on metaphysical issues, such as the necessary existence of God, infinite space, the extension and place of spirits, and the notion of substance. From 1731 to 1735, a spate of works appeared in criticism of Clarke's views on space. The authors of these critiques – including Isaac

99 Bodleian Library, University of Oxford, Rawlinson MS D 1092, fol. 130. Henry Dodwell maintains that the human soul is naturally mortal.
100 Leibniz to Caroline, November 1715; in H. G. Alexander (ed.), *The Leibniz–Clarke Correspondence* (Manchester: Manchester University Press, 1956), p. 11. Leibniz follows this with the observation that Locke and his supporters are uncertain about whether or not the soul is material.
101 Bertoloni Meli, 'Caroline, Leibniz, and Clarke'.
102 *Remarks Upon Some Writers* was first published in *The History of the Works of the Learned* (1743). The main part of the text also addresses the views of Daniel Waterland (1683–1740), who wrote an appendix to Edmund Law's *Enquiry into the Ideas of Space* (1734); William Warburton (1698–1779); the author of the *Divine Legation of Moses* (1737); Frances Hutcheson (1694–1746); Thomas Johnson (d. 1737), the anonymous author of the *Essay on Moral Obligation* (1731); and 'Philo-orthos' or George Johnston, the author of *The Eternal Obligation of Natural Religion*. One of the few writers Cockburn praises is John Balguy (1686–1748), a follower of Samuel Clarke.

Watts (1674–1748) and Edmund Law, the Bishop of Carlisle (1703–87) – are principally concerned with Clarke's Boyle Lectures of 1704 and 1705.[103] But they also comment on the exchange of letters between Clarke and Leibniz from 1715 to 1716.[104] Although Cockburn never mentions the correspondence by name, her views on space might be read as her opinions on this famous exchange. Cockburn takes Clarke's Newtonian position against the Leibnizian views of Law and Watts: she rejects Leibniz's claim that space is a mere relation; she supports Clarke's opinion that space is not just an idea in the mind; and she also agrees with his view that space is not the mere absence of matter. But she goes against Clarke in affirming that space should be treated like a *substance* (Clarke contends that space is an attribute of God). Out of Cockburn's responses to Clarke and his critics emerges a non-dualist metaphysics.

In the 'Cursory Thoughts', Cockburn addresses Law's lengthy notes to William King's *Essay on the Origin of Evil* (1731).[105] Law believes that space is nothing more than an idea – a purely mental construct. Cockburn, on the other hand, maintains that space has a real existence outside the mind because it is one of the particulars from which the idea of extension is abstracted. She agrees with Locke that the idea of space is acquired through the senses,[106] and comes *before* the general idea of extension. She says that unless one supports George Berkeley's idealism – a theory that Cockburn finds untenable – one must accept that material things exist outside of the mind because the senses tell us so; and we must accept the same in relation to space. Moreover, it is not possible to perceive of material bodies in motion unless we maintain that space is real. On this point, John Yolton summarises Cockburn as saying that 'Space is needed for motion; bodies move; therefore, there is space.'[107]

Cockburn notes that the only plausible argument for denying the real existence of space would be on the grounds that 'we know not in what class of beings to place it'.[108] Isaac Watts presents such an argument in his *Philosophical Essays* (1733).[109] But Cockburn maintains that ignorance of the nature or essence of space should not lead us to deny that it

---

[103] *A Demonstration of the Being and Attributes of God* (published in 1705), and *A Discourse Concerning the Unchangeable Obligations of Natural Religion* (1706).
[104] For further details on the history of the Leibniz–Caroline–Clarke correspondence, see Alexander, 'Introduction' to *The Leibniz–Clarke Correspondence*, pp. ix–lvi.
[105] Cockburn refers to the 1734 second edition of this translation.
[106] Locke, *Essay*, II.xiii.2.   [107] Yolton, *Thinking Matter*, p. 87, n. 2.
[108] Cockburn, *Remarks Upon Some Writers*, in *The Works*, vol. I, p. 390.
[109] Isaac Watts, *Philosophical Essays upon various subjects: with some remarks on Mr Locke's Essay on the human understanding*, with an introduction by John Yolton, reprint of 1742 edition (Bristol: Thoemmes Press, 1990), pp. 28–9.

exists, especially when we cannot expel the idea from our imagination. Philosophers go wrong, she says, when they inquire whether space is a spirit or a body. These categories of substance need not be exhaustive. In defence of this point, Cockburn appeals to Locke's assertion that

> Either this *Space* is something or nothing; if nothing be between two Bodies, they must necessarily touch; if it be allowed to be something, they ask, whether it be Body or Spirit? To which I answer by another Question, Who told them, that there was, or could be nothing, but solid Beings, which could not think; and thinking beings that were not extended? Which is all they mean by the terms *Body* and *Spirit*.[110]

Locke's next point is that, granted we have only an obscure idea of substance, space may or may not be a substance.[111] In accordance with this view, Cockburn maintains that there is 'no absurdity in supposing, that there may be other substances, than either spirits or bodies' – and one of these could be space.[112] Hence she directly challenges the typical Cartesian division of substances.

Cockburn gives a further argument in support of this view, drawing together the ideas of Cudworth, Locke, and Joseph Addison (1672–1719).[113] Cockburn's one explicit reference to Cudworth appears in a footnote, where she refers to him as an 'eminent author' who argues from eternal truths and immutable natures to the existence of an eternal mind as necessary support for 'eternal *abstract ideas*'.[114] There are also indirect references to Cudworth earlier in the work, when Cockburn draws on Law's notes.[115] In particular, Cockburn alludes to one passage in the *True Intellectual System*, where Cudworth refers to 'a *Scale or Ladder of Perfections*, in Nature, one above another, as of Living and Animate Things, above *sensless* and *Inanimate*; of *Rational* things above *Sensitive*'.[116] This 'gradual ascent' of beings eventually ends with God, the most perfect of all beings.

[110] Locke, *Essay*, II.xiii.16, p. 173. Cockburn quotes an almost identical passage put forward in Law's 'Notes'; see Cockburn, *Remarks Upon Some Writers*, in *The Works*, vol. 1, pp. 390–1.
[111] Locke, *Essay*, II.xiii.17, p. 174.
[112] Cockburn, *Remarks Upon Some Writers*, in *The Works*, vol. 1, p. 391.
[113] These authors are quoted in Law's notes.
[114] Cockburn, *Remarks Upon Some Writers*, in *The Works*, vol. 1, p. 435, n. a. Cockburn refers to John Norris in the same footnote. Masham's final letter to Leibniz draws on the same argument to defend Cudworth against Pierre Bayle's accusations. Like Masham in this letter, Cockburn asks 'Where can ideas exist but in some mind?' (*Remarks Upon Some Writers*, in *The Works*, vol. 1, p. 436).
[115] Law includes extensive quotations from Cudworth's *True Intellectual System*. Watts also refers to Cudworth's views in his *Philosophical Essays*.
[116] Cudworth, *True Intellectual System*, p. 648; William King, *An Essay on the Origin of Evil. By William King, late Lord Archbishop of Dublin. Translated from the Latin, with large Notes; tending to explain and vindicate some of the Author's Principles Against the Objections of Bayle, Leibnitz, the Author of a Philosophical*

Cudworth supports his theory with the claim that the mind cannot be derived from matter, since something less perfect cannot be the origin of something more perfect.[117] Similarly, in volume 519 of the *Spectator*, Addison observes that 'The whole Chasm in Nature, from a Plant to a Man, is filled up with diverse kinds of Creatures, rising one over another, by such a gentle and easy ascent.'[118] He refers to a passage in Locke's *Essay* on this same topic (III.vi.12), in which Locke says that it is not inconceivable 'that there may be many species of spirits as much separated and diversified one from another by distinct properties whereof we have no ideas, as the species of sensible things are distinguished one from another by qualities which we know and observe in them'.[119] This opinion is probable given that we see 'no chasms, or gaps' in the natural world.[120]

Cockburn applies similar suggestions about 'a gradual progress in nature' to the problem of the ontological status of space. She believes that our observation of a chain of beings suggests that there is 'some being to fill up the vast chasm betwixt body and spirit; otherwise the gradation would fail, the chain would seem to be broken'.[121]

What a gap betwixt *senseless material*, and *intelligent immaterial substance*, unless there is some being, which, by partaking of the nature of both, may serve as a link to unite them, and make the transition less violent? And why may not space be such a being? Might we not venture to define it, *an immaterial unintelligent substance*, the place of bodies, and of spirits, having some of the properties of both.[122]

Cockburn suggests that we treat space as a substance like both body and spirit. We are ignorant about the true nature of souls and bodies, according to Cockburn, and yet we affirm that they exist – we should do likewise with space. Moreover, the 'gradual ascent of beings' in

---

Enquiry concerning Human Liberty; and others, edited by Edmund Law (London: W. Thurlbourne, 1731), pp. 70–1, n. XI.

[117] On this topic, see Sarah Hutton, 'Cudworth, Boethius and the Scale of Nature', in *The Cambridge Platonists in Philosophical Context*, edited by G. A. J. Rogers (Dordrecht, Boston, and London: Kluwer Academic Publishers, 1997), pp. 93–100.

[118] Quoted in King, *Origin of Evil*, p. 94, n. 35.   [119] Locke, *Essay*, III.vi.12, pp. 446–7.

[120] On this point, Locke appears to have been influenced by Cambridge–Platonist ideas. His next passage is reminiscent of Cudworth:

And when we consider the infinite power and wisdom of the Maker, we have reason to think that it is suitable to the magnificent harmony of the universe, and the great design and infinite goodness of the Architect, that the species of creatures should also, by gentle degrees, ascend upward from us towards his infinite perfection, as we see they gradually descend from us downwards. (Locke, *Essay*, III.vi.12, pp. 446–7)

[121] Cockburn, *Remarks Upon Some Writers*, in *The Works*, vol. I, p. 391.   [122] *Ibid.*

nature provides us with good reason to affirm that space is a real entity; it is most probable that space is an immaterial unintelligent substance, partaking in the attributes of both body and spirit, and therefore linking 'the intelligent and material world together by an easy gradation'.[123] In this way, Cockburn combines Lockean philosophy with a Cambridge–Platonist conception of nature to develop an independent metaphysical position.

Cockburn's views about 'extended spirits' also bear a close resemblance to the philosophy of Henry More. In the correspondence with Leibniz, Samuel Clarke speaks of space as 'the place...of all ideas'.[124] But Cockburn rejects this view as too obscure, in favour of the claim that 'space is the place of spirits'. Isaac Watts claims that allowing spirits to be in a place is problematic for the notion of spirit in general: if we allow this, then we must also allow that spirits are extended, and then, 'if so, they must have some *shape or figure*, and consequently be *divisible*'.[125] Cockburn does not accept these implications. Such difficulties arise only if one supposes that spirits are extended in the same manner as bodies;

but may not beings, of whose nature we have but a partial knowledge, have some other kind of extension, consistent with that indivisibility, which we suppose essential to thinking substances? Is not space an instance of extension, or expansion,[126] without figure or indivisibility, to those, who allow it any being?[127]

Henry More claims that the soul can be extended and yet indivisible, and he also regards empty space as something extended but immaterial, a notion that apparently had a significant impact on Newton's thought.[128] Like More, Cockburn maintains that the idea that spirits are in no place is 'utterly inconceivable'. She says that 'perhaps there are few truths more clear and evident than this, that whatever has a real existence must exist *somewhere*; nor does any difficulty or inconsistency appear greater to me, than the suppsition [*sic*] of any being really existing, yet existing *no where*'.[129] Although we are ignorant about *how* spirits can be located

[123] *Ibid.*, p. 400.
[124] 'Dr. Clarke's Fourth Reply', in Alexander (ed.), *The Leibniz–Clarke Correspondence*, p. 50.
[125] Cockburn, *Remarks Upon Some Writers*, in *The Works*, vol. 1, p. 392.
[126] Locke suggests that the term 'extension' be applied to solid bodies alone, while the term 'expansion' be restricted to space in general (*Essay*, 11.xiii.26, pp. 179–80).
[127] Cockburn, *Remarks Upon Some Writers*, in *The Works*, vol. 1, p. 392.
[128] On connections between Newton and More, see chapter 10 in A. Rupert Hall, *Henry More and the Scientific Revolution* (Cambridge and New York: Cambridge University Press, 1996), pp. 202–23. See also Max Jammer, *Concepts of Space: The History of Theories of Space in Physics*, with a foreword by Albert Einstein (Cambridge, Mass.: Harvard University Press, 1954), pp. 38–47.
[129] Cockburn, *Remarks Upon Some Writers*, in *The Works*, vol. 1, p. 392.

in space, it is better to affirm that they are somewhere, because to do otherwise, is to 'go beyond our clear and distinct perceptions' and 'to turn from sensible ideas'.[130] It is impossible, according to Cockburn, to imagine a 'conscious active power' exerting its influence, and yet not actually *being somewhere*.[131]

Cockburn's remarks are reminiscent of Damaris Masham's letter to Leibniz (20 October 1705), where she claims that she is not 'able to conceive an existence of that which is *No Where*'.[132] Masham justifies this view with appeal to Locke's criterion of truth and certainty: wherever she has no idea of a thing, or a demonstration of its truth, she says, she cannot give her assent. Cockburn likewise turns to the Lockean criteria in her affirmation of extended yet indivisible souls. She claims that there is no need to go beyond our ideas when it comes to extended yet indivisible souls, 'extension not seeming to me inconsistent with indivisibility, the allowed property of thinking beings'.[133] According to Cockburn, space can also be regarded as an extended, yet indivisible entity, without involving us in a contradiction.

In opposition, Edmund Law and Isaac Watts maintain that there cannot be 'an immaterial being, without the power of thinking'.[134] But Cockburn dismisses their claims by noting that we are ignorant of whether or not 'a power of thinking may be the substance of spirit'.[135] She re-affirms her point in the *Defence* of Locke, that 'from what we know of the human soul... thinking cannot be the substance or essence of it; and that it may continue to be, though it should sometimes cease to act'.[136] Cockburn supports Locke's view that the human soul is *most probably* immaterial; and she affirms, with appeal to Locke, that God cannot be material.[137] But, according to Cockburn, none of this prevents us from affirming that some immaterial beings (*i.e.* space) may not think: 'from the strongest proofs, that all thinking beings must be immaterial, it does not follow, that every immaterial being must think; thinking not being a necessary consequence of immateriality'.[138]

In her article on Cockburn's moral philosophy, Martha Brandt Bolton observes that in the latter part of Cockburn's career, she moves away from Lockean philosophy and 'openly advocates a more Platonist metaphysics,

---

[130] *Ibid.*, p. 393.
[131] This view is supported with appeal to Locke's chapter on 'Identity and Diversity' (*Essay*, II.xxvii.1, p. 209). Spirits must also have a place, according to Cockburn, in order to be distinguished from one another.
[132] Masham to Leibniz, 20 October 1705; Hanover, MS 612, fols. 8ᵛ–9.
[133] Cockburn, *Remarks Upon Some Writers*, in *The Works*, vol. 1, p. 394.   [134] *Ibid.*, p. 395.
[135] *Ibid.*, p. 396.   [136] *Ibid.*, pp. 396–7.   [137] *Ibid.*, p. 399.   [138] *Ibid.*

positing moral truths as eternal objects of God'.[139] There are several
Cambridge–Platonist aspects to Cockburn's metaphysical thought, including her appeal to 'a scale of beings', and her argument for extended
yet indivisible spirits. Cockburn also uses similar arguments to Cudworth
to show that 'the reflections we make on the operations of our own
minds... lead us to the supreme mind, where all truth, and the abstract
nature of all possible things, must eternally and immutably exist'.[140] In
all of Cockburn's works, she is steadfastly anti-voluntarist, 'the notion
of founding morality on arbitrary will is carefully rejected; and the nature of God, or the divine understanding, and the nature of man, all
along supposed to be the true grounds of it'.[141] Like Cudworth and
Conway, Cockburn disassociates her views from those of Spinoza. In
Remarks Upon Some Writers, she rejects the idea that God exists by chance
because it lends arms to 'the followers of Spinoza', who claim that that
'the material world, and every existing substance, was eternal, absolutely
without any ground or reason of existence'.[142] Cockburn also supports
Clarke's opposition to 'Mr. Hobbs's principles' in her response to Thomas
Rutherforth's *Essay on the Nature and Obligations of Virtue* (1744), titled
Remarks upon the Principles and Reasonings of Dr. Rutherforth's Essay (1747).[143]
She is especially opposed to any theory of moral obligation founded upon
self-interest.

Yet despite these typical 'Cambridge' themes, Cockburn cannot be
labelled a Platonist in any strong sense of the term. In her metaphysical
views, and especially those on substances, Cockburn is a reasonably
consistent Lockean. She is indebted to Locke for the claim that we cannot
know the essence of material or immaterial substances, the view that the
soul may not always think, and the disassociation between the ideas
of matter and extension. More accurately, Cockburn brings together
Clarke's general ideas on space, Locke's conception of substances, and
More's view that souls are extended. John Henry notes that to most
seventeenth-century thinkers it is the case that 'if it is matter it is extended
and if it is extended it is matter'.[144] Henry More's philosophy was the
first to undermine this perception, and John Locke's ontological views
take these ideas to their natural conclusion. Cockburn's metaphysical

[139] Brandt Bolton, 'Some Aspects of the Philosophy of Catharine Trotter', 570.
[140] Cockburn, *Defence of Locke*, in *The Works*, vol. 1, p. 56.   [141] *Ibid.*, pp. 61–2.
[142] Cockburn, *Remarks Upon Some Writers*, in *The Works*, vol. 1, p. 386.
[143] Cockburn, *Remarks upon the Principles and Reasonings of Dr. Rutherforth's Essay*, in *The Works*, vol. 11,
p. 39.
[144] Henry, 'A Cambridge Platonist's Materialism', 177.

views are a further contribution to the downfall of Cartesianism leading up to (and following) Locke's *Essay*.

At the beginning of the seventeenth century, Margaret Cavendish lamented her isolation from both male and female intellectuals. By the end of the century, women philosophers could feel that they were part of a growing, albeit somewhat marginalised, group of thinkers. An awareness of other women's ideas, and the concerns of women in general, permeates Catharine Trotter Cockburn's work: her writings share the philosophical views of Astell, Masham, Elizabeth Burnet, and Chudleigh; she acknowledges the mentorship of Caroline; and she defends the equal moral and intellectual rights of women. Although Cockburn is not a remarkably original thinker, in the sense that Conway and Cavendish are, she is far from being the unquestioning disciple of Locke and Clarke: her writings reveal that she could develop independent and unique positions on *both* moral and metaphysical matters.

In Cockburn's metaphysical writings we see the end of the Cartesian influence in England. Her views on material and spiritual substances, some of which follow Locke, Cudworth, and More, are profoundly anti-Cartesian. In her early work, the *Defence of Locke*, Cockburn supports Locke's supposition about 'thinking matter' against its negative religious implications. She also supports the view that the soul may not always think, another of Locke's most anti-Cartesian ideas. These claims are developed in *Remarks Upon Some Writers*, a work in which Cockburn also puts forward a Cambridge–Platonist metaphysical outlook. Space, she suggests, should be treated like a substance with both physical and mental properties; space also provides a meeting point for extended bodies and extended souls. In this way, Cockburn's thought is a natural progression from the anti-dualist tendencies of Elisabeth, Cavendish, Conway, and (to a lesser extent) Astell and Masham. Her philosophy is one in which the intelligent and material worlds are linked together by an 'easy gradation', and where the typical attributes of matter and spirit are blurred: for all we know, systems of matter could be given the power of thought, the soul may be extended and yet indivisible, and the soul does not always think.

Conclusion

There is a prevailing opinion that women philosophers of the seven-teenth century were positively inspired by the new Cartesian conception of reason. But the writings of a number of early modern women show that a reverence for reason and dualist theories of the soul and body do not necessarily go hand in hand. Profoundly influenced by the Cambridge Platonists, these women are critical of Cartesian meta-physics and the theories it influenced, such as occasionalism, and pre-established harmony. In the 1640s, Elisabeth of Bohemia challenges Descartes' account of soul–body interaction, and develops a more ex-tensive definition of the soul and the soul–body relationship. Following in her footsteps, Margaret Cavendish and Anne Conway are opposed to the real distinction between soul and body; to the view that the soul is unextended, indivisible, and penetrable, and that material things lack life, self-motion, and perception. Although Conway's cosmology is commonly labelled as 'spiritualist', her system is not much different from Cavendish's 'materialist' philosophy. Both Conway and Cavendish defy typical seventeenth-century classifications by ascribing material at-tributes to spirit, and spiritual properties to matter. Mary Astell and Damaris Masham oppose the view that there is no genuine interaction between the soul and body. Despite their philosophical differences, they criticise the occasionalist philosophy of John Norris because it makes material things superfluous features of God's creation. Astell suggests that there might be a 'sensible congruity' between the soul and body, something like Henry More's theory of a vital congruity between the body and the plastic part of the soul. In her letters to Leibniz, Masham goes even further to suggest that all substances are extended, and that it is possible that God could give matter the power to think. Cockburn is likewise sceptical about the idea of 'substance', and suggests that the categories of 'soul' and 'body' may not be exhaustive.

These women each have a different response to dualist theorists of their time, yet each is critical of any theory in which there is a radical separation between material and immaterial substances, and in which matter is rendered causally impotent or purposeless. Furthermore, many of these women – in varying ways – avoid negative associations between materiality and femaleness. Cavendish subverts the typical alignment of women and the body; Conway advocates an interdependent relationship between female/material and male/spiritual principles; and Astell, Masham, and Cockburn reject the common stereotype of women as mere machines or bodies, devoid of rationality.

In *The Man of Reason*, Genevieve Lloyd says that 'the denigration of the "feminine" is one of the most salient aspects of the maleness of the philosophical tradition'.[1] The contributions of female philosophers of the past reveal that the history of philosophy can have positive implications for women. By being 'impertinent', or by 'meddling' in what is beyond the feminine province, these women are able to raise serious philosophical objections, and to offer their own unique, independent contributions to the philosophical enterprise of their time. Although they are inspired by the popular Cartesian conception of 'natural reason', their reverence for reason does not entail an unquestioning acceptance of dualist theories of the soul and body.

In the writings of Elisabeth, Cavendish, Conway, Astell, Masham, and Cockburn, those metaphysical categories now culturally associated with the 'feminine', such as matter, nature, and the body, are not derogated, ignored, or suppressed. Whether they reject dualism outright, or simply defend the possibility of genuine soul–body interaction, each writer raises the status of matter by emphasising its connection or affinity with the intellectual world.

---

[1] Lloyd, *The Man of Reason*, p. 107.

Bibliography

PRIMARY SOURCES

Alexander, H. G. (ed.), *The Leibniz–Clarke Correspondence* (Manchester: Manchester University Press, 1956).

Anonymous, *An Account of the causes of some particular rebellious distempers: viz. the scurvey, cancers in women's breasts, &c. vapours, and melancholy, &c. weaknesses in women, &c. . . . by an eminent practitioner in physick, surgery and chymistry* (London: 1670).

The Athenian Gazette: or Casuistical Mercury, Resolving all the most Nice and Curious Questions Proposed by the Ingenious of Either Sex (1691), vols. II and III.

Arnauld, Antoine, and Pierre Nicole, *Logic or the Art of Thinking*, translated and edited by Jill Vance Buroker (Cambridge: Cambridge University Press, 1996).

Astell, Mary, *The Christian Religion, As Profess'd by a Daughter Of The Church of England. In a Letter to the Right Honourable, T.L. C.I.* (London: R. Wilkin, 1705).

Astell: Political Writings, edited by Patricia Springborg (Cambridge: Cambridge University Press, 1996).

A Serious Proposal to the Ladies, Parts I and II, edited by Patricia Springborg, modern edition (London: Pickering and Chatto, 1997).

Astell, Mary, and John Norris, *Letters Concerning the Love of God, Between the Author of the Proposal to the Ladies and Mr. John Norris: Wherein his late Discourse, shewing That it ought to be intire and exclusive of all other Loves, is further cleared and justified* (London: J. Norris, 1695).

Atherton, Margaret (ed.), *Women Philosophers of the Early Modern Period* (Indianapolis: Hackett Publishing, 1994).

Barclay, Colonel D., *Reliquiae Barclaianae: Correspondence of Colonel D. Barclay and Robert Barclay of Urie and his son Robert, including Letters from Princess Elisabeth of the Rhine, the Earl of Perth, the Countess of Sutherland, William Penn, George Fox and others* (London: Winter and Bailey, 1870).

Burnet, Elizabeth, *A Method of Devotion: Or, Rules for Holy and Devout Living, with Prayers on Several Occasions, and Advice and Devotions for the Holy Sacrament. The Second Edition, To which is added Some Account of her Life, by T. Goodwyn*, second edition (London: Joseph Downing, C. Smith and A. Barker, 1709).

Burnet, Thomas, *Remarks upon an Essay Concerning Humane Understanding: in a Letter address'd to the Author* (London: M. Wotton, 1697).

Second Remarks upon an Essay Concerning Humane Understanding, in a Letter address'd to the Author: being a Vindication of the First Remarks against the Answer of Mr. Lock at the End of his Reply to the Lord Bishop of Worcester (London: M. Wotton, 1697).

Third Remarks upon an Essay concerning Humane Understanding, in a Letter address'd to the Author (London: M. Wotton, 1699).

Remarks on John Locke, edited by George Watson (Doncaster: Brynmill, 1989).

Cavendish, Margaret, *Poems, and Fancies: Written By the Right Honourable, The Lady Newcastle*, facsimile reprint of 1653 edition (Menston: Scolar Press, 1972).

The Philosophical and Physical Opinions, Written by her Excellency, the Lady Marchionesse of Newcastle (London: J. Martin and J. Allestrye, 1655); reissued as *Grounds of Natural Philosophy* (London: A. Maxwell, 1668).

The Worlds Olio. Written By the Right Honorable, the Lady Margaret Newcastle (London: J. Martin and J. Allestrye, 1655).

Philosophical Letters: Or, Modest Reflections Upon some Opinions in Natural Philosophy, Maintained By several Famous and Learned Authors of this Age, Expressed by way of Letters: By the Thrice Noble, Illustrious, and Excellent Princess, The Lady Marchioness of Newcastle (London: privately published, 1664).

Observations Upon Experimental Philosophy. To which is added, The Description of A New Blazing World. Written By the Thrice Noble, Illustrious, and Excellent Princesse, The Duchess of Newcastle (London: A. Maxwell, 1666).

The Life of the Thrice Noble, High and Puissant Prince William Cavendishe (London: A. Maxwell, 1667).

A Collection of Letters And Poems: Written by several Persons of Honour and Learning, Upon divers Important subjects, to the Late Duke and Dutchess of Newcastle (London: Langly Curtis, 1678).

The Blazing World and Other Writings, edited with an introduction by Kate Lilley (Harmondsworth: Penguin, 1994).

Grounds of Natural Philosophy: Divided into Thirteen Parts: With an Appendix containing Five Parts, with an introduction by Colette V. Michael, facsimile reprint of 1668 edition (West Cornwall, CT: Locust Hill Press, 1996).

Observations upon Experimental Philosophy, edited by Eileen O'Neill, first modern edition (Cambridge: Cambridge University Press, 2001).

Christina, Queen of Sweden, *The Works of Christina Queen of Sweden. Containing Maxims and Sentences, In Twelve Centuries; and Reflections on the Life and Actions of Alexander the Great* (London: Wilson and Durham, 1753).

Chudleigh, Mary, *The Poems and Prose of Mary, Lady Chudleigh*, edited by Margaret J. M. Ezell (New York and Oxford: Oxford University Press, 1993).

Cockburn, Catharine Trotter, *The Works of Mrs. Catharine Cockburn, Theological, Moral, Dramatic, and Poetical*, edited by Thomas Birch, 2 vols. (London: J. and P. Knapton, 1751).

Olinda's Adventures: Or the Amours of a Young Lady, with an introduction by Robert Adams Day (Los Angeles: Augustan Reprint Society no. 138, 1969).

The Plays of Mary Pix and Catharine Trotter, edited by Edna L. Steeves (New York and London: Garland Publishing, 1982), vol. II.

Conway, Anne, *The Principles of the Most Ancient and Modern Philosophy*, with an introduction by Peter Loptson (Amsterdam: Martinus Nijhoff, 1982).

The Principles of the Most Ancient and Modern Philosophy, translated and edited by Allison P. Coudert, and Taylor Corse (Cambridge: Cambridge University Press, 1996).

Cudworth, Ralph, *The True Intellectual System of the Universe: The First Part; Wherein, All the Reason and Philosophy Of Atheism is Confuted; And Its Impossibility Demonstrated*, facsimile reprint of 1678 edition (Stuttgart-Bad Cannstatt: Friedrich Frommann Verlag, 1964).

A Treatise Concerning Eternal and Immutable Morality, edited and introduced by Sarah Hutton (Cambridge: Cambridge University Press, 1997).

Descartes, René, *Descartes: Philosophical Letters*, translated and edited by Anthony Kenny (Oxford: Clarendon Press, 1970).

Descartes: His Moral Philosophy and Psychology, translated, with an introduction and conceptual index, by John J. Blom (New York: New York University Press, 1978).

The Philosophical Writings of Descartes, translated by John Cottingham, Robert Stoothoff, and Dugald Murdoch, 3 vols. (Cambridge: Cambridge University Press, 1985–91).

Oeuvres de Descartes, edited by Charles Adam and Paul Tannery, new edition (Paris: Librairie Philosophique J. Vrin, 1996), vols. III–V.

Drake, Judith, *An Essay In Defence of the Female Sex. In which are inserted the Characters Of A Pedant, A Squire, A Beau, A Vertuoso, A Poetaster, A City-Critick, and c. In a Letter to a Lady. Written by a Lady*, unabridged republication of 1696 edition (New York: Source Book Press, 1970).

Glanvill, Joseph, *The Vanity of Dogmatizing: Or Confidence in Opinions Manifested in a Discourse of the Shortness and Uncertainty of our Knowledge, And its Causes; With some Reflexions on Peripateticism; And An Apology for Philosophy* (London: E C for Henry Eversden, 1661).

Greer, Germaine, Susan Hastings, Jeslyn Medoff, and Melinda Sansone (eds.), *Kissing the Rod: An Anthology of Seventeenth-Century Women's Verse* (New York: The Noonday Press, 1988).

Hobbes, Thomas, *Leviathan, Or The Matter, Forme, and Power of a Common-wealth Ecclesiasticall and Civil*, reprint from the 1651 edition (Oxford: Clarendon Press, 1929).

Elements of Philosophy. The First Section, Concerning Body, in *The English Works of Thomas Hobbes of Malmesbury*, edited by William Molesworth, reprint of 1839 edition, 11 vols. (London: Scientia Aalen, 1962), vol. I.

King, William, *An Essay on the Origin of Evil. By William King, late Lord Archbishop of Dublin. Translated from the Latin, with large Notes; tending to explain and vindicate some of the Author's Principles Against the Objections of Bayle, Leibnitz, the Author of a Philosophical Enquiry concerning Human Liberty; and others*, edited by Edmund Law (London: W. Thurlbourne, 1731).

Leibniz, Gottfried Wilhelm, *The Monadology and Other Philosophical Writings*, translated and edited by Robert Latta (London: Oxford University Press, 1951).

Die Philosophischen Schriften von Gottfried Wilhelm Leibniz, edited by C. I. Gerhardt (Berlin: Georg Olms Hildesheim, 1960), vol. III.

Philosophical Papers and Letters, a selection translated and edited, with an introduction by Leroy E. Loemker, second edition (Dordrecht: Reidel Pub. Co., 1969).

Leibniz's New System and Associated Contemporary Texts, translated and edited by R. S. Woolhouse and Richard Francks (Oxford: Clarendon Press, 1997).

Locke, John, 'Remarks Upon some of Mr. Norris's Books, Wherein he asserts F. Malebranche's Opinion of Our Seeing all things in God', in *A Collection of Several Pieces of Mr. John Locke*, second edition (London: R. Francklin, 1739).

An Essay Concerning Human Understanding, edited by Peter H. Nidditch (Oxford: Clarendon Press, 1979).

The Correspondence of John Locke and Edward Clarke, edited by Benjamin Rand, reprint of 1927 edition (New York: Plainview, 1975).

The Correspondence of John Locke, edited by E. S. de Beer, 8 vols. (Oxford: Clarendon Press, 1976–82).

Malebranche, Nicolas, *Oeuvres complètes de Malebranche*, edited by A. Robinet (Paris: J. Vrin, 1958–84), vols. 18–19.

The Search After Truth, translated and edited by Thomas M. Lennon and Paul J. Olscamp (Cambridge: Cambridge University Press, 1997).

Masham, Damaris, *A Discourse Concerning the Love of God* (London: Awnsham and John Churchil, 1696); translated into French by Pierre Coste as *Discours sur L'amour Divin* (Amsterdam: Pierre de Coup, 1715).

Occasional Thoughts in Reference to a Vertuous or Christian Life (London: A. and J. Churchil, 1705).

More, Henry, *An Antidote Against Atheism, Or, An Appeal to the Naturall Faculties of the Minde of Man*, with a new introduction by G. A. J. Rogers, facsimile reprint of 1655 second edition (Bristol: Thoemmes Press, 1997).

The Immortality of the Soul; So farre forth as it is demonstrable from the Knowledge of Nature and the Light of Reason, facsimile reprint of 1659 edition (Bristol: Thoemmes Press, 1997).

Nicolson, Marjorie Hope, *The Conway Letters: The Correspondence of Anne, Viscountess Conway, Henry More and Their Friends, 1642–1684*, revised with an introduction and new material, edited by Sarah Hutton (Oxford: Clarendon Press, 1992).

Norris, John, *The Theory and Regulation of Love. A Moral Essay. In Two Parts. To which are added Letters Philosophical and Moral between the Author and Dr Henry More* (Oxford: Henry Clements, 1688).

Reflections upon the Conduct of Human Life: With reference to the Study of Learning and Knowledge. In a Letter to the Excellent Lady, the Lady Masham (London: S. Manship, 1690).

Practical Discourses Upon several Divine Subjects (London: S. Manship, 1693 and 1698), vols. III and IV.

An Essay Towards the Theory of the Ideal or Intelligible World (London: S. Manship, 1701 and 1704), parts I and II.

Osborne, Dorothy, *Letters to Sir William Temple*, edited with an introduction by Kenneth Parker (Harmondsworth: Penguin, 1987).

Patrides, C. A. (ed.), *The Cambridge Platonists* (London: Edward Arnold, 1969).

Penn, William, *The Papers of William Penn*, edited by Mary and Richard Dunn (Philadelphia: University of Pennsylvania Press, 1981), vol. I.

Pepys, Samuel, *The Diary of Samuel Pepys*, edited by Robert Latham and William Matthews (London: Bell, 1974), vols. VIII and IX.

Poulain de la Barre, François, *The Woman as Good as the Man; Or, the Equality of Both Sexes*, edited with an introduction by Gerald M. MacLean (Detroit: Wayne State University Press, 1988).

Schurman, Anna Maria van, *Whether a Christian Woman Should be Educated and Other Writings from Her Intellectual Circle*, edited and translated by Joyce L. Irwin (Chicago and London: The University of Chicago Press, 1998).

Spinoza, Baruch (or Benedict), *Tractatus Theologico-Politicus*, translated by Samuel Shirley, with an introduction by Brad S. Gregory, second edition (Leiden: Brill, 1991).

Thomas, Elizabeth, and Richard Gwinnett, *Pylades and Corinna: or, Memoirs of the Lives, Amours, and Writings of Richard Gwinnett and Mrs Elizabeth Thomas* (London: Edmund Curll, 1731).

The Honourable Lovers: Or, The Second and Last Volume of Pylades and Corinna. Being the Remainder of Love Letters, and other Pieces, (In Verse and Prose,) Which passed between Richard Gwinnett . . . And Mrs. Elizabeth Thomas . . . To Which is added, A Collection of Familiar Letters, between Corinna, Mr. Norris, Capt. Hemington, Lady Chudleigh, Lady Pakington, and c. (London: E. Curll, 1732).

Warnock, Mary (ed.), *Women Philosophers* (London: J. M. Dent, 1996).

Watts, Isaac, *Philosophical Essays upon various subjects: with some remarks on Mr Locke's Essay on the human understanding*, with an introduction by John Yolton, reprint of 1742 edition (Bristol: Thoemmes Press, 1990).

Wollstonecraft, Mary, *A Vindication of the Rights of Woman*, edited with an introduction by Miriam Brody (Harmondsworth: Penguin, 1992).

Worthington, John, *The Diary and Correspondence of Dr. John Worthington*, edited by James Crossley (Manchester: The Chetham Society, 1847).

Young, Edward, *Love of Fame, The Universal Passion. In Seven Characteristical Satires*, third edition (London: J. Jonson, 1730).

SECONDARY SOURCES

Acworth, Richard, *The Philosophy of John Norris of Bemerton (1657–1712)* (New York: Georg Olms Verlag, 1979).

Adams, Robert Merrihew, *Leibniz: Determinist, Theist, Idealist* (New York and Oxford: Oxford University Press, 1994).

Aiton, E. J., *Leibniz: A Biography* (Bristol: Adam Hilger, 1985).

Åkerman, Susanna, *Queen Christina of Sweden and Her Circle: The Transformation of a Seventeenth-Century Philosophical Libertine* (Leiden: E. J. Brill, 1991).
'Kristina Wasa, Queen of Sweden', in *A History of Women Philosophers*, edited by Mary Ellen Waithe (Dordrecht: Kluwer Academic Publishers, 1991), vol. III, pp. 21–40.
Alcover, Madeleine, *Poullain de la Barre: une aventure philosophique* (Paris-Seattle-Tubingen: Papers on French Seventeenth-Century Literature, 1981).
Antony, Louise M., and Charlotte Witt (eds.), *A Mind of One's Own: Feminist Essays on Reason and Objectivity* (Boulder and Oxford: Westview Press, 1993).
Atherton, Margaret, 'Cartesian Reason and Gendered Reason', in *A Mind of One's Own: Feminist Essays on Reason and Objectivity*, edited by Louise M. Antony and Charlotte Witt (Boulder and Oxford: Westview Press, 1993), pp. 19–34.
Ayers, Michael, *Locke: Epistemology and Ontology*, 2 vols. (London and New York: Routledge, 1993).
Ballard, George, *Memoirs of Several Ladies of Great Britain (who have been celebrated for their writings or skill in the learned languages, arts and sciences)*, with an introduction by Ruth Perry (Detroit: Wayne State University Press, 1985).
Battigelli, Anna, 'Political Thought/Political Action: Margaret Cavendish's Hobbesian Dilemma', in *Women Writers and the Early Modern British Political Tradition*, edited by Hilda L. Smith (Cambridge: Cambridge University Press, 1998), pp. 40–55.
Margaret Cavendish and the Exiles of the Mind (Lexington: University Press of Kentucky, 1998).
Bertoloni Meli, D., 'Caroline, Leibniz, and Clarke', *Journal of the History of Ideas* 60:3 (1999), 469–86.
Blaydes, Sophia B., 'Nature is a Woman: The Duchess of Newcastle and Seventeenth Century Philosophy', in *Man, God, and Nature in the Enlightenment*, edited by Donald C. Mell, Theodore E. D. Braun and Lucia M. Palmer (East Lansing, MI: Colleagues Press, 1988), pp. 51–64.
Blaze de Bury, Marie, *Memoirs of the Princess Palatine, Princess of Bohemia* (London: Richard Bentley, 1853).
Bordo, Susan, 'The Cartesian Masculinization of Thought', *Signs: Journal of Women in Culture and Society* 11:3 (1986), 439–56.
The Flight to Objectivity: Essays on Cartesianism and Culture (Albany: State University of New York Press, 1987).
(ed.), *Feminist Interpretations of René Descartes* (University Park, Pennsylvania: Pennsylvania State University Press, 1999).
Bowerbank, Sylvia, 'The Spider's Delight: Margaret Cavendish and the "Female" Imagination', *English Literary Renaissance* 14 (1984), 392–408.
Brandt Bolton, Martha, 'Some Aspects of the Philosophy of Catharine Trotter', *Journal of the History of Philosophy* 31:4 (1993), 565–88.
Broad, Jacqueline, 'Mary Astell (1666–1731)', *British Philosophers, 1500–1799*, edited by Philip B. Dematteis and Peter S. Fosl, in *Dictionary of Literary Biography* 252 (2002), 3–10.

'Review of Margaret Atherton's *Women Philosophers of the Early Modern Period*', *Australasian Journal of Philosophy* 75:2 (1997), 248–9.

Brown, Stuart, 'Leibniz and More's Cabbalistic Circle', in *Henry More (1614–1687) Tercentenary Studies*, edited by Sarah Hutton (Dordrecht: Kluwer Academic Publishers, 1990), pp. 77–96.

'Malebranche's Occasionalism and Leibniz's Pre-established Harmony: an "Easy Crossing" or an Unbridgeable Gap?', in *Nicolas Malebranche: His Philosophical Critics and Successors*, edited by Stuart Brown (Assen, the Netherlands: Van Gorcum, 1991), pp. 81–93.

Butler, Melissa A., 'Early Liberal Roots of Feminism: John Locke and the Attack on Patriarchy', *The American Political Science Review* 72:1 (1978), 135–50.

Carroll, Robert, *The Common-Sense Philosophy of Religion of Bishop Edward Stillingfleet, 1635–1699* (The Hague: Nijhoff, 1975).

Cassirer, Ernst, *The Platonic Renaissance in England*, translated by James P. Pettegrove (Edinburgh: Thomas Nelson and Sons, 1953).

Clark, Constance, *Three Augustan Women Playwrights* (New York: Peter Lang, 1986).

Clucas, Stephen, 'The Atomism of the Cavendish Circle: A Reappraisal', *The Seventeenth Century* 9:2 (1994), 247–73.

'The Duchess and Viscountess: Negotiations between Mechanism and Vitalism in the Natural Philosophies of Margaret Cavendish and Anne Conway', *In-Between: Essays and Studies in Literary Criticism* 9:1 (2000), 125–36.

'Variation, Irregularity and Probabilism: Margaret Cavendish and Natural Philosophy as Rhetoric', in *A Princely Brave Woman: Essays on Margaret Cavendish, Duchess of Newcastle*, edited by Stephen Clucas (Aldershot: Ashgate, forthcoming), pp. 199–209.

Colie, Rosalie L., 'Lady Masham's letter to Jean le Clerc of 12th of January 1705', *History of Ideas Newsletter* 1:4 (1955), 13–18; 2 (1956), 9–11, 35–7, 81–8.

Light and Enlightenment: A Study in the Cambridge Platonists and the Dutch Arminians (Cambridge: Cambridge University Press, 1957).

Connor, Margarette R., 'Catharine Trotter: An Unknown Child', *American Notes and Queries* 8:4 (1995), 11–14.

Coudert, Allison P., 'A Cambridge Platonist's Kabbalist Nightmare', *Journal of the History of Ideas* 36 (1975), 633–52.

'Henry More and Witchcraft', in *Henry More (1614–1687) Tercentenary Studies*, edited by Sarah Hutton (Dordrecht: Kluwer Academic Publishers, 1990), pp. 115–36.

The Impact of the Kabbalah in the Seventeenth Century: The Life and Thought of Francis Mercury van Helmont (1614–1698) (Leiden: Brill, 1999).

Craig, Edward (ed.), *Routledge Encyclopedia of Philosophy*, 10 vols. (London and New York: Routledge, 1998).

Crawford, Patricia, 'Women's Published Writings 1600–1700', in *Women in English Society: 1500–1800*, edited by Mary Prior (London: Methuen, 1985), pp. 211–31.

De Baar, Mirjam, Machteld Lowensteyn, Marit Monteiro, and A. Agnes Sneller (eds.), *Choosing the Better Part: Anna Maria van Schurman (1607–1678)*, translated by Lynne Richards (Dordrecht and London: Kluwer, 1996).

Duran, Jane, 'Anne Conway: A Seventeenth Century Rationalist', *Hypatia* 4:1 (1989), 64–79.

Eck, Caroline van, 'The First Dutch Feminist Tract? Anna Maria van Schurman's Discussion of Women's Aptitude for the Study of Arts and Sciences', in *Choosing the Better Part: Anna Maria van Schurman (1607–1678)*, edited by Mirjam De Baar, *et al.* (Dordrecht and London: Kluwer, 1996), pp. 43–54.

Ehrenpreis, Irvin, 'Letters of Advice to Young Spinsters', in *The Lady of Letters in the Eighteenth Century* (Los Angeles: 1969).

Ezell, Margaret J. M., *The Patriarch's Wife: Literary Evidence and the History of the Family* (Chapel Hill and London: The University of North Carolina Press, 1987).

Fleming, Alison, 'Catherine Trotter – "the Scots Sappho" ', *Scots Magazine* 33 (1940), 305–14.

Frankel, Lois, 'Damaris Masham: A Seventeenth-Century Feminist Philosopher', *Hypatia* 4:1 (1989), 80–90.

'Damaris Cudworth Masham', in *A History of Women Philosophers*, edited by Mary Ellen Waithe (Dordrecht: Kluwer Academic Publishers, 1991), vol. III, pp. 73–85.

'Anne Finch, Viscountess Conway', in *A History of Women Philosophers*, edited by Mary Ellen Waithe (Dordrecht: Kluwer Academic Publishers, 1991), vol. III, pp. 41–58.

'The Value of Harmony', in *Causation in Early Modern Philosophy: Cartesianism, Occasionalism and Preestablished Harmony*, edited by Steven Nadler (University Park, Pennsylvania: Pennsylvania State University Press, 1993), pp. 197–216.

Gabbey, Alan, 'Anne Conway et Henry More', *Archives de Philosophie* 40 (1977), 379–404.

'Philosophia Cartesiana Triumphata: Henry More (1646–1671)', in *Problems of Cartesianism*, edited by Thomas M. Lennon, John M. Nicholas, and John W. Davis (Kingston and Montreal: McGill-Queen's University, 1982), pp. 171–250.

'Henry More and the Limits of Mechanism', in *Henry More (1614–1687) Tercentenary Studies*, edited by Sarah Hutton (Dordrecht: Kluwer Academic Publishers, 1990), pp. 19–35.

Gallagher, Catherine, 'Embracing the Absolute: the Politics of the Female Subject in Seventeenth-Century England', *Genders* 1:1 (1988), 24–39.

Garber, Daniel, 'Understanding Interaction: What Descartes Should Have Told Elisabeth', *Southern Journal of Philosophy* 21, Supplement (1983), 15–32.

Giglioni, Guido, 'Panpsychism *versus* Hylozoism: An Interpretation of Some Seventeenth-Century Doctrines of Universal Animation', *Acta Comeniana* 11 (1995), 25–44.

Gilligan, Carol, *In A Different Voice: Psychological Theory and Women's Development* (Cambridge, Mass.: Harvard University Press, 1982).

Godfrey, Elizabeth, (Jessie Bedford), *A Sister of Prince Rupert: Elizabeth Princess Palatine and Abbess of Herford* (London and New York: John Lane, 1909).

Gosse, Edmund, 'Catharine Trotter, the Precursor of the Bluestockings', *Transactions of the Royal Society of Literature* 34 (1916), 87–118.

Grant, Douglas, *Margaret the First: A Biography of Margaret Cavendish, Duchess of Newcastle 1623–1675* (London: Rupert Hart-Davis, 1957; Toronto: University of Toronto Press, 1957).

Hall, A. Rupert, *Henry More and the Scientific Revolution* (Cambridge and New York: Cambridge University Press, 1996).

Harris, Frances, 'Living in the Neighbourhood of Science: Mary Evelyn, Margaret Cavendish and the Greshamites', in *Women, Science and Medicine 1500–1700*, edited by Lynette Hunter and Sarah Hutton (Stroud: Sutton, 1997), pp. 198–217.

Harth, Erica, *Cartesian Women: Versions and Subversions of Rational Discourse in the Old Regime* (Ithaca and London: Cornell University Press, 1992).

'Cartesian Women', in *Feminist Interpretations of René Descartes*, edited by Susan Bordo (University Park, Pennsylvania: Pennsylvania State University Press, 1999), pp. 213–31.

Heil, John, *Philosophy of Mind: A Contemporary Introduction* (London and New York: Routledge, 1998).

Henry, John, 'A Cambridge Platonist's Materialism: Henry More and the Concept of Soul', *Journal of the Warburg and Courtauld Institute* 49 (1986), 172–95.

'Henry More Versus Robert Boyle: The Spirit of Nature and the Nature of Providence', in *Henry More (1614–1687) Tercentenary Studies*, edited by Sarah Hutton (Dordrecht: Kluwer Academic Publishers, 1990), pp. 55–76.

Hill, Bridget (ed.), 'Introduction' to *The First English Feminist:'Reflections Upon Marriage' and Other Writings by Mary Astell* (Aldershot: Gower Publishing Co., 1986).

Hunter, Lynette, 'Sisters of the Royal Society: The Circle of Katherine Jones, Lady Ranelagh', in *Women, Science and Medicine 1500–1700*, edited by Lynette Hunter and Sarah Hutton (Stroud: Sutton, 1997), pp. 178–97.

Hunter, Lynette, and Sarah Hutton (eds.), *Women, Science and Medicine 1500–1700* (Stroud: Sutton, 1997).

Hutton, Sarah, 'Damaris Cudworth, Lady Masham: Between Platonism and Enlightenment', *British Journal for the History of Philosophy* 1:1 (1993), 29–54.

'Ancient Wisdom and Modern Philosophy: Anne Conway, F. M. van Helmont and the Seventeenth-Century Dutch Interchange of Ideas', in *Quaestiones Infinitae* (Utrecht: Department of Philosophy, Utrecht University, 1994).

'Anne Conway Critique d'Henry More: L'Esprit et la Matiere', *Archives de Philosophie* 58:3 (1995), 371–84.

'Like Father Like Daughter? The Moral Philosophy of Damaris Cudworth, Lady Masham', presented at the South Eastern meeting of the American Philosophical Association in Atlanta, 28–30 December 1996.

'Of Physic and Philosophy: Anne Conway, F. M. van Helmont and Seventeenth-Century Medicine', in *Religio Medici: Medicine and Religion in Seventeenth-Century England*, edited by Ole Peter Grell and Andrew Cunningham (Aldershot, England: Scolar Press, 1996).

'Cudworth, Boethius and the Scale of Nature', in G. A. J. Rogers (ed.), *The Cambridge Platonists in Philosophical Context* (Dordrecht, Boston, and London: Kluwer Academic Publishers, 1997), pp. 93–100.

'In Dialogue with Thomas Hobbes: Margaret Cavendish's Natural Philosophy', *Women's Writing* 4:3 (1997), 421–32.

'Anne Conway, Margaret Cavendish and Seventeenth-Century Scientific Thought', in *Women, Science and Medicine 1500–1700*, edited by Lynette Hunter and Sarah Hutton (Stroud: Sutton, 1997), pp. 218–34.

'On an Early Letter by Anne Conway', in *Donne filosofia e cultura nel seicento*, edited by G. Totaro (Rome: Consiglio Nazionale delle Ricerche, 2000).

'Conway, Anne (*c.* 1630–79)', in Craig (ed.), *Routledge Encyclopedia of Philosophy*, vol. 11, pp. 669–71.

'Cockburn, Catharine (1679–1749)', in Craig (ed.), *Routledge Encyclopedia of Philosophy*, vol. 11, pp. 386–7.

Hutton, Sarah (ed.), *Henry More (1614–1687) Tercentenary Studies* (Dordrecht: Kluwer Academic Publishers, 1990).

Irwin, Joyce, 'Anna-Maria van Schurman: From Feminism to Pietism', *Church History* 46 (1977), 46–62.

'Anna-Maria van Schurman: The Star of Utrecht', in *Female Scholars: The Tradition of Learning before 1800*, edited by J. R. Brink (Montreal: Eden Press, 1980).

'Learned Woman of Utrecht: Anna-Maria van Schurman', in *Women Writers of the Seventeenth Century*, edited by Katharina Wilson and Frank Warnke (Athens and London: University of Georgia Press, 1989).

Jaggar, Alison, 'Liberal Feminism and Human Nature', in *Feminist Politics and Human Nature* (Totowa, New Jersey: Rowman and Littlefield, 1983).

James, Susan, *Passion and Action: The Emotions in the Seventeenth Century* (Oxford: Clarendon Press, 1997).

'The Philosophical Innovations of Margaret Cavendish', *British Journal for the History of Philosophy* 7:2 (1999), 219–44.

Jammer, Max, *Concepts of Space: The History of Theories of Space in Physics*, with a foreword by Albert Einstein (Cambridge, Mass.: Harvard University Press, 1954).

Johnston, Charlotte, 'Locke's *Examination of Malebranche* and John Norris', *Journal of the History of Ideas* 19 (1958), 551–8.

Johnstone, Albert A., 'The Bodily Nature of the Self or What Descartes Should have Conceded Princess Elizabeth of Bohemia', in *Giving the Body Its Due*, edited by Maxine Sheets-Johnstone (Albany: State University of New York Press, 1992), pp. 16–47.

Jones, Kathleen, *A Glorious Fame: The Life of Margaret, Duchess of Newcastle, 1623–1673* (London: Bloomsbury, 1990).

Kargon, Robert Hugh, *Atomism in England from Hariot to Newton* (Oxford: Clarendon Press, 1966).

Keller, Eve, 'Producing Petty Gods: Margaret Cavendish's Critique of Experimental Science', *English Literary History* 64 (1997), 447–71.

Keller, Evelyn Fox, *Reflections on Gender and Science* (New Haven and London: Yale University Press, 1985).

Kinnaird, Joan K., 'Mary Astell and the Conservative Contribution to English Feminism', *The Journal of British Studies* 19:1 (1979), 53–75.

Kirchberger, C., 'Elizabeth Burnet, 1661–1709', *Church Quarterly Review* 148 (1949), 17–51.

Knight, Joseph, 'Cavendish, Margaret', *Dictionary of National Biography*, vol. III, pp. 1264–6.

Kroll, Maria, *Sophie Electress of Hanover: A Personal Portrait* (London: Victor Gollancz, 1973).

Lamprecht, Sterling P., 'The Role of Descartes in Seventeenth-Century England', *Studies in the History of Ideas* 3 (1935), 181–240.

Le Doueff, Michèle, 'Women and Philosophy', *Radical Philosophy* 17 (1977), 181–209.

Hipparchia's Choice: An Essay Concerning Women, Philosophy, etc. (Oxford: Blackwell, 1989).

Lloyd, Genevieve, *The Man of Reason: 'Male' and 'Female' in Western Philosophy* (London: Methuen, 1984).

'Texts, Metaphors and the Pretensions of Philosophy', *The Monist* 69 (1986), 87–102.

Loptson, Peter, 'Introduction' to Anne Conway, *The Principles of the Most Ancient and Modern Philosophy* (Amsterdam: Martinus Nijhoff, 1982).

'Anne Conway, Henry More, and their World', *Dialogue* 34 (1995), 139–46.

Mathews, Freya, *The Ecological Self* (London: Routledge, 1994).

Mattern, Ruth, 'Descartes's Correspondence with Elizabeth: Concerning Both the Union and Distinction of Mind and Body', in *Descartes: Critical and Interpretive Essays*, edited by Michael Hooker (Baltimore and London: John Hopkins University Press, 1978), pp. 212–22.

McAlister, Linda Lopez (ed.), *Hypatia's Daughters: Fifteen Hundred Years of Women Philosophers* (Bloomington and Indianapolis: Indiana University Press, 1996).

McCracken, Charles, *Malebranche and British Philosophy* (Oxford: Clarendon Press, 1983).

McCrystal, John, 'Revolting Women: The Use of Revolutionary Discourse in Mary Astell and Mary Wollstonecraft Compared', *History of Political Thought* 14 (1993), 189–203.

MacKinnon, Flora Isabel, *The Philosophy of John Norris*, in Philosophical Monographs (Baltimore: Psychological Review Publications, 1910), vol. I.

Medoff, Jeslyn, 'The Daughters of Behn and the Problem of Reputation', in *Women, Writing, History 1640–1740*, edited by Isobel Grundy and Susan Wiseman (London: B. T. Batsford, 1992), pp. 33–54.

Merchant, Carolyn, 'The Vitalism of Anne Conway: Its Impact on Leibniz's Concept of the Monad', *Journal of the History of Philosophy* 17 (1979), 255–69.

The Death of Nature: Women, Ecology and the Scientific Revolution (San Francisco: Harper and Row Publishers, 1980).

Merrens, Rebecca, 'A Nature of "Infinite Sense and Reason": Margaret Cavendish's Natural Philosophy and the "Noise" of a Feminized Nature', *Women's Studies* 25 (1996), 421–38.

Mintz, Samuel I., 'The Duchess of Newcastle's Visit to the Royal Society', *The Journal of English and Germanic Philology* 51 (1952), 168–76.

The Hunting of Leviathan: Seventeenth Century Reactions to the Materialism and Moral Philosophy of Thomas Hobbes (Cambridge: Cambridge University Press, 1970).

Nadler, Steven, *Malebranche and Ideas* (Oxford: Oxford University Press, 1992).

(ed.), *Causation in Early Modern Philosophy: Cartesianism, Occasionalism and Preestablished Harmony* (University Park, Pennsylvania: Pennsylvania State University Press, 1993).

Nicolson, Marjorie, 'The Early Stage of Cartesianism in England', *Studies in Philology* 26 (1929), 356–74.

Nuovo, Victor, 'Cockburn, Catharine (1679?–1749)', in *The Dictionary of Seventeenth-Century British Philosophers*, edited by Andrew Pyle (Bristol: Thoemmes Press, 2000), pp. 191–4.

Nye, Andrea, 'Polity and Prudence: The Ethics of Elisabeth, Princess Palatine', in *Hypatia's Daughters: Fifteen Hundred Years of Women Philosophers*, edited by Linda Lopez McAlister (Bloomington and Indianapolis: Indiana University Press, 1996), pp. 68–91.

The Princess and the Philosopher: Letters of Elisabeth of the Palatine to René Descartes (Lanham: Rowman and Littlefield, 1999).

O'Donnell, Sheryl, 'Mr Locke and the Ladies: The Indelible Words on the Tabula Rasa', *Studies in Eighteenth-Century Culture* 8 (1979), 151–64.

' "My Idea in Your Mind": John Locke and Damaris Cudworth Masham', in *Mothering the Mind*, edited by Ruth Perry and Martine Brownley (New York: Holmes and Meier, 1984), pp. 26–46.

O'Neill, Eileen, 'Mind–Body Interaction and Metaphysical Consistency: A Defence of Descartes', *Journal of the History of Philosophy* 25 (1987), 227–45.

'Philosophical Ambition: The System of Nature in Margaret Cavendish's Corpus', presented at the 'Seventeenth-Century Women Philosophers' conference at the University of Massachusetts, Amherst, November 1997.

'Disappearing Ink: Early Modern Women Philosophers and their Fate in History', in *Philosophy in a Feminist Voice: Critiques and Reconstructions*, edited by Janet A. Kourany (Princeton: Princeton University Press, 1998), pp. 17–62.

'Women Cartesians, "Feminine Philosophy", and Historical Exclusion', in *Feminist Interpretations of René Descartes*, edited by Susan Bordo (University Park, Pennsylvania: Pennsylvania State University Press, 1999), pp. 232–57.

'Elisabeth of Bohemia (1618–80)', in Craig (ed.), *Routledge Encyclopedia of Philosophy*, vol. III, pp. 267–9.

'Cavendish, Margaret Lucas (1623–73)', in Craig (ed.), *Routledge Encyclopedia of Philosophy*, vol. I, pp. 260–4.

'Astell, Mary (1666–1731)', in Craig (ed.), *Routledge Encyclopedia of Philosophy*, vol. I, pp. 527–30.

'Schurman, Anna Maria Van (1607–78)', in Craig (ed.), *Routledge Encyclopedia of Philosophy*, vol. VIII, pp. 556–9.

Osborne, Christabel,'Masham, Damaris', in *Dictionary of National Biography*, vol. XII, p. 1298.

Osler, Margaret J., *Divine Will and the Mechanical Philosophy: Gassendi and Descartes on contingency and necessity in the created world* (Cambridge: Cambridge University Press, 1994).

Owen, Gilbert Roy, 'The Famous Case of Lady Anne Conway', *Annals of Medical History* 9 (1937), 567–71.

Passmore, John A., *Ralph Cudworth: An Interpretation* (Cambridge: Cambridge University Press, 1951).

Perry, Ruth, 'Radical Doubt and the Liberation of Women', *Eighteenth Century Studies* 18:4 (1985), 472–93.

The Celebrated Mary Astell: An Early English Feminist (Chicago: Chicago University Press, 1986).

'Mary Astell and the Feminist Critique of Possessive Individualism', *Eighteenth Century Studies* 23 (1990), 444–57.

Plumwood, Val, *Feminism and the Mastery of Nature* (London and New York: Routledge, 1993).

Popkin, Richard H., 'The Philosophy of Bishop Stillingfleet', *Journal for the History of Philosophy* 9 (1971), 303–20.

'The Spiritualistic Cosmologies of Henry More and Anne Conway', in *Henry More (1614–1687) Tercentenary Studies*, edited by Sarah Hutton (Dordrecht: Kluwer Academic Publishers, 1990), pp. 97–114.

Powicke, F. J., 'Henry More, Cambridge Platonist; and Lady Conway, of Ragley, Platonist and Quakeress', *Friends' Quarterly Examiner* 55 (1921), 199–220.

Pyle, Andrew (ed.), *The Dictionary of Seventeenth-Century British Philosophers* (Bristol: Thoemmes Press, 2000).

Richardson, R. C., 'The "Scandal" of Cartesian Interactionism', *Mind* 91 (1982), 20–37.

Richetti, John J., *Philosophical Writing: Locke, Berkeley, Hume* (Cambridge, Mass.: Harvard University Press, 1983).

Rogers, John, *The Matter of Revolution: Science, Poetry and Politics in the Age of Milton* (Ithaca and London: Cornell University Press, 1996).

Rogers, Katharine M., *Feminism in Eighteenth-Century England* (Urbana: University of Illinois Press, 1982).

Roothaan, Angela, 'Anna Maria van Schurman's "Reformation" of Philosophy', in *Choosing the Better Part: Anna Maria van Schurman (1607–1678)*, edited by Mirjam De Baar, *et al.* (Dordrecht and London: Kluwer, 1996), pp. 103–16.

Rosa, Susan, 'Ralph Cudworth in the *République des Lettres*: The Controversy about Plastick Nature and the Reputation of Pierre Bayle', *Studies in Eighteenth-Century Culture* 23 (1994), 147–60.

Rosenfield, Leonora Cohen, *From Beast-Machine to Man-Machine: Animal Soul in French Letters from Descartes to La Mettrie*, new and enlarged edition (New York: Octagon Books, 1968).

Sarasohn, Lisa T., 'A Science Turned Upside Down: Feminism and the Natural Philosophy of Margaret Cavendish', *Huntington Library Quarterly* 47 (1984), 289–307.

Saveson, J. E., 'Differing Reactions to Descartes Among the Cambridge Platonists', *Journal of the History of Ideas* 21 (1960), 560–7.

Schiebinger, Londa, *The Mind Has No Sex? Women in the Origins of Modern Science* (Cambridge, Mass.: Harvard University Press, 1989).

'Margaret Cavendish', in *A History of Women Philosophers*, edited by Mary Ellen Waithe (Dordrecht: Kluwer Academic Publishers, 1991), vol. III, pp. 1–20.

Seidel, Michael A., 'Poulain de la Barre's *The Woman as Good as the Man*', *Journal of the History of Ideas* 35:3 (1974), 499–508.

Shapiro, Lisa, 'Princess Elizabeth and Descartes: The Union of Soul and Body and the Practice of Philosophy', *British Journal for the History of Philosophy* 7:3 (1999), 503–20.

Simonutti, Luisa, 'Damaris Cudworth Masham: una Lady della Repubblica delle Lettere', in *Scritti in Onore di Eugenio Garin* (Pisa: Scuola Normale Superioire, 1987), pp. 141–65.

Skinner, Quentin, 'Thomas Hobbes and his Disciples in France and England', *Comparative Studies in Society and History* 8 (1965), 153–67.

Skwire, Sarah E., 'Women, Writers, Sufferers: Anne Conway and An Collins', *Literature and Medicine* 18:1 (1999), 1–23.

Sleigh, Robert, 'The Masham–Leibniz Correspondence: What does it tell us about Masham?', presented at the 'Seventeenth-Century Women Philosophers' conference in Amherst, Massachusetts, November 1997.

Smith, Florence M., *Mary Astell* (New York: Columbia University Press, 1916).

Smith, Hilda L., *Reason's Disciples: Seventeenth Century English Feminists* (Urbana: University of Illinois Press, 1982).

'Intellectual Bases for Feminist Analyses: The Seventeenth and Eighteenth Centuries', in *Women and Reason*, edited by Elizabeth D. Harvey and Kathleen Okruhlik (Ann Arbor: University of Michigan Press, 1992), pp. 19–38.

(ed.), *Women Writers and the Early Modern British Political Tradition* (Cambridge: Cambridge University Press, 1998).

Springborg, Patricia, 'Mary Astell (1666–1731), Critic of Locke', *American Political Science Review* 89 (1995), 621–33.

'Astell, Masham, and Locke: Religion and Politics', in *Women Writers and the Early Modern British Political Tradition*, edited by Hilda L. Smith (Cambridge: Cambridge University Press, 1998), pp. 105–25.

Squadrito, Kathleen M., 'Mary Astell's Critique of Locke's View of Thinking Matter', *Journal of History of Philosophy* 25 (1987), 433–9.

'Mary Astell', in *A History of Women Philosophers*, edited by Mary Ellen Waithe (Dordrecht: Kluwer Academic Publishers, 1991), vol. III, pp. 87–99.

Stephen, Leslie, 'Cockburn, Catharine (1679–1749)', in *Dictionary of National Biography*, vol. IV, pp. 639–40.

'Burnet, Thomas (1635?–1715)', in *Dictionary of National Biography*, vol. III, pp. 408–10.

Stephen, Leslie, and Sidney Lee (eds.), *The Dictionary of National Biography . . . From the Earliest Times to 1900* (Oxford: Oxford University Press, 1917).

Stevenson, Jay, 'The Mechanist–Vitalist Soul of Margaret Cavendish', *Studies in English Literature* 36 (1996), 527–43.

Stock, Marie Louise, *Poullain de la Barre: A Seventeenth-Century Feminist* (PhD diss.: Columbia University, 1961).

Stuurman, Siep, 'Social Cartesianism: François Poulain de la Barre and the Origins of the Enlightenment', *Journal of the History of Ideas* 58 (1997), 617–40.

'From Feminism to Biblical Criticism: The Theological Trajectory of François Poulain de la Barre', *Eighteenth-Century Studies* 33:3 (2000), 367–82.

Ten Eyck Perry, H., *The First Duchess of Newcastle and her Husband As Figures in Literary History* (Boston and London: Ginn and Company, 1918).

Thompson, Janna, 'Women and the High Priests of Reason', *Radical Philosophy* 34 (1983), 10–14.

Tollefsen, Deborah, 'Princess Elisabeth and the Problem of Mind–Body Interaction', *Hypatia* 14:3 (1999), 59–77.

Waithe, Mary Ellen, 'Catharine Trotter Cockburn', in *A History of Women Philosophers*, edited by Mary Ellen Waithe (Dordrecht: Kluwer Academic Publishers, 1991), vol. III, pp. 101–25.

(ed.), *A History of Women Philosophers*, 4 vols. (Dordrecht: Kluwer Academic Publishers, 1991).

Wallas, Ada, *Before the Blue Stockings* (London: G. Allen and Unwin, 1929).

Ward, Richard, *The Life of the Learned and Pious Dr Henry More*, edited with an introduction by M. F. Howard, facsimile reprint of 1911 edition (Bristol: Thoemmes Press, 1997).

Wartenberg, Thomas E., 'Descartes's Mood: The Question of Feminism in the Correspondence with Elisabeth', in *Feminist Interpretations of René Descartes*, edited by Susan Bordo (University Park, Pennsylvania: Pennsylvania State University Press, 1999), pp. 190–212.

Watson, Richard, *The Breakdown of Cartesian Metaphysics* (Atlantic Highlands, NJ: Humanities Press International, 1987).

Weinberg, Sue, 'Damaris Cudworth Masham: A Learned Lady of the Seventeenth Century', in *Norms and Values: Essays on the Work of Virginia Held*, edited by Joram Graf Haber (Lanham: Rowman and Littlefield, 1998), pp. 233–50.

Whitebrook, J. C., 'Samuel Cradock, Cleric and Pietist (1620–1706) and Matthew Cradock, First Governor of Massachusetts', *Congregational Historical Society Transactions* 5 (1911–12), 181–91.

Wiesner, Merry E., *Women and Gender in Early Modern Europe* (Cambridge: Cambridge University Press, 1993).

Willey, Basil, *The Seventeenth-Century Background: Studies in the Thought of the Age in Relation to Poetry and Religion* (London: Ark Paperbacks, 1986).

Wilson, Catherine, *Leibniz's Metaphysics: An Historical and Comparative Study* (Princeton: Princeton University Press, 1989).

Wilson, Margaret Dauler, 'Descartes on the Origin of Sensation', *Philosophical Topics* 19:1 (1991), 293–323.

Descartes (London and New York: Routledge, 1993).

'Animal Ideas', *Proceedings and Addresses of the American Philosophical Association* 69:2 (1995), 11.

Witt, Charlotte, 'Feminist Metaphysics', in *A Mind of One's Own: Feminist Essays on Reason and Objectivity*, edited by Louise M. Antony and Charlotte Witt (Boulder and Oxford: Westview Press, 1993), pp. 273–88.

Woolf, Virginia, *The Common Reader* (London: Hogarth Press, 1968).

Wright, John P., 'Hysteria and Mechanical Man', *Journal of the History of Ideas* 42 (1980), 233–47.

Yolton, John, *Thinking Matter: Materialism in Eighteenth Century Britain* (Minneapolis: University of Minnesota Press, 1983).

Zedler, Beatrice H., 'The Three Princesses', *Hypatia* 4:1 (1989), 28–63.

Index

Cockburn, Catharine Trotter (*cont.*)
  and S. Clarke, 141, 144, 145, 158–9, 162, 164
  and Cudworth, 160–1, 164
  dramatic career of, 143
  feminism of, 5, 146–50
  and Leibniz, 127, 144, 157–8
  on Leibniz–Clarke dispute, 145, 159
  and Locke, 141, 145, 147, 151–6, 160, 163, 164
  and Masham, 145, 147, 149, 163
  moral theory of, 143, 148–50
  and More, 162
  on reason, 143, 145, 146
  reputation of, 156–7
  on scale of beings, 160–2
  on souls, 153–6, 161–2
  on space, 158–62
  theology of, 149, 163, 164
  on 'thinking matter', 151, 155
  works
    Defence of Locke, 141, 151–5, 163
    Discourse Concerning a Guide in Controversies, 144
    Olinda's Adventures, 142
    Remarks upon the Principles and Reasonings of Dr. Rutherforth, 141, 164
    Remarks upon Some Writers, 158–64
    Revolution of Sweden, 146
    Unhappy Penitent, The, 143
    'Verses Occasioned by the Busts in the Queen's Hermitage', 147, 149
    Works of Mrs. Catharine Cockburn, 141
Cockburn, Patrick, 156
Colie, Rosalie L., 130
common sense, 119
Connor, Margarette R., 142
Conway, Anne, Viscountess, 65, 164
  biographical details of, 5, 67, 117
  on Cartesian conception of matter, 70–1, 75, 84
  M. Cavendish, diverges from, 72, 80–9
  M. Cavendish, similar to, 66, 71–80
  and Descartes, 67–8
  and Elisabeth, 27
  on female and male principles, 75, 78–80
  on final causes, 81–3
  and Hobbes, 66, 81
  and kabbalism, 68, 73, 77
  and Leibniz, 66, 127
  on love, 75–6, 78
  on mechanism, 71, 81
  monism of, 70, 75–8

and More, 66, 67, 69, 72–80
on perfection, 82–5
on soul–body interaction, 74–5, 77–8
on Spinoza, 66, 80–1
spiritualism of, 72–3
theology of, 70–2, 75, 80, 81, 83–6
and F. M. van Helmont, 68, 73
works
  Conway Letters, 67
  Principles of the Most Ancient and Modern Philosophy, 66, 68–9
Conway, Edward, 67
Conway, Heneage Edward, 67
'Corinna' *See* Thomas, Elizabeth
Corse, Taylor, 73
Coste, Pierre, 114
Coudert, Allison P., 27, 65, 68, 73
Covel, John, 117
Coventry, Lady Anne, 92
Cradock, Damaris, 117
Cradock, Elizabeth, 67
Crossley, James, 65
Cudworth, Damaris *See* Masham, Lady Damaris Cudworth
Cudworth, Ralph, 11, 117, 151, 160–1, 164
  on animals, 53
  and M. Cavendish, 53–4, 66, 87–8
  on God, 86, 106–7, 129–30
  and Masham, 114–17, 127, 130, 133, 160
  on mental causality, 82, 88
  See also Cambridge Platonism; plastic nature/spirit of nature
Culverwell, Nathanael, 11

Dacier, Anne, 147
death and annihilation, 72, 84
dependence, 25–6
Descartes, Catherine, 20, 54
Descartes, René
  anti-authoritarianism of, 18
  on beast-machine doctrine *See* animals
  on clear and distinct ideas, 26
  on dualism *See* soul and body
  on final causes, 82
  on gravity, 22
  judgement, his theory of, 26–7
  and method, 6, 7, 9, 19
  moral theory of, 30
  and neo-Stoicism, 24, 31
  on the pineal gland, 45–6
  popularity of, 40
  on primitive notions, 21–2, 32
  on qualities, 99

feminism of, 5, 115–16, 123, 135–40, 149
and Leibniz, 117, 118, 126–35, 160, 163
and Locke, 114–18, 120–2, 125, 133, 134,
    136
on love, 120–2
and Malebranche, 118, 126, 129, 138
and Norris, 114, 118, 129
on occasionalism, 119, 125–6
on plastic nature, 130
on pre-established harmony, 126, 129, 133
on sense and reflection, 121, 122
on substance, 133–4
teleological reasoning of, 137, 138, 140
theology of, 125–6, 129, 132, 133
and 'thinking matter', 134
works
    Discourse concerning the Love of God, 96, 114,
        118, 119
    Occasional Thoughts, 114, 117, 136, 149
Masham, Sir Francis, 116
Masham, Francis Cudworth, 116
materialism, 56, 59
    of M. Cavendish, 36, 42, 44, 50, 58,
        62, 63
    of Hobbes, 46, 47–9
Mathews, Freya, 6
matter
    Cartesian conception of, 70–1, 75, 84
    extension of, 99
    impenetrability of, 60, 76
    thinking, 134, 151–3, 155
    see also under specific philosophers; soul and body
Mattern, Ruth, 14, 22
mechanism, 11, 22, 45, 48–50, 56, 57, 71, 81,
    82, 96
    See also under animals
Medoff, Jeslyn, 143
Merchant, Carolyn, 39, 65, 66
Merrens, Rebecca, 39
Mersenne, Marin, 37, 38
mind *See* soul; intellect; reason
mind–body problem *See* soul and body
Mintz, Samuel I., 38, 47
miracles, 128, 129
Molanus, Gerhard Wolter, 135
Molyneux, William, 118
monads, 135
monasteries, 122, 124
More, Henry, 11, 28, 44, 92, 105, 106, 117, 133,
    151, 162
    on animals, 53
    and M. Cavendish, ch. 2 *passim*; 55–63,
        69–70
    and Conway, 66, 67, 69, 72, 73–80
    and Descartes, 27, 28, 52, 53

and Elisabeth, 27
on extended souls, 28, 57, 59, 67, 133, 164
and materialism, 56, 59
on mechanism, 56
spirit of nature *See* plastic nature/spirit of
    nature
on soul–body distinction, 28, 57, 67
works
    Account of Virtue, 92, 108
    Antidote Against Atheism, 43, 53, 56, 57, 67,
        79, 151
    Enchiridion Metaphysicum, 27
    Explanation of the Grand Mystery of Godliness,
        70
    Immortality of the Soul, 43, 56, 92, 106, 151
mothers, 24, 137, 138

Nadler, Steven, 100
nature
    as a woman, 58, 78, 88, 102
Newcastle, Margaret, Duchess of
    See Cavendish, Margaret, Duchess of
    Newcastle
Newcastle Circle, 37, 38, 42
Newton, Isaac, 162
Nicole, Pierre, 96
Nicolson, Marjorie Hope, 4, 27, 40, 67, 68
Norris, John, 54, 152, 157
    and Astell, 1, 90–3, 98–109, 114
    and Masham, 114, 118, 129
    diverges from Malebranche, 100
Nuovo, Victor, 141, 142
Nye, Andrea, 14, 15, 32

occasionalism, 11, 99–102, 119, 125–9
O'Donnell, Sheryl, 116
O'Neill, Eileen, 2, 13, 15, 17, 20, 23, 33, 39, 43,
    44, 45, 95
Osborne, Christabel, 115
Osborne, Dorothy, 38, 50
Osler, Margaret J., 86, 87
Owen, Gilbert Roy, 68

pain, 99, 100, 102
panpsychism, 88
pantheism, 81
passions, the, 31–3, 143
Passmore, John A., 108
Pepys, Samuel, 38
perfectionism, 82–5, 110
Perry, Ruth, 3, 4, 90, 91, 92, 94, 115, 137
personal identity, 154
pineal gland, 45–6
plastic nature/spirit of nature, 36, 55, 56,
    59–61, 70, 99, 106–7, 130–3